Grandma's Shoebox

Grandma's Shoebox

What I have learned along the way...
A Journal of Faith, Hope and Love...

By :
Deborah Gorman

Graphics & Design By:
Bradley Gorman
Tyson Roberts

Copyright © 2009 by Deborah Gorman
Published by St. Louis Legacy Books, a division of Virginia Publishing Co.
St. Louis, MO, www.STL-Books.com

My Dearest Kevin,

Where do I start, I guess to begin I will say Happy Father's Day. I am so glad that you are the "father" of the children that have come into this world because of the love that we share.

We have now been together for more than 30 years. We have definitely shared good times and hard times. When I look back over our life together I count my blessings because God gave me you. After all these years you still take my breath away.

It's funny how our memory works, the events that stay with us through out time. I vividly remember the birthday of each of our children. I look at them now all grown up making their own way. They also take my breath away!

Throughout these last 30 years I have laughed often, and cried too. There have been times when things were so hard I thought I would die. But, through it all I have always had your strong loving arms to hold me up and help me through.

God has sent us many lessons to learn, and we have shared each one of those lessons. Some were easy and others were a bit harder. There are pictures of our life scattered through our home. There are memories in our hearts that are ours alone.

When God placed us on this Earth, our plan was cast. He has our path all lined out for us. He never shows us our future; we only get to keep the memories of our past.

When I look at the pictures of our children from days that are now so long ago, they bring back so many memories of the joyous times I have had just being "Mommy." There is nothing so beautiful as the pitterpatter of those 6 little feet. There are times when I hold these pictures close to my heart and I long to rock each one of them just one more time till they fall asleep. There was nothing more joyous in my life than holding our babies in my arms close to my heart.

God gave me the perfect 3. Our precious, beautiful daughter Mindy, with her eyes of pure ocean blue, there were so many lessons I learned with her. First came "love," then came patience, then came more love and more patience. Through it all, she is the perfect image of the woman I dreamed she would be!

Then came Brad in the image of my Granddad. God was answering my prayers when he gave us Brad. Every day that we have shared makes my heart smile. Because my Granddad was such an important part of my past, Brad was just what I asked for in my prayers when I asked God to give my Granddad back to me. It was the first time in my life that I knew from the bottom of my heart that God really does listen to us through our hearts.

I asked again and along came Chris. Chris was always meant to be my baby. When I see Chris smile, I see a wave of light that shines clear through me. Chris must know that he is a part of my heart…and I long for him each and every day of my life. When he is gone, it's like a part of me is missing because when I see him smile, I know I can do anything. Any mother will tell you that one look at her baby will always make her heart smile. Chris, you are my ray of light. Please come home; I am just not me without you.

I don't know why the sky is blue, but I know one thing in my life that is always certain… and that, my dear husband, is you!
I would lay down my life for you.
I don't know exactly just what my future holds, but I always know that I will be with you. Knowing that if you will let me, I will hold your hand tightly in mine as we walk along the way.

Forever loving you, from the depths of my heart to yours,

Debbie

For the Memories
that you have given me, for those who are still on this Earth

My parents, John & Jackie

My In-Laws, Bob and Ann

My children – Mindy – Brad – Chris. You are the light of my life. I
hope that I have inspired you in ways that will keep the light forever
burning in your hearts.

To my "male friends" – Tommy, Kevin,Wayne, Greg, Randy, Dennis,
Vito,Chris, Rudy, and Mike. Thanks for being in my Heart, and
thanks for letting me be in yours.

To my brothers – Johnny, Mark, Jeff, Jude and Joe. With you guys in
my life I didn't need a "sister". Life with you in it will always be
filled with laughter.

To my extra sons – Kyle, Kenneth, Tony, Jarod, Nick, Matt, Tyson. I
really do love you just like one of my own.

To my "girl friends" - Karen, Carleen, Debbie, Ellen, Lynne, Sue E,
Sue Y, Lana, Kim, Lyn, Rhonda, Melinda, Donna, Holly, Carol, Kate,
Katie, Alyssa, Susan, Lorene, Stacy, Helen, MaryKay, Cherry, Sandy,
Vickie, Janet, Mary(Marilyn), Marybeth, Mary Lynn.

Time passes. Life happens.
Distance separates, children grow up.
Jobs come and go, love waxes and wanes.
Men don't do what they are supposed to do.
Hearts break, parents die.
Colleagues forget favors, careers end.

But, women are there, no matter how much time or how many miles
are between you.
A girlfriend is never farther away than needing her.
When you have to walk that lonesome valley and you have to walk it
by yourself...

The women in your life will be on the valley's rim, cheering you on,
praying for you, pulling for you, intervening on your behalf, and
waiting with open arms at the valley's end.

Sometimes, they will even break the rules and walk alongside of you,
or come in and carry you out.

Girlfriends, daughters, granddaughters, daughters in law, sisters,
sisters in law, mothers, grandmothers, aunties, nieces, cousins and
extended family all bless our life.

When we began this adventure called womanhood, we had no idea of
the incredible joys or sorrows that lay ahead, nor did we know how
much we would need each other each and every day.

Special Message

Welcome to Grandma's Shoebox and my heart! I hope that you will use this Family Journal to keep track of your life stories, so that you may pass them down to all those who hold a special place in your heart.

I wish that I would have finished this project while my Grandmothers were still alive, but my heart is still filled with their love, so what I can remember from them through my heart is a part of this project.

I have written this book and designed this journal for anyone to leave behind their heart's messages to their loved ones. I hope that over time you will fill it with messages from your Heart. I hope that someday your great, great, great, great etc...grandchildren will have a copy of your message and learn about you through their heart. It's never too late...to leave your mark on this world.

I also hope that after you read through the messages I have included, you will know that you can walk with Christ in your life every day and then you will know that there is a light of love to guide you always through out your life.

As a mother you are the common thread that weaves through your family's lives and keeps them bonded together. You are a true "unsung hero." Part of everyone's purpose on this Earth is to leave behind your message.

It was my Grandma's faith that was planted in me when I was just a child. She always told me that it doesn't matter what it is, if you really wanted to do something that your heart felt needed to be done you can do it. As long as there is life in your body you can get it done.

Your Family Journal is designed not only to share your good times, it's just as important to share your struggles. It is usually in times of struggle that your faith will be tested, and your soul will grow from the lesson you have learned. Our children and their children need to know the lessons of our hearts. They need to know that it really doesn't matter what it is, if you let Him, the Lord will take you through.

Introduction

I believe that throughout our life each one of us will be presented
with opportunities to change the world. For the majority of us it
may be something small that affects a select few people; our family,
friends, or maybe a complete stranger. For others, it may be something more substantial and earth-shaking. Whether large, small or
anything in between, I assure you, our efforts do make a difference.
If we can inspire just one individual even for a short period of time,
the world at that moment is a better place.
This is my way to make a difference in any heart that I can possibly
touch to better this world.
It would be nice if we could each sit down and take the time to
reach deep into our hearts and find the words that we desperately
long to share. It's in each of us, but sometimes trying to get what
we are feeling inside out into words, especially written words, is not
an easy task. It was no different for me. I do hope you will find the
verses and quotes in this journal to be thought provoking, eye
opening and powerful. But just to give you the effect that is in my
heart of the lessons that I have learned, I have included some of the
pictures that were left to me in Grandma's Shoebox.
This book was not designed to be a cover-to-cover read. It's not a
story. It really is a "Book of Thoughts to Think About". Over the
last 50 years I have found encouragement through books, music,
scripture, conversation with others, and always in the shoebox.
This journal is my way of passing along the bits and pieces of
everything that challenged my thoughts and inspired me when I
needed inspiration the most. I enjoyed reading every book that
appears in the bibliography section of this book. Each one of these
books took me one step closer to where I am today. They taught me
that it was really all up to me where I was to go in this life.
I figured out where I wanted to be years ago. I finally found my
way today. I finished what I started, I started with what I had, and
you are holding the finished project in your hands. I hope that it
brings you many, many, many years of joy and comfort, and I hope
that you find the love in your heart to leave behind your own message to the ones that you love.

I am delighted that my book has found its way into your hands. I trust that no matter what it is you are seeking, there is something for you just a page turn away. I hope that these words will help you find comfort, knowledge, faith and inspiration, but most of all - love. They were written for you.

This book was my opportunity to inspire. Each passage was written with the intent of sharing God's message. If it can add even a glimmer of faith to what you already believe then I have accomplished all that I wanted to do.

May your life be filled with days worth being thankful for, and may the moments in each of your days be blessed.

Remember, God hears your prayers and he really does answer them. I hope that you will enjoy the stories of my life that I have included within these precious pages. I pray that you will take the time to add your own.

(Ecclesiastes 3:1)

1 To every thing there is a season, and a time to every purpose under the heaven:

2 A time to be born, and a time to die; a time to plant, and a time to pluck up that which is planted;

3 A time to kill, and a time to heal; a time to break down, and a time to build up;

4 A time to weep, and a time to laugh; a time to mourn, and a time to dance;

5 A time to cast away stones, and a time to gather stones together; a time to embrace, and a time to refrain from embracing;

6 A time to get, and a time to lose; a time to keep, and a time to cast away;

7 A time to rend, and a time to sew; a time to keep silence, and a time to speak;

8 A time to love, and a time to hate; a time of war, and a time of peace.

I encourage you to keep your own journal as you read through this book. Fill the pages of your journal with all the special moments of your life.

When my Grandma died, our Family met at her home after the funeral luncheon. Now, keep in mind that for the previous 2 to 3 years my Grandmother put a piece of masking tape on all of her "special treasures", and she wrote a name on each one of them. So, that day at her house was like a treasure hunt. I know that she was watching us the same way she used to watch us all at Christmas time. Her heart was always filled with joy and her eyes with love. She left behind one more special Christmas with Grandma for all of us to share.

To some, my Grandma was a simple woman. She was never rich, but she was extremely wealthy with the love of her Family. I saw my Grandma almost every day of my life, and every day that I walked through her doorway it was always the same: I was met with a heart filled with joy and her beautiful brown eyes filled with love. I was lucky. My Grandma left me her heart when she left her Special Shoebox and her Bible. She left me a message straight from her soul. Within the pages of her Bible I found so many hidden treasures tucked between the pages. I hold it close to my heart every day. It's like getting to hug her one more time each and every day. So I encourage you to leave behind your heart. It's amazing what effect it can have on your loved ones after you are gone. There are moments within all of us that will remain forever etched in our hearts. It is very important that you share these memories with the ones who put them there.

Stepping into this next generation

I have heard people say that God answers prayers and I believe this to be true. I think that there are many others of all kinds of "faith" that believe in a form of prayer. I have also heard at least a million times from my Grandma; who just kept reminding me that it was coming from our Father, the Lord, the God Almighty, creator of Heaven and Earth, from whom all things are given to us.

I have experienced many lessons in my life, and I can tell you honestly that I believe. If God chooses to pour out his blessings on me for believing in Him then I will gratefully accept them. I will accept each of them in my heart. I truly know that life with Him in my heart is better than life without.

I hope to someday teach this lesson to my grandchildren. I will speak of Him often in my home and I will always make sure that my family knows where to find Him.

You must know the importance of you. You have a purpose. You must never stop learning. That is what the Bible describes as progressing along the way.

In order to feel the gift of joy you must be in constant communication with the Lord. I try very hard to understand the wisdom of the words of scripture. I do this because they were passed down for a reason, from generation to generation. They are in fact the journey of many lives. They are our Journal of Life...Life's Instruction Book. I hope that my family will do the same. I hope that they can find it in their hearts to put aside a little time each day to be thankful for their blessings.

It all comes down to this. Your story, your circumstances, your timing may not be as dramatic as someone else's, but the risks are exactly the same. There comes a time in everyone's life when a decision is required. And that decision, should you make it, will have a far-reaching effect on generations to come.

There is a thin thread that intertwines you to hundreds of thousands of lives. Your actions and even one simple decision that you make can literally change the world.

Debbie

PS: Let your journal someday be filled with your own "Great Last Words" to share with your family. Be sure you add some of your favorite family photos to keep your tribe alive.

In His Will is Our Peace

NOVENA IN HONOR OF OUR LADY OF THE MIRACULOUS MEDAL

PRAYER

O Lord Jesus Christ Who has been pleased to glorify by countless miracles the Immaculate Conception of the Virgin Mary Thy Mother, grant that always imploring her intercession we may attain to everlasting joys. Amen.

O Mary conceived without sin,
Pray for us who have recourse to Thee.

OUR LADY OF TEARS

Grandma's Shoebox

♥

Table of Contents

♥What I Found Inside That Little Box♥

Chapter 1

My Grandma's Heart - The Pictures in the Box

. *faith* . **HOPE** . love . mind . **BODY** . *spirit* .

My Grandma was what I would call a "devout Catholic". Maybe in today's world, I would also call her a "devout Christian woman." She was raised in a large Catholic family, by a mother who deeply believed in God and Jesus.

As a child growing up, I used to spend my entire summer vacation at my grandparents' home in DeSoto, Missouri. Her sisters, my great aunties, would also have their grandchildren for the summer. I would spend every day playing with my cousins and getting a lot of good quality time with my Grandma and my aunties. They were much like you would expect sisters to be. There was always a lot of laughter between them and they always seemed to be having a wonderful day when they were together. While all the kids were running around playing, they were always in the house doing things together. They played pinochle, bridge, spades and canasta. They also baked a lot.

My Grandma and her sisters all lived within a couple of blocks of each other. I think this was because none of them knew how to drive a car. I can remember my Grandma saying that one of them really should get a license so they would not be so dependent on their spouses. They had in fact all driven a tractor so it couldn't be much more difficult than that. But they never did. They walked to each other's homes all the time. They walked to the grocery store a few times per week. In the cold winter months, one of their husbands would pick them all up and take them to the store. It was really quite a simple way of life. We stayed busy every day of the summer, sort of like an extended vacation. We swam in my Grandma's pool, we went to the river and had picnics, and walked in to town anytime we wanted. It was just fun for us everyday.

. *faith* . **HOPE** . love . mind . **BODY** . *spirit* .

Grandma's Shoebox

Every morning my Grandma and her sisters met in front of the Catholic church, Saint Rose of Lima. Before going inside they would give each other little pieces of paper. When I asked her what they were doing she explained that on those pieces of paper was the request that they would be praying for that day. They never missed a day of Mass. Grandma took me with her each morning if I was willing to go. I remember asking her why she went every day, when most people just go on Sunday. This is what she said to me: "When two or more gather in his name, he hears your prayers faster, and I believe that a person should make time every day for God. This has been the way that my mother did it, and my sisters and I have just always done it too. Maybe someday you will understand and you will do it too." Today, many years later, I can fully understand why my Grandma practiced her faith the way that she did. The power of prayer cannot be overemphasized for permanent, satisfying prosperity. The person who prays daily is certain to succeed, because he is attuning himself to the richest, most successful force in the universe. Jesus promised, "All things whatsoever ye shall ask in prayer, believing, ye shall receive." (Matthew 21:22)

Jesus asked, "How much more shall my Heavenly Father give you when you come to him with an open heart?"

The Power of a Sincere Heart

When you pray, think. Think well what you are saying, and make your thoughts into things that are solid. In that way, your prayers will have strength, and that strength will become a part of you in mind, body and spirit.

To offer a prayer that will reach Heaven and the heart of God:

faith . **HOPE** . love . mind . **BODY** . *spirit* .

Keep it simple. Keep it pure. Keep it you.

The purpose of prayer is not to change God's mind, which always knows your wholeness and deservingness. The purpose of prayer is to change your mind so you can see through the eyes of God.

♥

I never saw my Grandma get upset or overly aggravated with anyone or any situation. She always gave it up to God and let him help her out. From what I can remember, this worked very well for her. There were the occasional times when my Uncle Joe (He is just 2 years older than me and the person that I have always thought of as the funniest guy in the world) wouldn't do something he was supposed to do and she would get on him a little. I remember one day I was out in the pool and my Grandma came running after Uncle Joe, wearing her slip. She had a little whisk broom in her hand and she was shaking it at him. My uncle Joe started running around the pool in circles, and my Grandma was trying to catch up with him. Then he jumped up on the diving board, did a huge cannonball near the edge of the pool where she was standing and completely soaked her with water. My Grandma was laughing so hard she ran into the house to go to the bathroom. That was an everyday event with my Grandma. She always saw the humor in every situation.

My Grandma had 3 sons, John, Jude, and Joseph. She would never have given her children a name that was not in the Bible. She collected pieces of forget-me-nots. In that shoebox there are many prayers to St. Jude, St. Joseph and St. John. She lived every day of her life as a strong Christian woman. She left behind a wonderful example of what a good mother, wife, and grandmother should be. But most of all she was a great example of what a Christian should be. She taught me that true prayers join our human heart with the heart of God. When you pray consistently to God, your heart yields more and more love, peace and aliveness.

.faith. HOPE. love. mind. BODY. spirit.

Grandma's Shoebox

faith . **HOPE** . love . mind . **BODY** . *spirit* .

Chapter 1 - My Grandma's Heart

♥

I hope that you will enjoy the pictures that I have included throughout this entire book. Every one of these pictures came out of "The Shoebox." My Grandma never threw away a picture if it showed Mary, Joseph or Jesus. These pictures were so much a part of my Grandma's life, and they are the things that she looked at day after day that brought beauty into her life.

The pictures that I have in Grandma's Shoebox were the pictures she carried with her in her soul. My Grandma did not believe that you should ever discard a picture of Jesus, The Blessed Mother Mary, or Joseph. When these pictures made their way into your hands it was for a reason. If she received a picture on a Christmas card or a special note, she put the picture in the shoebox and added it to her collection. Mind you, she did not keep the entire card, just the picture. Whenever she needed a little pick-me-up or just time to sit and reflect, you would see her sitting with her shoebox on her lap. She would look at all the beautiful pictures she had collected over the years, and she would read all her favorite verses that bought her so much joy.

♥

Grandma never had much money; her home was not filled with beautiful paintings to display to the world. She found beauty in her beliefs, and she kept them safely tucked away in her little shoebox. Now these same little pictures sit in the same little shoebox, and they are the most beautiful pictures of my life. I sit with Grandma's box on my lap and I do the same things that she did. I read the verses she left marked in her booklets, I say the same Novenas, and I stare deeply at those pictures. It gives me an enormous amount of comfort knowing that her little hands held each one of these pictures with loving care.

♥

. *faith* . **HOPE** . love . mind . **BODY** . *spirit* .

Grandma's Shoebox

I believe that she knew just what she was doing when she gave that little shoebox to me. She knew how much I loved her, and she knew how much I enjoyed looking at the pictures with her when I was just a little girl. I think she might have known that I would share the contents of the box with anyone who would listen.

So, my Grandma and I are still together, and this is our way to make a difference in the world. I stare at these pictures and I see the beauty in her eyes, I feel the love in her heart, and I benefit from the wisdom of her soul. My Grandma was a Catholic for a reason. She saw the beauty in the faith, the prayers and the rituals. She knew that her prayers would be answered.

Our hope is that you will create the same feelings with the ones that you love. Don't let time get away from you. Time is all that we have here. Create your beautiful memories and pass them down to those you love.

♥

The following are some of the things that my Grandma used to say to me whenever we looked through the shoebox together:

"Did you know that when you pray and you end your prayer with the word "Amen" the word Amen means 'Be it unto me'?"

So when you are focusing your prayers on your progress, be sure to end them with a positive 'Amen'.

♥

"The world demonstrates an ancient truth: You will believe that others do to you exactly what you think you did to them."

So always follow the Golden Rule and "do unto others as you would have them do unto you".

faith . **HOPE** . love . mind . **BODY** . *spirit* .

"Every decision that you make stems from what you think you are and represents the value that you put upon yourself."

♥

God wants you to succeed in your goals and dreams, and if you believe it, you can do it. You can succeed at whatever you try to do if you follow God's laws of life. When you finally learn to turn to your Bible for guidance, you will find all the answers to help you overcome all of your hurdles and barriers. You will realize that your ambitions and dreams can all come true.

The first thing that you have to do if you want to succeed at anything in life is "Seek ye first the kingdom of God, and his righteousness; and all these things shall be added unto you." (Matthew 6:33)

God's laws are simple; they are the paths that you must follow to get to your destination, no matter what that destination is. If it is prosperity, peace and happiness, you must obey these laws. He has placed every good thing in this world for you. He has also placed the power to gain it in your heart.

If you really want to be happy, then you must first help to make others happy. If you want to be prosperous, then you must first help others to become prosperous. These are God's laws, His rules for life. When you take them to heart and start to fully understand them, you will see some truly life-changing events.

"For whosoever will save his life shall lose it: but whosoever shall lose his life for my sake, the same shall save it." (Luke 9:24)

You must think of other people first, and you must give of your own life. You have to help others with their hopes and dreams in order to obtain yours.

faith . **HOPE** . love . mind . **BODY** . *spirit*.

Grandma's Shoebox

faith . **HOPE** . love . mind . **BODY** . *spirit* .

Chapter 1 - My Grandma's Heart

♥

Your best thinking is what got you here. You can apply that to all the events and situations in your life. Our best thinking is exactly where all of our so-called problems exist. If we couldn't think about them anymore, they would not exist. We can change our very best thinking and begin to see the mistakes of that thinking. Then we can realize that a connection to God is what heals or eliminates our problems.

So how do we stop that error? Very simple: We correct it, and it goes away. That is, we bring truth to the presence of the error, and the error disappears. You cannot send problems out of your life by attacking them or trying to better understand them. Instead, you can correct the error in your thinking that produces the problem in the first place. Once you bring a correction to the problem it no longer has any substance or validity, and it fades away completely from your life.

How do you find the truth in the error? Now that might be known as the $64,000 question. We have always heard the saying, "The Truth Shall Set You Free." What exactly does that mean? Does it mean that you have to "fess up" to the errors of your ways? Does it mean that you need to seek forgiveness from someone other than our Father? I believe that every person has to "right their wrongs" if they really want to let it go and move on with their life. If you go day after day living a lie, it begins to eat away at you, and then so many things in your life start to go wrong.
So, really, it's just best to get it out in the open. Don't dwell on it. Find a friend, confide in them, and let them help you. If you are lost, go to someone who can help put you back on the right path. If that means owning up to something you regret doing, then just do it and get it over with. If you don't, it could haunt you for the rest of your life.

. *faith* . **HOPE** . love . mind . **BODY** . *spirit* .

Grandma's Shoebox

There is a God who made you for a reason, and your life has deep, insightful meaning! We discover that meaning and purpose only when we make God the reference point of our lives. The only accurate way to understand ourselves is by what God is and by what he does for us.

♥

Here is the secret for dealing with those close to you who exhibit hatred. First, remember that hatred is a reaction to aggravated love. Then, silently repeat to yourself over and over, "Lord, make me an instrument of thy peace; where there is hatred, let me sow love."

♥

Use your gift, but use it in the way that it was given. Your life must have balance. Too much of any one behavior might require that you be swatted back on the path. Use your gift, don't abuse it. Whatever it is, it came to you from your "Father." It is the path he has chosen for you. We can't all be doctors and Indian chiefs. Every gift is special, it was meant just for you. The test is still the same for everyone: How will you use this gift that has been given to you? Look for these answers; they are the ones that will bring you the greatest joy.

♥

Discernment is not simply about resisting evil, self absorption, or destructiveness. It is about foundational identity. It is about who we know ourselves to ultimately be. It's about paying attention to the ways in which the limited power we exert, the modest respect we demand, and the resources that we take for granted provide us with our primary sense of meaning. To what extent do we "know" ourselves? Are we simply church members, respectable citizens, conscientious parents, homeowners or employees and not at all as beloved daughters and sons of God? We are beloved not because of what we do. We are beloved because of who we are.

faith . **HOPE** . love . mind . **BODY** . *spirit* .

Chapter 1 - My Grandma's Heart

♥

Learn first who you are as a child of the Father. Then you will know yourself as whatever you want to be. As long as ye are one! It's when you lose this thought that crisis happens in your life. Just know that this is just his way of lining up his ducklings. It's all a part of nature. God tries to keep all of us in line at whatever age or level we are experiencing. If you keep getting out of line, it's only natural that he would swat you a little harder trying to get you back in line and on course. So if you are experiencing any difficulties, get back on his path.

♥

Gifts are those abilities that seem to arise from within you without any training or conscious development. Perhaps they are even inborn. Using them energizes us, and compels us at some deeper level.

On one hand, using our natural or inborn gifts, whatever they may be, engages our joy, creativity and energy. Skills, on the other hand, are learned and deliberately developed.

When we use those gifts we may "wear out but we will never burn out." That's because in using our gifts we are following God's call. We gratefully use the gifts, given to us by God, to be who we are called to be; we don't try to be something we are not.

You can begin releasing the power to produce greater good in your life and affairs when you realize that your mind is your world. When you rule your mind, you rule your world. When you choose your thoughts, you choose your results.

♥

faith. **HOPE**. love. mind. **BODY**. *spirit*.

Grandma's Shoebox

There is no need to panic and give up when you find yourself bombarded or flooded with negative experiences. You just have to know that a cleansing is taking place. That which is no longer for your highest and best good is being cleansed, released and dissolved from your life – whether you want it to be or not. Greater good and greater blessings are on their way! For example, the experience of ill health, in which you seemed flooded with pain and weakness is a time when your body is attempting to throw off, release and dissolve that which is no longer of any use by the mind or body.

A flood experience is good. It is a purifying, balancing process that is helping you get ready for greater good. Often after prolonged emotional stress in one's human relationships, the whole picture changes and greater happiness comes than you have previously known. Your flood experiences are for good. That is the success attitude that you need to know when it seems much of the past or present is being swept away from you on a floodtide of negative experiences that may seem beyond your control.

Flood experiences come to you in the pretext or appearance of confusion, loss, disappointment, financial crisis; in harmony; or even betrayal in human relationships. However, a flood of such circumstances is not an unfortunate experience at all. It is a time when balance and stability are taking place. It is a time to release, let go and let the new good come forth in ways you may not have even dreamed possible. When you recognize these flood experiences for what they are, you will no longer be overwhelmed by them. You can rejoice, knowing you are being saved, and healed, and that divine adjustments are taking place. Greater good always comes to you after these severe periods, if you dare to expect it! Now, remember this, it's what got you here, and if you are back on the right path, stay there!

faith . HOPE . love . mind . BODY . *spirit*.

Chapter 1 - My Grandma's Heart

♥

Words may help you to understand something. Experience allows you to know.

♥

What you are here to do is as important a contribution as anyone else's, be it to raise your children in the best way you can, make a contribution through your job, or help and heal others.
All life has a purpose once it gets here! You need to figure out what your purpose is and then run with it, do the best you can and know that while you are doing it, you are making a difference.
My Grandma lives on in the hearts of those whom she loved, but now she will live on a little longer with the words of this book. She picked me to pass on her message and to share her faith.

♥

Life seeks energy, awareness and love. Every situation teaches you more about who you are. With every problem that comes your way, you learn and become stronger. Share your lessons with all those that you love. You don't need to reinvent the wheel, but there's always room for improvement in any life. A lesson spared is a lesson shared.

♥

There is absolutely no reason to be around anyone who makes you feel bad about yourself. Always choose to be with those who empower and motivate you. Be with people who love you just the way you are.

♥

In your day-to-day life, it is important to know that you do not owe anyone your time or energy. They are the greatest gifts you have been given, and how you use them will determine how much you will evolve in this lifetime. Use them wisely!

faith . **HOPE** . love . mind . **BODY** . *spirit* .

Your time and energy are your most precious gifts. When you choose to give them away you can't get them back. Spend time with those you love and help them along the way.

♥

We are all here for a reason and a purpose, even though we may not be fully aware of it. Our purpose in life is often related to our talents, but is much more important. Your life purpose is what you are here to achieve.

Your purpose may well be something that you have always known, but have for some reason ignored and kept in the back of your mind. Live your purpose. Live your life to the fullest and make every day as beautiful as it can be. Enjoy what you have; think about how wonderful it is to have these blessings. Enjoy your gifts.

♥

There was one birthday card that Grandma saved in her shoebox - and guess what! It was from me.

faith. **HOPE**. love. mind. **BODY**. *spirit*.

Grandma's Shoebox

Chapter 2

Pieces of her soul -
The religion in the box

There was no doubt that my Grandma was a very devout Catholic. All of the things that she left me in her shoebox surely tell me so. She believed in her faith, and she studied it her entire life. She tried very hard to pass it on to her family. She did this most of the time by leading by example. She never missed Mass, she said her rosary daily, and she prayed every day in the way that she was taught to do so.

I never noticed if my Grandparents were going through any "hard times." Maybe I was just too young to know.

♥

Inside this little box was a small hardbound book. The golden letters on the cover of the book read, Four Thousand Questions and Answers. When you open the book, the inside page says that there are 4000 questions and answers on the Bible. Grandma was doing the exact same thing that I have found myself doing for the last 30+ years: She was finding her way home through her beliefs. She was doing just what the Lord instructed us all to do: Study, research and learn. Finding your way to determine your beliefs is not always a simple task. I believe that my Grandma was just simply "learning her way home." I think that is an easier task for someone raised in a faithful home than someone who was not. Sometimes, it doesn't matter how we are raised, we have to figure it out for ourselves. That is exactly what we are told to do - figure it out!

♥

My Grandma was using all the resources available to educate her soul, and all of the pieces that helped her along the way were safely tucked away. I hold them here with me today. I have read hundreds of books trying to find my way. I have always had a very strong longing in my soul. I realize now that I have done things very similar to my Grandma. The walls of my bedroom are filled with the books that have touched my soul. In front of the books on the shelves are the trinkets that I have collected along the way. I hope that someday my children and grandchildren will realize the wisdom that is being left behind for them with the contents of those shelves.

♥

I know exactly what my Grandma was trying to convey to me with her Shoebox. It was her way of saying "here is my heart, here is what I believe, do with it what you can and someday remember me." There is not a day that goes by that I do not think about my Grandma. I can close my eyes and see her just as plain as day. Sometimes I can even smell the lilac powder that she used to wear. Grandma had the faith to move mountains. She found her way home, and she made her way in this world through that same Faith that took her home.

I miss her every day of my life; the long talks, the joy and laughter that she put deep in my heart. When I need to be near her, or find myself just wanting to visit with her again, you can bet that I go to the Shoebox and I find her there. I know that she is in my heart forever; but if I just want to hold a little piece of her, I can pick up anything out of the box.

♥

faith . HOPE . love . mind . BODY . *spirit* .

Chapter 2 - Pieces of Her Soul

There have been times when I was just simply feeling down and my hands were guided to a particular prayer or verse. That is when I know that she is watching me a little closer. My hands have always been guided to what I needed to learn.

CHAPTER 3

-GOD-
The Adoration in the Box

My Prayer…His Answer…
For all that I Believe…
For all that I Love…
For all of those who have given me a piece of their Heart…

Father, please, I ask you this with all of my Heart. Forgive me for the sins that are of my past. Continue please to guide my way. Lord, I thank you for the beauty and the blessings that you have given me as you continue to light my way.

Please, on this beautiful day; hear the cries of my heart this day as always. I look up to you every time I need a hand, for you alone hold the keys to my heart. Please take just a moment and send your love down on me. I am asking for your love and forgiveness for any pain I may have caused. Please, dear Father, open your heart to me.

If you have the time, please hold me gently in your arms and let me feel your heart. For it is there I will find the answers for the path that you have chosen for me. Please pick me up one more time. I will dedicate my life to you. I will give you proper thanks and praise.

I hear you say, "You are forgiven, just share the way…" "Through the darkness my child just look for the light…I will be there to guide you…I will light your way. You must keep my light shining along your way with the heart that you have been blessed with deep inside you…don't keep this love all for yourself…share it with those that you love along your way...Open your heart, find your way…you will always be able to feel my heart…"

"What is love…when you write, write your love letters from deep in your heart. Every hand that reaches out to you, you must reach back from your heart."

. *faith* . **HOPE** . love . mind . **BODY** . *spirit* .

Grandma's Shoebox

Father, please take my hand and hold it tight. And dear Father please don't let me go…for I will reach out to those along my way and I will shine your light always, for I know that I am not alone.

You, God my Father believes in me as I believe in you…you hear only the cries of our heart…for you are made of pure love…I am a part of you…you have blessed me with a heart full of love…I can only believe that you hear my prayers and that with your love I really can move mountains. So I ask you now with the faith of a mustard seed…help me move my mountains…

I hear you say… "My child, you must work from your heart and not from your head because it is love that will always help you find your way. You've got to feel this…I am telling you this for all of your life's purposes…you must follow the ways of your heart…"

Dear Father, we all want to make our way in this world…we all want our voices to be heard…we all struggle just trying to be someone… "Dearest child…when you learn to just be me…as you are an important part of me…then you will always know true love along your way…it is when you look back and see your own light shining through all the others that you have touched along the way…then you know that when you look back for the life you live and the life you give…you have been loved all along the way…"

So as I sit back and say my prayers, I ask always to know how to love and to give it away. I put all my faith and hope in you dear father. I believe that somebody really is out there watching over me and all of this world, and that somebody always has been you. "When you put your faith in thee it is amazing what can be seen…" "Keep building along your path as you make your way. Remember when you follow your heart, you follow your dreams.

faith . **HOPE** . love . mind . **BODY** . *spirit* .

Chapter 3 - God

I will always put happiness back in your heart. All you have to do is ask. Just ask me, please, and let me feel your heart. Then you will always find the beauty that is waiting there to be seen. When you work the plan that fills your heart you will always see color everywhere."

"You will find your silver lining in every cloudy day. Please know that I am always with you lighting your way. It is when you feel down that you will see. That I have always been there with you, just waiting for you to see. I will never leave you. I have always been in your heart. You have nothing to be afraid of there really is nothing that you should fear."

Father, I hear you. I will do my best each and every day. And when I grow weary I will find you along my way. "Remember, my child, to give me just a little bit of your time out of each and every day. As you would say this to your own children, I now say this to you. Place your hand on your heart…you must feel this…you must feel me filling up your heart with my love for you. I believe in you…and all I really want to do is to help you believe in you too"

Father, is it really that simple? Is that all I need to do?

"Someone is always out there reaching. Some can't seem to move ahead. They are paralyzed with fear. It is really at those times that all I want to do is to help each and every one of you. I will hold you up. I will help you stand. I will always be that still small voice that shouts to your heart. I believe in you. Let me show you that there are so many ways that you can go when we both believe…"

Father, I Believe,
Debbie

. *faith* . **HOPE** . love . mind . **BODY** . *spirit* .

Grandma's Shoebox

♥

What we believe about God shapes who we are and all that we become. What have you become? Are you allowing yourself to be guided from within? If you keep your Heart in touch with God, you will soon discover that when he wants to get your attention he will grab you there.

♥

Elohim – Genesis 1:1 – In the beginning God created Heaven and Earth. Elohim (e-lo-Heem) one of the oldest designations for divinity in the world. Elohim is used more than 2500 times in the Bible. "Genesis" is a word that means Birth…to begin. To be created in the image of God. (Genesis 1:26-28) Be thankful that you were created in his image.

When you pray, ask God to renew your sense of wonder, and express your gratitude for all the things that he has made.

Ask God, the one who made you to remake your sense of wonder with his creative powers.

♥

You must be following your heart for he has chosen our path. If you follow Him he will guide you the entire way you go. You just need to follow his signs and clues along your way.

God wants you to succeed in your goals and dreams. You can do this, you can succeed at whatever you try to do if you will follow God's laws of life. When you finally learn to turn to your Bible for guidance you will find all the answers to help you overcome all of your hurdles and barriers. You will realize that your ambitions, and your dreams can all come true.

Find the right place to worship and praise and go there often in his name.

♥

The Many Different Names of God in the Bible

Ab, Abba, Pater – Father
Adonay – Master Lord
El Chay – Living God
El Kanna
Elohim – God the Mighty Creator
El Elyon – God the Most High
El Olam – The Everlasting and Eternal God
El Roi – The God who sees me
El Shadday – God Almighty
Esh Oklah – Jealous God, Fire Consuming
Hashem – The Name
Machseh – Magen – Maon – Strong Tower, Refuge, Dwelling Place,
Shield Fortress
Melek – King
Miqweh Yisrael – Hope of Israel
Qedosh Yisrael – Holy one of Israel
Shophet – Judge
Yahweh – Lord
Yahweh Nissi – The Lord My Banner
Yahweh Roi - The Lord is My Shepherd
Yahweh Rophe – The Lord who Heals
Yahweh Shalom – The Lord of Peace
Yahweh Shammah – The Lord is there
Yahweh Tsebaoth – The Lord of Hosts
Yahweh Tisdqenu – The Lord our Righteousness
Yahweh Tsuri – The Lord My Rock
Yahweh Yireh – The Lord will Provide

. *faith* . **HOPE** . love . mind . **BODY** . *spirit* .

42

(Genesis 28:10-22)

10And Jacob went out from Beersheba, and went toward Haran.

11And he lighted upon a certain place, and tarried there all night, because the sun was set; and he took of the stones of that place, and put them for his pillows, and lay down in that place to sleep.

12And he dreamed, and behold a ladder set up on the earth, and the top of it reached to heaven: and behold the angels of God ascending and descending on it.

13And, behold, the LORD stood above it, and said, I am the LORD God of Abraham thy father, and the God of Isaac: the land whereon thou liest, to thee will I give it, and to thy seed;

14And thy seed shall be as the dust of the earth, and thou shalt spread abroad to the west, and to the east, and to the north, and to the south: and in thee and in thy seed shall all the families of the earth be blessed.

15And, behold, I am with thee, and will keep thee in all places whither thou goest, and will bring thee again into this land; for I will not leave thee, until I have done that which I have spoken to thee of.

16And Jacob awaked out of his sleep, and he said, Surely the LORD is in this place; and I knew it not.

17And he was afraid, and said, How dreadful is this place! this is none other but the house of God, and this is the gate of heaven.

18And Jacob rose up early in the morning, and took the stone that he had put for his pillows, and set it up for a pillar, and poured oil upon the top of it.

19And he called the name of that place Bethel: but the name of that city was called Luz at the first.

20And Jacob vowed a vow, saying, If God will be with me, and will keep me in this way that I go, and will give me bread to eat, and raiment to put on,

21So that I come again to my father's house in peace; then shall the LORD be my God:

. faith . HOPE . love . mind . BODY . spirit .

Chapter 3 - God

22And this stone, which I have set for a pillar, shall be God's house: and of all that thou shalt give me I will surely give the tenth unto thee.

(Genesis 35:1-8)

1And God said unto Jacob, Arise, go up to Bethel, and dwell there: and make there an altar unto God that appeared unto thee when thou fleddest from the face of Esau thy brother.

2Then Jacob said unto his household, and to all that were with him, Put away the strange gods that are among you, and be clean, and change your garments:

3And let us arise, and go up to Bethel; and I will make there an altar unto God, who answered me in the day of my distress, and was with me in the way which I went.

4And they gave unto Jacob all the strange gods which were in their hand, and all their earrings which were in their ears; and Jacob hid them under the oak which was by Shechem.

5And they journeyed: and the terror of God was upon the cities that were round about them, and they did not pursue after the sons of Jacob.

6So Jacob came to Luz, which is in the land of Canaan, that is, Bethel, he and all the people that were with him.

7And he built there an altar, and called the place Elbethel: because there God appeared unto him, when he fled from the face of his brother.

8But Deborah, Rebekah's nurse died, and she was buried beneath Bethel under an oak: and the name of it was called Allonbachuth.

When you pray, ask God to increase your desire to bless others with the gifts he has given you. Ask Elohim for what you need, believing in both his power to bless and his desire to care for you.

♥

. *faith* . HOPE . love . mind . BODY . *spirit* .

Grandma's Shoebox

Prayer is more than just words, but prayer begins and ends with words. As the great religions of the world have always known, the word is God in action.

(Psalm 102:25-27)

25 Of old hast thou laid the foundation of the earth: and the heavens are the work of thy hands.

26 They shall perish, but thou shalt endure: yea, all of them shall wax old like a garment; as a vesture shalt thou change them, and they shall be changed:

27 But thou art the same, and thy years shall have no end.

No matter what happens to us or the world around us, God always remains the same. He is perfect; nothing could be added to him or taken away from him.

When you pray, ask him for his help to let you perceive his greatness; this way you can stop projecting your own feelings on him. Let the Lord, who never changes, steady your world today. Whatever course or path that you must take, whatever changes you must confront, let them take you to Him. He is a strong God and you can lean on Him forever.

♥

Ask only for what you truly need from your Heart. God really can change your situation, but you must follow your heart all the way home.

The first thing that you must do if you really want to succeed at anything in life is "Seek ye first the Kingdom of God, and his righteousness, and all these things shall be added unto you."

Your heart always takes you home.

faith . **HOPE** . love . mind . **BODY** . *spirit*

Chapter 3 - God

Words of truth are sharp as a two-edged sword (Hebrews 4:12) and quickly cut through negation and dissolve it, thereby releasing the omnipresent good. The Hindu scriptures pointed this out: "If a man speaks or acts with a pure, affirmative thought, happiness follows him." The Egyptian creation story emphasized the power of affirmative words for creating, just as does our own Genesis story of creation: "It was the Egyptian god who made the world, speaking it into existence. That which flows from his mouth happens, and that which he speaks comes into being." The Greeks said the word is filled with cosmic power. In India, the spoken word of affirmation is considered the greatest power in the world. The Chinese have long believed that words are so powerful that no piece of paper containing written words should ever be destroyed, even when it is no longer of value.

♥

(Isaiah 40:28-29)

28Hast thou not known? hast thou not heard, that the everlasting God, the LORD, the Creator of the ends of the earth, fainteth not, neither is weary? there is no searching of his understanding.

29He giveth power to the faint; and to them that have no might he increaseth strength.

A promise is only as good as the person making the promise. Our Creator is absolutely trustworthy.

Pray that God will turn your darkness into light.

(Psalm 18:28)

28For thou wilt light my candle: the LORD my God will enlighten my darkness.

♥

Although you perceive yourself as weak and frail, with wasted hopes and devastated dreams, born but to die, to weep and suffer pain, hear this: "All Power is given unto you in Earth and Heaven. There is nothing you cannot do."

faith . **HOPE** . love . mind . **BODY** . *spirit* .

Grandma's Shoebox

God never strays, only humans can stray off God's path. He is the same always, throughout all of time-past, present, future.

♥

El Roi – The Lord our God who knows everything about us. (Genesis 16:1-16)

1Now Sarai Abram's wife bare him no children: and she had an handmaid, an Egyptian, whose name was Hagar.

2And Sarai said unto Abram, Behold now, the LORD hath restrained me from bearing: I pray thee, go in unto my maid; it may be that I may obtain children by her. And Abram hearkened to the voice of Sarai.

3And Sarai Abram's wife took Hagar her maid the Egyptian, after Abram had dwelt ten years in the land of Canaan, and gave her to her husband Abram to be his wife.

4And he went in unto Hagar, and she conceived: and when she saw that she had conceived, her mistress was despised in her eyes.

5And Sarai said unto Abram, My wrong be upon thee: I have given my maid into thy bosom; and when she saw that she had conceived, I was despised in her eyes: the LORD judge between me and thee.

6But Abram said unto Sarai, Behold, thy maid is in thine hand; do to her as it pleaseth thee. And when Sarai dealt hardly with her, she fled from her face.

7And the angel of the LORD found her by a fountain of water in the wilderness, by the fountain in the way to Shur.

8And he said, Hagar, Sarai's maid, whence camest thou? and whither wilt thou go? And she said, I flee from the face of my mistress Sarai.

9And the angel of the LORD said unto her, Return to thy mistress, and submit thyself under her hands.

10And the angel of the LORD said unto her, I will multiply thy seed exceedingly, that it shall not be numbered for multitude.

faith . **HOPE** . love . mind . **BODY** . *spirit* .

11 And the angel of the LORD said unto her, Behold, thou art with child and shalt bear a son, and shalt call his name Ishmael; because the LORD hath heard thy affliction.

12 And he will be a wild man; his hand will be against every man, and every man's hand against him; and he shall dwell in the presence of all his brethren.

13 And she called the name of the LORD that spake unto her, Thou God seest me: for she said, Have I also here looked after him that seeth me?

14 Wherefore the well was called Beerlahairoi; behold, it is between Kadesh and Bered.

15 And Hagar bare Abram a son: and Abram called his son's name, which Hagar bare, Ishmael.

16 And Abram was fourscore and six years old, when Hagar bare Ishmael to Abram.

When you pray, ask God to increase your awareness of his presence in your life. God knows when even the smallest sparrow falls to the ground. Don't hesitate to ask him to hear your cries for help. Psychology, as well as religion, agrees that you should use a lot of verbal prayer. Psychology insists that the spoken word has more suggestive power, is more likely to reach and improve the deeper psychic levels of the mind, than mere inarticulate thought. Psychology insists that verbal prayer is very powerful for cleansing and improving the mind and emotions, because psychology has found that your centers of speech are closely connected with your mental life. Thus, when you speak forth good words, you improve your mental life.

Ishmael – The Hearing God

faith . **HOPE** . love . mind . **BODY** . _spirit_ .

Grandma's Shoebox

(Genesis 21:1-21)

1And the LORD visited Sarah as he had said, and the LORD did unto Sarah as he had spoken.

2For Sarah conceived, and bare Abraham a son in his old age, at the set time of which God had spoken to him.

3And Abraham called the name of his son that was born unto him, whom Sarah bare to him, Isaac.

4And Abraham circumcised his son Isaac being eight days old, as God had commanded him.

5And Abraham was an hundred years old, when his son Isaac was born unto him.

6And Sarah said, God hath made me to laugh, so that all that hear will laugh with me.

7And she said, Who would have said unto Abraham, that Sarah should have given children suck? for I have born him a son in his old age.

8And the child grew, and was weaned: and Abraham made a great feast the same day that Isaac was weaned.

9And Sarah saw the son of Hagar the Egyptian, which she had born unto Abraham, mocking.

10Wherefore she said unto Abraham, Cast out this bondwoman and her son: for the son of this bondwoman shall not be heir with my son, even with Isaac.

11And the thing was very grievous in Abraham's sight because of his son.

12And God said unto Abraham, Let it not be grievous in thy sight because of the lad, and because of thy bondwoman; in all that Sarah hath said unto thee, hearken unto her voice; for in Isaac shall thy seed be called.

13And also of the son of the bondwoman will I make a nation, because he is thy seed.

faith . HOPE . love . mind . BODY . *spirit*.

14And Abraham rose up early in the morning, and took bread, and a bottle of water, and gave it unto Hagar, putting it on her shoulder, and the child, and sent her away: and she departed, and wandered in the wilderness of Beersheba.

15And the water was spent in the bottle, and she cast the child under one of the shrubs.

16And she went, and sat her down over against him a good way off, as it were a bow shot: for she said, Let me not see the death of the child. And she sat over against him, and lift up her voice, and wept.

17And God heard the voice of the lad; and the angel of God called to Hagar out of heaven, and said unto her, What aileth thee, Hagar? fear not; for God hath heard the voice of the lad where he is.

18Arise, lift up the lad, and hold him in thine hand; for I will make him a great nation.

19And God opened her eyes, and she saw a well of water; and she went, and filled the bottle with water, and gave the lad drink.

20And God was with the lad; and he grew, and dwelt in the wilderness, and became an archer.

21And he dwelt in the wilderness of Paran: and his mother took him a wife out of the land of Egypt.

Thank God for hearing your prayers. Open your eyes to the works of the Lord, increase your faith even when you feel nothing but despair. In the final analysis, the practice of prayer is the ultimate secret to success on all levels of life.

(Psalm 33:13-22)

13The LORD looketh from heaven; he beholdeth all the sons of men.

14From the place of his habitation he looketh upon all the inhabitants of the earth.

15He fashioneth their hearts alike; he considereth all their works.

faith . **HOPE** . love . mind . **BODY** . *spirit* .

Grandma's Shoebox

16There is no king saved by the multitude of an host: a mighty man is not delivered by much strength.

17An horse is a vain thing for safety: neither shall he deliver any by his great strength.

18Behold, the eye of the LORD is upon them that fear him, upon them that hope in his mercy;

19To deliver their soul from death, and to keep them alive in famine.

20Our soul waiteth for the LORD: he is our help and our shield.

21For our heart shall rejoice in him, because we have trusted in his holy name.

22Let thy mercy, O LORD, be upon us, according as we hope in thee.

When you pray, cry out to the Lord from whose eyes nothing is hidden. Scripture makes it very clear that God never sleeps. While alone with nature, the ancient people knew the great secrets of the universe. They felt there was a miracle consciousness, which when discovered and tapped, could perform miracles in an instant. I believe it!

♥

Blessings = Faith   Faith = Blessings

You can't have one without the other.
Faith is to believe what one has not seen. The reward of faith is to see what one has believed.

Develop your convictions, your certainty in God. Look around; this world can be a beautiful place. You can find beauty in your world. You can find peace and happiness. It's out there; just keep your faith and believe.

faith . **HOPE** . love . mind . **BODY** . *spirit* .

Chapter 3 - God

♥

If life's challenges are making you weak, the best solution to any problem is to strengthen your commitment in Christ.

By refusing to dwell on a problem and turning it over to God, you are allowing the divine consciousness of love and peace to flow into you. This spiritual awareness brings the solution to the problems you are mulling over and over in your mind.

(Psalm 121:3, 5-8)

3He will not suffer thy foot to be moved: he that keepeth thee will not slumber.

5The LORD is thy keeper: the LORD is thy shade upon thy right hand.

6The sun shall not smite thee by day, nor the moon by night.

7The LORD shall preserve thee from all evil: he shall preserve thy soul.

8The LORD shall preserve thy going out and thy coming in from this time forth, and even for evermore.

(Matthew 6:3-4)

3But when thou doest alms, let not thy left hand know what thy right hand doeth:

4That thine alms may be in secret: and thy Father which seeth in secret himself shall reward thee openly.

(Deuteronomy 12:28)

28Observe and hear all these words which I command thee, that it may go well with thee, and with thy children after thee for ever, when thou doest that which is good and right in the sight of the LORD thy God.

faith . **HOPE** . love . mind . **BODY** . *spirit* .

(Matthew 5:8)

8Blessed are the pure in heart: for they shall see God.

When you pray to El Shadday, you are invoking the name of the Lord for whom nothing is impossible.

Creative imagination is a form of prayer. Jesus was speaking of creative imagination when he said, "What things so ever ye desire, when ye pray, believe that ye receive them, and ye shall have them." In other words, if you can imagine receiving your desires, they will come into your experience.

(Genesis 17:1-8, 15-18)

1And when Abram was ninety years old and nine, the LORD appeared to Abram, and said unto him, I am the Almighty God; walk before me, and be thou perfect.

2And I will make my covenant between me and thee, and will multiply thee exceedingly.

3And Abram fell on his face: and God talked with him, saying,

4As for me, behold, my covenant is with thee, and thou shalt be a father of many nations.

5Neither shall thy name any more be called Abram, but thy name shall be Abraham; for a father of many nations have I made thee.

6And I will make thee exceeding fruitful, and I will make nations of thee, and kings shall come out of thee.

7And I will establish my covenant between me and thee and thy seed after thee in their generations for an everlasting covenant, to be a God unto thee, and to thy seed after thee.

8And I will give unto thee, and to thy seed after thee, the land wherein thou art a stranger, all the land of Canaan, for an everlasting possession; and I will be their God.

15And God said unto Abraham, As for Sarai thy wife, thou shalt not call her name Sarai, but Sarah shall her name be.

faith . **HOPE** . love . mind . **BODY** . *spirit* .

Chapter 3 - God

16And I will bless her, and give thee a son also of her: yea, I will bless her, and she shall be a mother of nations; kings of people shall be of her.

17Then Abraham fell upon his face, and laughed, and said in his heart, Shall a child be born unto him that is an hundred years old? and shall Sarah, that is ninety years old, bear?

18And Abraham said unto God, O that Ishmael might live before thee!

Our Lord has made an everlasting covenant with us. (Galations 3:7)
7Know ye therefore that they which are of faith, the same are the children of Abraham.

(Psalm 91: 1-2,14)
1He that dwelleth in the secret place of the most High shall abide under the shadow of the Almighty.

2I will say of the LORD, He is my refuge and my fortress: my God; in him will I trust.

14Because he hath set his love upon me, therefore will I deliver him: I will set him on high, because he hath known my name.

Give thanks for the Lord's blessings. When you pray, ask God to increase your trust in him in the days and months to follow. God's love is everlasting, and his patience endures forever. If you have to cry out for God's help two hundred times a day to defeat a particular temptation, he will still be eager to give mercy and grace, so come boldly. Ask him for the power to do the right thing and expect him to provide it.

♥

God always puts the sweet summer memories in your heart...He will always take you back...you can always start again.

faith. **HOPE**. love. mind. **BODY**. *spirit*.

When you pray, you should talk to God like you are talking to a dear friend. Prayer is not magic; it is speaking with our Father. If all of your wishes were "granted" and every problem solved, then what lessons would you be learning here on earth? Sometimes the answer to your prayer is the solution to your problem.

♥

When you read the Bible you must research the information that you are reading. God wants you to figure it out for yourself…that is how you find your way home.

In the Bible there are many accounts of a desert. The desert times are the time of transition and testing. God's people were in the desert and challenged to trust and to obey his words when He promised to lead them to the promise land. Learn what it means to rest in the shadow of the Almighty God. Study Psalm 91.

(Psalm 91: 1-16)

1He that dwelleth in the secret place of the most High shall abide under the shadow of the Almighty.

2I will say of the LORD, He is my refuge and my fortress: my God; in him will I trust.

3Surely he shall deliver thee from the snare of the fowler, and from the noisome pestilence.

4He shall cover thee with his feathers, and under his wings shalt thou trust: his truth shall be thy shield and buckler.

5Thou shalt not be afraid for the terror by night; nor for the arrow that flieth by day;

6Nor for the pestilence that walketh in darkness; nor for the destruction that wasteth at noonday.

7A thousand shall fall at thy side, and ten thousand at thy right hand; but it shall not come nigh thee.

8Only with thine eyes shalt thou behold and see the reward of the wicked.

faith . HOPE . love . mind . BODY . *spirit* .

Chapter 3 - God

9Because thou hast made the LORD, which is my refuge, even the most High, thy habitation;

10There shall no evil befall thee, neither shall any plague come nigh thy dwelling.

11For he shall give his angels charge over thee, to keep thee in all thy ways.

12They shall bear thee up in their hands, lest thou dash thy foot against a stone.

13Thou shalt tread upon the lion and adder: the young lion and the dragon shalt thou trample under feet.

14Because he hath set his love upon me, therefore will I deliver him: I will set him on high, because he hath known my name.

15He shall call upon me, and I will answer him: I will be with him in trouble; I will deliver him, and honour him.

16With long life will I satisfy him, and shew him my salvation.

Can you call to mind a period or time in your life when you experienced God's care and protection in your life? In July 2008 as I write these words, my life is going through an extreme transition…I will share what I think will interest you, and most important, how I have been protected.

In April 2005, I ended a business partnership that began in 1994. I owned 50% of a mortgage company with my husband's cousin. After being in business for 11 + years together, we were no longer able to see eye to eye on many issues. I wanted out. To get out, I think I would have done just about anything. During the short-term relationship that was created through our contract, the company was "defrauded" by a real estate agent who was falsifying documents to obtain loans for homes that he was selling. Our company did 50+ loans with this agent. Please know that we were not a "large" company.

faith . **HOPE**. love . mind . **BODY** . *spirit*.

Within a matter of months, foreclosures began on these loans. The borrowers did not have the income to cover the loan, and they never made their payments. For 3 years, we have been battling this issue with one of the largest banks in the country. They are in the process of suing my ex-partner for more than two million dollars. In turn, my ex-partner is suing me. It is without question the biggest nightmare in my life to date.

When I was served with the court documents for the lawsuit, I got up from my desk and went home. I was just simply ill. I was ill with fear, I was ill with the thought of 2 million dollars, I was petrified of going to federal court with any issue. My daughter, who is a new young attorney, told me that the cost of federal court alone would be devastating. Everything that I had worked for over the past 30 years would be lost. My family would go through some extremely difficult times because of this issue.

If you take into consideration the current economic conditions of the US real estate and mortgage industry you know that there is no way I can survive this crisis. My life is about to be changed drastically and I am about to head down another path.
I could not eat, I could not sleep, I could not focus…I was lost. So I did what I have always done. I prayed, and I prayed, and I prayed. I cried and I ask for help from the only person that I knew could help me. I have done multiple novenas; I have spent hours and hours meditating on this issue. I have studied scripture and spirituality for more than 30 years and I knew that my answers were going to be found there. I just needed to find them. The first thing that popped into my head was to start with what I had. However, I wasn't sure just what that was. I knew that I was asking constantly for help. I just wanted the problem to go away and get out of my life.

faith . **HOPE** . love . mind . **BODY** . *spirit* .

I even went out and bought a few lottery tickets just in case that was going to be the answer to my prayers. Needless to say, I didn't win. So I prayed some more…I got the same answer again…start with what you already have.

I was sitting outside one Saturday afternoon in my back yard, and I was meditating. I kept focusing on "start with what I have." I finally said out loud, "Lord, please help me…I'm not sure what I have…I am so stressed and so upset that my mind is not picking up on what you think I already have. So if you don't mind, would you just put the thought into my head…because I am really struggling here." Then it hit me like a ton of bricks. The next thought in my head was FINISH YOUR BOOK. I started this book 10 years ago. I would work on it on the weekends in the winter months and whenever I was able to go on vacation. I have not been on a vacation for more than three years, so I had not done much work on my book.

I read at least 2 books a week, and I do a lot of research, but I had not spent much time putting my notes in order. A few years back I had even looked into a "ghost writer" to help me get organized. That was not the path for me. By the time I could have organized my notes for them, I could have finished the book.

I still own my mortgage company, and I have 10+ people still employed by my company. But as of today, July 28, 2008, I think its days are numbered. So instead of drowning in my sorrows of ending my mortgage career, I am finishing my book. I'm not afraid of what the future holds. I believe with all of my heart that God is watching over me throughout this tragic event in my life.

The Bible tells us that God the Almighty will always be a refuge for

faith . **HOPE** . love . mind . **BODY** . *spirit* .

us in the midst of a personal desert period. My husband is taking anti-depressants. I am praying and finding my strength in the Lord. One way or another, I know I will survive. My ex-partner and I did not commit the fraud that was done on those files. We were the victims of an evil man. I do not believe that God will make us pay the price for the sins of another. But in the meantime, it's important to keep the faith in my heart alive and move forward.

On September 9, 2008 my prayers were partially answered. I was notified that the judge would not allow my ex-partner to bring me into his federal law suit. This doesn't mean that my problems are gone, but it does mean that my prayers were heard.

♥

God wants you to know him and to love him. He is full of wisdom and infinite love for you. He has the power to give you wisdom and love. So many times, people have prayed for one thing only to be given something far greater by a much wiser Father. So if you don't get exactly what you asked for, don't be disappointed, sometimes you weren't asking for enough.

When I am praying, I always ask for God to hear the cries of my heart. I am always looking for the sign that I know he hears me. There are times when I actually feel the softest breath upon my skin, and then I know that he is listening.

♥

Don't let there be any weeds on your path to faith in God.

You can't sit back and wonder why am I not the other guy? Why does everything seem to happen to me? Nothing in life is not without God's plan. He is the Master Teacher. He does have a plan for everyone. The question is, are you a part of his plan? Are you on the path to God? Or are you on a path to destruction? You are either with him or against him! When you reach a certain level of belief and faith, you realize that there is no "in-between." When that

. *faith* . **HOPE** . love . mind . **BODY** . *spirit* .

Chapter 3 - God

happens, you take control of your "fate" and your destiny; you have found your faith. You know that all things are possible. Just go to the messages from your Father to get your answers.

♥

You must know and feel that God is in the world around you and within you. He is your friend at all times. His friendship never changes. It is eternal. A friendship with God is the secret for peace and joy in your life. It is also the secret to achievement. When you have a close friendship with God you will know how to carry your burdens and not be overwhelmed by them.

(Psalm 33:13-22)

13The LORD looketh from heaven; he beholdeth all the sons of men.

14From the place of his habitation he looketh upon all the inhabitants of the earth.

15He fashioneth their hearts alike; he considereth all their works.

16There is no king saved by the multitude of a host: a mighty man is not delivered by much strength.

17An horse is a vain thing for safety: neither shall he deliver any by his great strength.

18Behold, the eye of the LORD is upon them that fear him, upon them that hope in his mercy;

19To deliver their soul from death, and to keep them alive in famine.

20Our soul waiteth for the LORD: he is our help and our shield.

21For our heart shall rejoice in him, because we have trusted in his holy name.

22Let thy mercy, O LORD, be upon us, according as we hope in thee.

♥

.faith . HOPE . love . mind . BODY . spirit .

Grandma's Shoebox

You can have a conversation with your Father; just open up your heart first, and then your mind will follow. I know that I have had many, and there is nothing like it in this world when you feel his presence with you. God puts desire into your soul! True desire is to know him, to feel his presence, to get that feeling that what "that book, the Bible, says is true."

If you don't understand, keep going within and asking. Going within, means going to God. You will find him there; just allow yourself to look. He is there. Even when the going gets really rough, He is there, He's just waiting on you to call on him. The best way to call him is through your heart. Some people call this "soul search-ing." When you have a longing that is being unfulfilled in your soul, eventually it will cry out to you, "STOP. Take me home."
That is when you will start back on your search for God. He will be calling on each and every one of us in His own way. For some it may be financial problems, for others it could be the lack of love in your life. What's worse? Well, I guess that depends on who you ask. If you are going through financial difficultie,s then for you that is worse. Guess what: that's OK! The answer isn't always love in the first degree. There are many levels to love. When you find what level you are dealing with, it is love that will solve your problems. But that love is really coming from your Father's heart. It doesn't matter what version of the "Book" you are reading; love does solve all things.

(Deuteronomy 7:13)
And he will love thee, and bless thee, and multiply thee: he will also bless the fruit of thy womb, and the fruit of thy land, thy corn, and thy wine, and thine oil, the increase of thy kine, and the flocks of thy sheep, in the land which he sware unto thy fathers to give thee.

faith . **HOPE** . love . mind . **BODY** . *spirit* .

♥

Learn first who you are as a child of the Father. Then you will know yourself as whatever you want to be. "As long as ye are one!" It's when you lose this thought that crisis happens in your life. Just know that is just his way of lining up his ducklings. It's all a part of nature. God tries to keep all of us in line at whatever age or level we are experiencing. If you keep getting out of line, it's only natural that he would eventually have to swat you a little harder trying to get you back on the right path. If you are experiencing any major difficulties make sure you are finding your way back on the right path.

♥

Example of God's intervention:
He does not take away our problems; he gives us the resources to cope with them. When you are researching your resources you will find him there.

♥

To accomplish our mission, we must think with the mind of God, Love with the heart of God, and act with the strength of God.

♥

Those who believe in a personal God, force their eyes back. They consider caring for the poor and disabled courageous rather than absurd or meaningless. Survival of the fittest is a problem to cure, not a reality to accept. God cares for the needy through the heroic, through those willing to sacrifice themselves on behalf of another.

(Deuteronomy 15:11)
11For the poor shall never cease out of the land: therefore I command thee, saying, Thou shalt open thine hand wide unto thy brother, to thy poor, and to thy needy, in thy land.

It takes a tribe to raise a child. We all play a part or a role in the tribe. It's not all about you and it never will be. It's all about each other,

faith . **HOPE** . love . mind . **BODY** . *spirit* .

Grandma's Shoebox

knowing that to God "everybody matters." If it matters to him, it should matter to you.

♥

Man has accomplished some terrific things. But it is God who gave us the inclination and capacity to do so.

(Deuteronomy 4:1)
  1Now therefore hearken, O Israel, unto the statutes and unto the judgments, which I teach you, for to do them, that ye may live, and go in and possess the land which the LORD God of your fathers giveth you.

(Deuteronomy 4:40)
  40Thou shalt keep therefore his statutes, and his commandments, which I command thee this day, that it may go well with thee, and with thy children after thee, and that thou mayest prolong thy days upon the earth, which the LORD thy God giveth thee, for ever. "The Lord giveth, and he can take it away…"

♥

Deep within every human soul lives a desire for justice. It belongs in your soul, not in your hands. Be careful with this lesson. The hurdles could be really bumpy. God sees all and he knows all things. Let it go, and let God deal with it.

(Passage 2 Chronicles 9:8)
  8Blessed be the LORD thy God, which delighted in thee to set thee on his throne, to be king for the LORD thy God: because thy God loved Israel, to establish them for ever, therefore made he thee king over them, to do judgment and justice.

♥

Forgive those as they forgive… that's an early chapter in the book of

faith . **HOPE**. love . mind . **BODY** . *spirit* .

life. If you really care the way God wants you to…then you can find forgiveness in your heart.

(Acts 26:18)
18To open their eyes, and to turn them from darkness to light, and from the power of Satan unto God, that they may receive forgiveness of sins, and inheritance among them which are sanctified by faith that is in me.

♥

Our good nature can only do for us what it can do through us! It has been lying down on the job, awaiting our recognition of it. If our divine nature worked with no recognition from us, we would be automated with no freedom of expression or power of choice. And that is exactly what man was given in the beginning: freedom of choice and dominion over everything in the universe. It has been up to man since the beginning of time to claim and use that freedom and dominion. It's still up to him today. Some things will never change.

(Genesis 1:26)
26And God said, Let us make man in our image, after our likeness: and let them have dominion over the fish of the sea, and over the fowl of the air, and over the cattle, and over all the earth, and over every creeping thing that creepeth upon the earth.

♥

For nothing happens by accident in God's world, and there is no such thing as coincidence.

♥

I tell you now that the answer is within. Every Heart which sincerely asks, "Which is the path to God?" is shown. Come to me along the path of your heart, not through a journey of the mind. You will never find me in your mind. In order to truly know God, you have to be out of your mind.

faith . **HOPE** . love . mind . **BODY** . *spirit* .

Grandma's Shoebox

(Exodus 4:14)

14And the anger of the LORD was kindled against Moses, and he said, Is not Aaron the Levite thy brother? I know that he can speak well. And also, behold, he cometh forth to meet thee: and when he seeth thee, he will be glad in his heart.

♥

When you find a child growing up amid injustice, you can know that before his birth his soul chose those circumstances through which to evolve, ultimately to fulfill its divine destiny. You can know that such a soul is a strong soul who will often go on to a better adult life than will other youngsters around him who are facing less strenuous challenges. How true it is that "Out of the mud, comes the lily." As you read the biographies of great people who have made splendid contributions to mankind, you often find a history of obvious injustice in their early lives. Instead of feeling sorry for children in the midst of injustice, affirm: "The hidden law of justice is at work for you, making all things right."

(Isaiah 59:9)

9Therefore is judgment far from us, neither doth justice overtake us: we wait for light, but behold obscurity; for brightness, but we walk in darkness.

♥

When you hear of a person dying an "untimely death", it seems unjust, especially if a spouse and young children are left behind. But the soul decides when it will leave this world and under what circumstances. So there is truly no injustice. Always the power of choice has been exercised, though perhaps subconsciously. The soul is fulfilling its divine destiny in some way that you cannot see or understand humanly. Man is like an iceberg; in reality we see only a small part of his entire being.

♥

faith . **HOPE** . love . mind . **BODY** . *spirit* .

Chapter 3 - God

Love never dies. It lives on through eternity. Your heart always stays connected to all those you love and who love you. You take your love with you everywhere that you go.

(Jude 1:21)
 21Keep yourselves in the love of God, looking for the mercy of our Lord Jesus Christ unto eternal life.

If you follow your heart you will stay connected. You will know that you are connected when you feel like all the stars are lined up right. It comes down to just one moment, one breathtaking moment in your life. When you take that breath, the breath of life that was given to you from God the Father, you will believe. There will be no question of Faith. You will believe! Once you feel yourself on that path, I promise you this, you will never want to fall off of it again.

♥

The pictures that I have included in this book all came from my Grandma's shoebox. She took the time to cut them out and put them in her special box. There were many times in my life that she would show me the pictures in her shoebox. These are the pictures of faith that are forever etched in my memory. It's high time I put them in a special place in my home and stop keeping them in my heart all to myself. There is beauty in the Lord; it's all in the eyes of the beholder.

♥♥♥♥♥♥♥

. faith . HOPE . love . mind . BODY . spirit .

Grandma's Shoebox

Why I Go to Bald Head Island

It brings me closer to the Lord. When it comes to needing to get away from the world for a while and capture a little slice of heaven on earth for a while, that is what Bald Head does for me.

Of all my favorite memories of this world, this captures them for me. It saves them in my heart, and it forces me to pray and ask for forgiveness and to say thank you for all the blessings that have come my way. It is a place that is filled with emotions, of being able to let go and let God. I hope that someday one of my great-great-grandchildren will open this book and go experience it for themselves. If I can make my dreams come true I will leave this memory behind for you.

faith . HOPE . love . mind . **BODY** . *spirit* .

Chapter 3 - God

Chapter 4

Jesus in My Heart

"For God so loved the world that He gave His only begotten Son, that whosoever believeth in Him should not perish, but have everlasting life."

♥

The way that you receive God's blessings is to live your life as close as possible to the way that Jesus Christ said you are to live.

♥

You can overcome a lot of problems, and find that you will have happiness and prosperity when you develop your faith in at least these two things:

 1. In the beginning, God created the world filled with abundance and happiness, that He loves you and He wants you to have your fair share of happiness and abundance.

2. Jesus Christ is the Son of God, and he was sent here to save you from sin and to show you the way of life eternal and life abundant.

♥

Fill your heart with love; let your life become alive again…
I do not know where I would be today without the faith that I hold in my heart.

♥

"For whosoever will save his life shall lose it, but whosoever shall lose his life will save it. But he that giveth his life shall find it a hundredfold."

♥

Jesus taught, "As a man thinketh, so shall it be," he was reminding us that we must keep our mind on our hopes, not our fears. We must focus on our heart's desires rather than our nightmares.
Forget it, it's over, move on, get over it, it's done for the day. Some problems stick around a little longer than others; sometimes this is

faith . **HOPE** . love . mind . **BODY** . *spirit* .

because others are learning on the same lesson plane. It's not always a private tutorial. Think about it, there really are no coincidences.

♥

If adversity moves us to rediscover ourselves and the God within us, it becomes an important ally. Pain and challenge are the universe's way of getting our attention so we can shift direction from loss to success. "Make your mess your message" is an old saying of my Grandmother's. Don't keep your problems all to yourself. Share them with others. God is trying to answer your prayers. When you get the solution to those problems, be sure you share your blessings too!

♥

If you can get through your problems, then you can help others get through theirs.
If you have issues, put them out there, ask for forgiveness when necessary, and then count your blessings, because help is on the way.

♥

When confronted with a situation that appears to make us fall to pieces or seems impossible, step back for a moment, close your eyes, and mentally envision perfection behind the situation. Go to that inner place where there is no problem, and believe in that consciousness. Then step into the vision of how different things would (and will) be when the problem has been handled, and it will. "This too shall pass." To live in a heavenly world, we must see through heavenly vision.

♥

The Father had already developed the plan and Jesus's responsibility was to carefully obey his Father's will. Jesus's own words say it best: "I tell you the truth, the Son can do nothing by himself; he can do only what he sees his Father doing, because whatever the Father does

. faith . HOPE . love . mind . BODY . spirit .

Chapter 4 - Jesus in My Heart

the Son also does. For the Father loves the Son and shows him all he does. Yes, to your amazement he will show him even greater things than these….By myself I can do nothing, I judge only as I hear, and my judgment is just, for I seek not to please myself but him who sent me" (John 5:19-20, 30 NIV).

Whenever and wherever he saw his Father at work, Jesus immediately joined him.

You can search your whole life through, sooner or later you will find out it all comes down to this!

The son shows him all he does, he really does see all! Would you always do what you are doing if you knew your Father were watching? Learn the lesson. It may be a hard one, but it must be learned.

♥

Whenever two people begin thinking about an objective in a harmonious way, there is double mind power at work, so that increased energy and ideas are released upon the objective. Jesus was speaking of this power when He said: "If two of you shall agree on earth as touching anything that they shall ask, it shall be done for them of my Father which is in heaven." (Matthew 18:19)

♥

Both of your genius powers—intuition and creative imagination —respond best to harmonious minds. Your genius powers are delicate powers that come forth forcefully only under receptive conditions of mind and atmosphere.

♥

He taught us a lesson of love. He taught that we need not be attached to any one career or job or accomplishment, but only to remember that everything in life is a blessing and that fulfillment and peace are always available to us.

Sometimes careers do change; you will make a turn on your path. It's not always a straight shot on your map. There will be curves and bumps along the way. You just have to enjoy the ride, and follow the path with great expectation to find the end. Eventually the search will lead us back to our true mission and the road home. In time we will remember who sent us and why.

♥

God's friendship is clearly understood and pointed out when Jesus said to his Disciples: "When ye pray say Father." Just the word Father paints a completely different picture of God. You can be dear friends with your "Father"; you can go to your "Father" for help and guidance in any situation. He is the one you can also go to for comfort when you need to tell your problems to someone, no matter how large or small they may be. If you really want to know "God" as your friend, put aside 10 minutes a day for your "Father." In this short period you will be amazed at what happens when you let his Spirit in, and His friendship will then follow.

A Chinese philosopher once said: "Go often to the house of your 'friend' lest weeds spring up in the path and you cannot find the way."

♥

Think about it. Before Jesus can comfort us, before He can help us and heal us, we must have the attitude that we are willing to be helped! He cannot make us happy unless we want to be happy.

♥

Only your way of thinking can conceal the truth from you or reveal the truth to you. As a man thinketh in his heart, so shall he be. To repeat; there is no partition between you and your source. I and my father are one.

There is power in one; one person can make a difference in this world. The world is full of examples of people who do. You can make a difference in the world, in the acts of kindness that you share, in the way that you chose to treat all the people in your life.

. *faith* . **HOPE** . love . mind . **BODY** . *spirit* .

Chapter 4 - Jesus in My Heart

If you make the choice to be kind instead of angry, if you make the choice to love instead of being cruel, all these things make a difference in the life of the other person.

When you chose to give words of hope and encouragement to someone else, God rewards you with what you give. If you could read the hearts and minds of others you might find that they want the same things in life as you: for their serious problems to be solved, for their homes to be happy and joyous, and for all that they know and love to be healthy.

In order to make this world a better place it only has to start with only one person and it starts in your heart. It then moves to the choices you make in your mind. Once in your mind it becomes the example you set for others, it becomes what you try to teach your children so that they will live a life that you know God wants them to live.

When your heart changes to live a life of kindness and generosity those who view you as a mentor learn to do the same, and before long you have touched the lives of hundreds or thousands of people.

There is a song on the radio that says: "She just might be an angel." Every time I hear this song it makes me think about the angels that God places here on earth. My point about this song is in one particular verse that talks about giving to a man on the street.

When I see someone standing on the street corner with a cardboard sign that says: "Help", then I give. I give because my heart aches for their souls. I will stop at a green light to give, hoping that maybe it will inspire the people behind me to do the same thing. I always ask God to bless this soul and help them to find their way so that they don't have to struggle too long.

♥

One day when my daughter was about 8 or 9 years old there was a man standing on the corner of a very busy intersection, his card board sign said: "My family is homeless, please help me feed them."

I was reaching in my purse to give him some money and my little girl came across the seat with all the money she had in her purse and tears were rolling down her cheeks. She gave him all that she had to help make his life a little better. As we pulled away with the cars behind us honking, she asked me, "Why can't we just take that man and his family home with us? Nobody should be homeless, especially little children."

Later that same evening there was a documentary on TV about some people who were actually making a living by begging on the streets. My daughter looked at me knowing she had just given all of her money away that day to a man on the streets.

This is what I told her: God is watching all of us, all the time. You do each day what you feel in your heart is the right thing to do. Today God saw you give a gift straight from your heart and he smiled. If the person who took the gift was not really in need, then God saw that, too. One day he will have to seek forgiveness for his own soul. But what you did today was a beautiful thing. Don't ever stop giving from your heart. When your heart tells you, or compels you to give, then follow the signs from your heart. Maybe, just maybe, the man on the street corner was one of God's angels, and every car in the line was being tested today. If that was the case you got an "A."

♥

"In my Father's house are many mansions…"

The thoughts we think, the prayers we offer, the good we do in this world lives on, influencing and affecting not only our souls after death, but also the world we leave behind. In other words, nothing ever dies.

When you leave this earthly plain, how will you be remembered? Then how will you be recognized when you get home?

♥

faith . **HOPE**. love . mind . **BODY** . *spirit* .

Chapter 4 - Jesus in My Heart

Paul told Timothy, "Reflect on what I am saying, for the Lord will give you insight into all this."

If you really want to improve your life, memorizing scripture may be the most important habit you can begin.

Writing down your thoughts is the best way to clarify them. Reflect, think, take time…you will find your own answers. He will put them there for you to discover.

♥

If you truly desire to change your relationship, that change begins with the intention to change it. How it will change depends upon the intention that you set.

If you are not aware of all of your intentions, the strongest one will win. Know what is going on in your life at all times. Keep your life's journal, that way you can ask forgiveness and count your blessings each and everyday. Then offer your words in that journal to the Lord your Father.

You create your reality with your intentions.

♥

Say to yourself often: "THROUGH THE POWER OF CHRIST IN ME, MY LIFE CAN BE AS WONDERFUL AS I WANT IT TO BE!" Whether it seems to be literally true or not, begin to think of yourself as glorious, splendid, beloved, strong, well, and capable. Begin to think of the world as a beautiful place in which to live, work, grow, and play. Affirm often for others, especially those who trouble you: "THROUGH THE POWER OF CHRIST IN YOU, YOUR LIFE CAN BE AS WONDERFUL AS YOU WANT IT TO BE!" You will be surprised how this simple, delightful way of thinking will

. faith . HOPE . love . mind . BODY . spirit .

resurrect--bring back to notice, restore to life--your good. Also, declare often for any situation that troubles you: "I APPRAISE THIS SITUATION AS GOOD."

Jesus asked us to do things in remembrance of him. "The Lord Jesus on the night he was betrayed took bread, and when he had given thanks, he broke it, and said "this is my body which is for you. Do this in remembrance of me." In the same way he took the cup, "This is the new covenant in my blood. Do this, as often as you drink it, in remembrance of me." How are you remembering him? When you take the sacraments on Sunday, you are saying, "I will do things in remembrance if how Jesus lived his life. I will try to live my life close to the way he lived his…WWJD…what would Jesus do?"

♥

Your spiritual growth will contribute to your mastery of living, allowing you to live with more joy, aliveness, and love. Any energy you spend on growth will come back to you multiplied. The more you work on your spiritual growth, the more easily you will manifest what you want. Every moment spent loving others, growing, and expressing your aliveness will create enormous gains.

To grow spiritually it is important to know you create your own reality. A major turning point in your growth comes when you begin to take responsibility for everything that happens.

You create your reality through your thoughts, emotions, beliefs, and intent, which determine your vibration and thus the people, objects, events, and circumstances you attract to your life. Your emotions and your intent determine how fast you get what you are thinking about. Everything in your life comes from a thought or feeling you have, for your inner world of thoughts and feelings creates your outer world of events, objects, and relationships. Because you create your own

faith . HOPE . love . mind . BODY . *spirit* .

Chapter 4 - Jesus in My Heart

reality, you can choose any reality you want.

♥

The fact is that the greatest discovery of all ages is that all things apparently have their source in the invisible, intangible ether. What Jesus taught so profoundly in symbols about the riches of the kingdom of the heavens has now been proven to be true.

According to the Greek, the language in which the New Testament has come down to us, Jesus did not use the word "heaven" but the word "heavens" in His teaching. He was not telling us of the glories of some faraway place called "heaven" but was revealing the properties of the "heavens" all around us, called both "space" and "ether" by physicists. He taught not only its dynamic but also its intelligent character, and said that the entity that rules it is within man: "The kingdom of God is within you." He not only described this kingdom of the heavens in numerous parables but made its attainment by man the greatest object of human existence. He not only set this as man's goal but attained it Himself, thereby demonstrating that His teaching is practical as well as true
Heaven is a plane of existence, accessible to all, depending upon your state of divinity.

♥

. *faith* . **HOPE** . love . mind . **BODY** . *spirit* .

Grandma's Shoebox

Chapter 5

Honor Thy Father And Thy Mother

faith . **HOPE** . love . mind . **BODY** . _spirit_ .

What does it mean to honor your Father and Mother? Are you doing this?

(Exodus 34:28)

28And he was there with the LORD forty days and forty nights; he did neither eat bread, nor drink water. And he wrote upon the tables the words of the covenant, the Ten Commandments.

(Deuteronomy 4:13)

13And he declared unto you his covenant, which he commanded you to perform, even Ten Commandments; and he wrote them upon two tables of stone.

(Deuteronomy 10)

1 At that time the LORD said unto me, Hew thee two tables of stone like unto the first, and come up unto me into the mount, and make thee an ark of wood.

2 And I will write on the tables the words that were in the first tables which thou brakest, and thou shalt put them in the ark.

3 And I made an ark of shittim wood, and hewed two tables of stone like unto the first, and went up into the mount, having the two tables in mine hand.

4 And he wrote on the tables, according to the first writing, the ten commandments, which the LORD spake unto you in the mount out of the midst of the fire in the day of the assembly: and the LORD gave them unto me.

5 And I turned myself and came down from the mount, and put the tables in the ark which I had made; and there they be, as the LORD commanded me.

6 And the children of Israel took their journey from Beeroth of the children of Jaakan to Mosera: there Aaron died, and there he was

buried; and Eleazar his son ministered in the priest's office in his stead.

7 From thence they journeyed unto Gudgodah; and from Gudgodah to Jotbath, a land of rivers of waters.

8 At that time the LORD separated the tribe of Levi, to bear the ark of the covenant of the LORD, to stand before the LORD to minister unto him, and to bless in his name, unto this day.

9 Wherefore Levi hath no part nor inheritance with his brethren; the LORD is his inheritance, according as the LORD thy God promised him.

10 And I stayed in the mount, according to the first time, forty days and forty nights; and the LORD hearkened unto me at that time also, and the LORD would not destroy thee.

11 And the LORD said unto me, Arise, take thy journey before the people, that they may go in and possess the land, which I sware unto their fathers to give unto them.

12 And now, Israel, what doth the LORD thy God require of thee, but to fear the LORD thy God, to walk in all his ways, and to love him, and to serve the LORD thy God with all thy heart and with all thy soul,

13 To keep the commandments of the LORD, and his statutes, which I command thee this day for thy good?

14 Behold, the heaven and the heaven of heavens is the LORD's thy God, the earth also, with all that therein is.

15 Only the LORD had a delight in thy fathers to love them, and he chose their seed after them, even you above all people, as it is this day.

16 Circumcise therefore the foreskin of your heart, and be no more stiffnecked.

17 For the LORD your God is God of gods, and Lord of lords, a great God, a mighty, and a terrible, which regardeth not persons, nor taketh reward:

. faith . HOPE . love . mind . BODY . spirit .

Chapter 5 - Honor Thy Father And Thy Mother

18He doth execute the judgment of the fatherless and widow, and loveth the stranger, in giving him food and raiment.

19Love ye therefore the stranger: for ye were strangers in the land of Egypt.

20Thou shalt fear the LORD thy God; him shalt thou serve, and to him shalt thou cleave, and swear by his name.

21He is thy praise, and he is thy God, that hath done for thee these great and terrible things, which thine eyes have seen.

22Thy fathers went down into Egypt with threescore and ten persons; and now the LORD thy God hath made thee as the stars of heaven for multitude.

♥

The Fifth Commandment

A Commandment with a Promise

"Honor thy father and thy mother: that thy days may be long upon the land which the LORD thy God giveth thee," (Exodus 20:12). "Honor thy father and thy mother, as the LORD thy God hath commanded thee; that thy days may be prolonged, and that it may go well with thee, in the land which the LORD thy God giveth thee," (Deuteronomy 5:16). "Ye shall fear every man his mother, and his Father . . . ," (Leviticus 19:3). "Children, obey your parents in the Lord: for this is right. Honor thy father and thy mother; which is the first commandment with promise; that it may be well with thee, and thou mayest live long on the earth. And, ye Fathers, provoke not your children to wrath: but bring them up in the nurture and admonition of the Lord," (Ephesians 6:1-4). "Children, obey your parents in all things: for this is well pleasing unto the Lord. Fathers, provoke not your children to anger, lest they be discouraged," (Colossians 3:20-21).

faith . HOPE . love . mind . **BODY** . *spirit*.

"My son, hear the instruction of thy father, and forsake not the law of thy mother," (Proverbs 1:8). "A wise son maketh a glad father: but a foolish man despiseth his mother," (Proverbs 15:20). "Children's children are the crown of old men; and the glory of children are their fathers," and, "A foolish son is a grief to his father, and bitterness to her that bare him," (Proverbs 17:6, 25). "A foolish son is the calamity of his father," and, "He that wasteth his father, and chaseth away his mother, is a son that causeth shame, and bringeth reproach," (Proverbs 19:13, 26). "Hearken unto thy father that begat thee, and despise not thy mother when she is old," (Proverbs 23:22). "Correct thy son, and he shall give thee rest; yea, he shall give delight unto thy soul," (Proverbs 29:17). "For whom the Lord loveth He chasteneth, and scourgeth every son whom He receiveth," (Hebrews 12:6).

Not a Light Thing to Disobey Parents

"Cursed be he that setteth light by his father or his mother. And all the people shall say, Amen," (Deuteronomy 27:16). "And he that smiteth his father, or his mother, shall be surely put to death," And "he that curseth his father, or his mother, shall surely be put to death," (Exodus 21:15, 17). "For every one that curseth his father or his mother shall be surely put to death: he hath cursed his father or his mother; his blood shall be upon him," (Leviticus 20:9). "If a man have a stubborn and rebellious son, which will not obey the voice of his father, or the voice of his mother, and that, when they have chastened him, will not hearken unto them: Then shall his father and his mother lay hold of him, and bring him out unto the elders of his city, and unto the gate of his place; And they shall say unto the elders of his city, This our son is stubborn and rebellious, he will not obey our voice; he is a glutton, and a drunkard. And all the men of his city shall stone him with stones, that he die: so shalt thou put evil away from among you; and all Israel shall hear, and fear," (Deuteronomy 21:18-21).

faith . **HOPE** . love . mind . **BODY** . *spirit* .

Without Family Affection

"Thou shalt rise up before the hoary head, and honour the face of the old man, and fear thy God: I am the LORD," (Leviticus 19:32). "There is a generation that curseth their father, and doth not bless their mother," (Proverbs 30:11). "And I will give children to be their princes, and babes shall rule over them. And the people shall be oppressed, every one by another, and every one by his neighbor: the child shall behave himself proudly against the ancient, and the base against the honorable . . . . As for my people, children are their oppressors, and women rule over them," (Isaiah 3:4-5, 12). "This know also, that in the last days perilous times shall come. For men shall be lovers of their own selves, covetous, boasters, proud, blasphemers, disobedient to parents, unthankful, unholy, Without natural affection," (II Timothy 3:1-5).

"For God commanded, saying, Honor thy father and mother: and, He that curseth father or mother, let him die the death. But ye say, Whosoever shall say to his father or his mother, It is a gift, by whatsoever thou mightest be profited by me; And honor not his father or his mother, he shall be free. Thus have ye made the commandment of God of none effect by your tradition," (Matthew 15:4-6 [see also Mark 7:10-13]). ". . . what shall I do to inherit eternal life? . . . Thou knowest the commandments, . . . Honor thy father and thy mother," (Luke 18:18-20).

" . . . There is no man that hath left house, or parents, or brethren, or wife, or children, for the kingdom of Gods sake, Who shall not receive manifold more in this present time, and in the world to come life everlasting," (Luke 18:29-30). "If any man come to me, and hate not [love less by comparison] his father, and mother, and wife, and children, and brethren, and sisters, yea, and his own life also, he cannot be my disciple," (Luke 14:26).

♥

faith . HOPE . love . mind . **BODY** . *spirit* .

Some prosperous older parents seem to take no time or interest in their grandchildren. They may not even be aware of their selfishness and lack of love. They could be very happy enriching the lives of their grandchildren and others. Grandchildren need love and concern, not just money and gifts. If such people would only wake up, they would realize that showing love for others results in happiness for themselves.

Some fathers do not know how to relate to their children or show love and affection. Their children have a void in their lives because of the absence of fatherly love.

And there are fathers who provoke their children to wrath. They whip their children for every small matter, giving them no affection, and telling them "you'll never amount to a hill of beans." So the children begin to act as if this were true. They never see love and never learn how to give it.

Some parents are workhorses. The father struggles to succeed in making a living. He becomes frustrated and feels depressed and defeated, then turns around and imposes strict rules on his son, dealing out strict discipline when the son disobeys. And there is the teenage daughter with emotional problems, needing the counsel of a wise, loving mother. She doesn't get it because the mother is likewise struggling for material things. The Almighty is "visiting the iniquity of the fathers upon the children unto the third and fourth generation. . .," (Exodus 20:5).

Other parents want to "get rid" of their children for a few weeks vacation, and are happy when their children grow up and leave home so they can live their own lives. Some grandparents continue to selfishly pursue their own interests, forgetting their children and grandchildren. Some children abandon their parents to nursing homes. "May the kingdom come to bring the hearts of the children to the fathers, and the hearts of the fathers to their children" (Malachi 4:5-6).

♥

. faith . HOPE . love . mind . BODY . spirit .

Chapter 5 - Honor Thy Father And Thy Mother

The fifth commandment is the first with a promise: a long and happy life. It points to the divine family of God and living forever in one big happy family. Let us prepare for that time now by learning to honor our parents, and to be honorable parents.

♥

(Exodus 20:12)
12Honour thy father and thy mother: that thy days may be long upon the land which the LORD thy God giveth thee.
(Exodus 21:15)
15And he that smiteth his father, or his mother, shall be surely put to death.
(Leviticus 20:9)
For every one that curseth his father or his mother shall be surely put to death: he hath cursed his father or his mother; his blood shall be upon him.

♥

Thou Shalt Honor Thy Father and Mother
Martin Luther

The first work is that we honor our own father and mother. And this honor consists not only in respectful demeanor, but in this: that we obey them, look up to, esteem and heed their words and example, accept what they say, keep silent and endure their treatment of us, so long as it is not contrary to the first three Commandments. In addition, when they need it, that we provide them with food, clothing and shelter. For not for nothing has He said: "Thou shalt honor them"; He does not say: "Thou shalt love them," although this also must be done. But honor is higher than mere love and includes a certain fear, which unites with love, and causes a man to fear offending them more than he fears the punishment. Just as there is fear in the honor we pay a sanctuary, and yet we do not flee from it as from a punishment, but draw near to it all the more. Such a fear mingled with love is the true honor; the other fear without any love is that which we have toward things which we despise or flee from, as we fear the hangman or punishment. There is no honor in that, for it is a fear without all love, nay, fear that has with it hatred and enmity. Of this we have a proverb of St. Jerome: What we fear, that we also hate. With such a fear God does not wish to be feared or honored, nor to have us honor our parents; but with the first, which is mingled with love and confidence.

♥

Recently one of my children asked me if I regretted having to take care of my parents financially. I could hardly believe that they would ask me this question. I looked at her and said the only thing that I regret is that I cannot do more.

When my mother was 59 she had a massive stroke. A couple of years later, my father had a brain tumor. They would never be able to work again. I don't come from a wealthy family, but I do come from a loving mother and father, and I would never turn my back on them. Whatever my circumstances are, taking care of them has always been very important to me. When I was a young girl, I needed them and they were always there for me. I owe them my life. No matter what I did as a child they were the people who taught me that you never turn your back on your family.

Sure, sometimes it's hard. But it's never something that I regret. It is an honor for me to take care of them. It's how I was raised. It's a very important lesson that I learned early in my life. My Grandmother on my mothers side always had someone living with her; my Great Grandmother lived on a farm and her daughter and son-in-law lived with her. My family has always taken care of each other. It's

. *faith* . **HOPE** . love . mind . **BODY** . *spirit* .

what family does. When it comes to love you don't count the cost. What counts is what you have in your heart.

♥

"Show honor to your parents and pay homage to them. This will cause blessings to descend upon you from the clouds of the bounty of your Lord, the Exalted, the Great."
Baha'i Faith
Baha'u'llah
in the Family Life compilation, pp. 386-38

♥

Honor your father and your mother, that your days may be long in the land which the Lord your God gives you.
Christianity & Judaism
Exodus 20:12

♥

Now, filial piety is the root of all virtue. And the stem out of which grows all moral teaching... our bodies--to every hair and bit of skin--are received by us from our parents, and we must not presume to injure or wound them: this is the beginning of filial piety. When we have established our character by the practice of the filial course, so as to make our name famous in future ages, and thereby glorify our parents: this is the end of filial piety. It commences with the service of parents; it proceeds to the service of the ruler; it is completed by the establishment of [good] character.
Confucianism
Confucianism. Classic on Filial Piety 1

♥

Do not neglect the works due to the gods and the fathers! Let your mother be to you like unto a god! Let your father be to you like unto a god!
Hinduism
aittiriyaka Upanishad 1.11.2

faith . **HOPE** . love . mind . **BODY** . *spirit* .

♥

Thy Lord has decreed... that you be kind to parents. Whether one or both of them attain old age in your lifetime, do not say to them a word of contempt, nor repel them, but address them in terms of honor. And, out of kindness, lower to them the wing of humility, and say, "My Lord! bestow on them Thy mercy even as they cherished me in childhood."
Islam
Qur'an 17.23

♥

One companion asked, "O Apostle of God! Who is the person worthiest of my consideration?" He replied, "Your mother." He asked again, "And second to my mother?" The Prophet said, "Your mother." The companion insisted, "And then?" The Messenger of God said, "After your mother, your father."
Islam
Hadith of Bukhari and Muslim

♥

There are three partners in man, God, father, and mother. When a man honors his father and mother, God says, "I regard it as though I had dwelt among them and they had honored me."
Judaism
Talmud, Kiddushin 30b

♥

Do not despise the breath of your fathers,
But draw it into your body.
That our roads may reach to where the life-giving road of our sun
father comes out,
That, clasping one another tight,
Holding one another fast,
We may finish our roads together;

faith . HOPE . love . mind . BODY . *spirit* .

Chapter 5 - Honor Thy Father And Thy Mother

That this may be, I add to your breath now.
To this end:
May my father bless you with life;
May your road reach to Dawn Lake,
May your road be fulfilled.

-Native American Zuni Prayer

♥

Attend strictly to the commands of your parents and the instructions of your teachers. Serve your leader with diligence; be upright of heart; eschew falsehood; and be diligent in study; that you may conform to the wishes of the heavenly spirit.
Shinto
Oracle of Temmangu

Son, why do you quarrel with your father,
Due to him you have grown to this age?
It is a sin to argue with him.
Sikhism
Adi Granth, Sarang, M.4, p. 1200

♥

It seems very clear to me that taking care of my parents, and loving them with all my heart is what God wants me to do. For me this is not a test, it's an honor. I plan to continue to do this until the day that we leave this earth for a better place.

♥

It's hard to be wealthy when you are the caretaker of the elderly in your family. All my life, I watched my father take care of all the elderly people in his family and my mother's family. He was always the one who got the phone calls in the middle of the night, and he always flew as quickly as he could to assist them.

faith . **HOPE** . love . mind . **BODY** . *spirit* .

Grandma's Shoebox

He missed a lot of work days taking the elderly people in his family to and from hospitals and doctors. Money has never been important to my father, but his family has always been the most important thing in his life. When it's time to leave this earth none of us will be taking any money with us. But we will be taking the love of our family with us throughout eternity.

♥

. faith . **HOPE**. love . mind . **BODY** . spirit.

Chapter 5 - Honor Thy Father And Thy Mother

.*faith* . **HOPE** . love . mind . **BODY** . *spirit* .

Chapter 6

Lessons from Mom

The essence of something is the function you want this item to perform, the purposes you will use it for, or what you think it will give you.

♥

Never take it for granted that you only have one way to go. As you open your mind to consider your numerous opportunities, new ideas will come to you.

♥

The purpose you give each thing within your world is what makes it what it is to you. Your purpose should always be central to a good life and making improvements all the time. Are you improving yourself?

♥

Truth is that which does not contaminate you, but empowers you.

♥

Your life metaphor: It's the view of life that you hold, consciously or unconsciously, in your mind. It is your description of how life works and what you expect from it.

Your unspoken life metaphor influences your life more than you realize.

Put simply, if your thoughts are in the gutter, chances are the circumstances happening in your life are in the gutter too!
We all have the same parts, or at least at one point we were all supposed to start out that way. The degree to which you choose to develop and use your mind is the degree to which you will succeed. But the SUBJECT to study is FAITH.

♥

What you want wants you. This statement is so much more profoundly and overwhelmingly true than most people realize.

faith . **HOPE** . love . mind . **BODY** . *spirit* .

Grandma's Shoebox

It doesn't matter what you want, first you must ask for it. Did you know that God answers your prayers in one of four ways? Sometimes he says yes, sometimes no. Sometimes the answer is wait, and then often the answer is, "Here is something better for you." But if what you really want is for the good of others and yourself, then our loving Father will not fail to answer the soul sincerely asks anytime, anywhere. Everyone who seeks and everyone who asks will be given something in answer to their prayer.

When we are confronted with obstacles and we struggle, then we lose our awareness of God. Understanding isn't a given, it is earned. When we encounter roadblocks in life, it is because we've lost sight of our path to God. Prayer is the map that leads us out of the wilderness and connects us to God.

When you pray, you should talk to God as if you are talking to a dear friend. Prayer is not magic; it is speaking with our Father. If all of your wishes were "granted" and every problem solved, then what lessons would you be learning here on earth? Sometimes the answer to your prayer is the solution to your problem.

God wants you to know him and to love him. He is full of wisdom and infinite love for you. He has the power to give you wisdom and love. So many times people have prayed for one thing only to be given something far greater by a much wiser Father. So if you don't get exactly what you asked for, don't be disappointed. Sometimes you weren't asking for enough.

Sometimes your prayers are not answered because you have not done your part. God helps those who "help themselves" and answers your prayers only after you have tried all that you can do to help yourself.

faith . HOPE . love . mind . BODY . *spirit* .

Chapter 6 - Lessons from Mom

When you want something, it has to be for the better of more than just yourself. It can't be just for you. You have to really want it for others, and then he will say yes. When it is for selfish reasons, he says no.

When God says "Wait" that means that at that moment he is probably having a problem pounding something into your head! When you figure out what that is, then he says, "Yes, you have learned your lesson and you may move on to the next level, and you will never have to deal with that again. "For this is my gift, my gift that I give unto you." And when that happens, you usually find that there was something wonderful waiting ahead for you. All you had to do was: 1. Believe 2. Share your beliefs and blessings with your family. You can't just share your beliefs; you also have to share your blessings.

I have probably heard and read a million times that when you pray you should speak to God as if you were talking to your "Earthbound" dad. Don't start your prayers, "Dear Lord"; start them, "Dear Father", now I understand why. Entering into the next generation, I know there will be times in life that my children will need a voice in the night. There are many times in life when it hurts, when you don't always know what to do, but you do the best you can until you find your way.

♥

All the stories that you hear about "the good life" are about what we are all hoping to live. Listen to the song: "I'm Proud of the House We Built". What do you get out of that song?
Stop. Think. God has a deeper message.
The answer is being proud of the house you build and the life that you live. Think about it, really think, and know that it all comes down to who's there for you in the end and why they are there.

faith. **HOPE**. love. mind. **BODY**. *spirit*.

Get it in your head that we are all at different levels of this thing we call life, but it is our responsibility to make sure that we survive. That was the first lesson, and we must pass our knowledge on. I believe that "our" generation has been a little lax in that area, especially lately.

I've heard the phrase, "New Catholic". I'm still trying to figure out just what that means. Are they saying that there are old traditions that no longer apply? There is extreme beauty in the Catholic faith, and all of its rituals. There is power in prayer, and even more power in focused and concentrated prayer.

It really isn't OK to think about God just on Sundays or whatever day of the week you worship. You need to feel him in your heart every day. That's just a fact. But that doesn't mean you won't have lessons, because you will. He will bring you through them in a way that they do not hurt you.

So when you pray, know first in your heart that what you are asking for must be genuine, for the good of your family and others. You must be prepared to share your blessing, for the good of God and all his church! I understand the lesson and I will pass it on. I will change the things I have done wrong and follow a better path. I know all things begin in my mind with my thoughts, so I know that he will place a thought in my mind that will lead to my next level of success in this world.

Ask your Father as if you were 3 and you wanted a puppy or a kitten. Then feel as you would feel if He said yes! Maybe that explains my love for puppies; it mirrors that feeling. So God bless all of us who have mastered that lesson. But by all means pray, count your blessings each and every day, and ask forgiveness at the end of each day for each and every wrong that you did. Stop trying to shorten your prayer. Just face up to what you did, ask for forgiveness and learn from it.

faith . **HOPE** . love . mind . **BODY** . *spirit* .

Chapter 6 - Lessons from Mom

Try not to ask God for forgiveness for the same sin over and over again. Because if you do, you need a little tutoring from someone who has already passed that course! Go get it from a loving, caring grandparent, someone you can trust to guide you on your correct path. We are supposed to be on a path of righteousness. I understand that this means use my mind and think "right" and I will do right! Do a better job of sharing his message with others. I believe that the world needs a right way of thinking. Teach your family and those that come across your path that they should be sharing their blessings. If you do more wrong than right you will not be feeling God's love. It's just the same as if you misbehave as a child, and your Parents are at their wits' end with you and try to get you to behave and get back on the right path.

♥

Never lose your sense of adventure, your desire to learn and grow with each new day. Get in touch with your deepest feelings, your most honest and sincere thoughts. Keep your pursuit of self-knowledge joyful.

♥

You may have memories of situations you deemed were meant to embarrass or destroy you, when in fact they were meant to teach you what you needed to learn to lead you to a success you now enjoy.

♥

Beliefs stem from the experience, testimony and demonstration of others who in one way or another have attempted to persuade you of their truths. All your institutional religious training, holy books, and theological dogma may be valid and extremely forthright. Nevertheless they are usually presented as the truth for all, including you. The pressures to believe may have been almost insurmountable if you were assigned these beliefs at birth and raised on them. I am not suggesting that religious training is wrong. However, I do think any method of conditioning people to accept beliefs about God creates doubt, because beliefs do not come from any conscious contact or direct experience of God. To create a knowing that supplies you with faith, you must establish a direct experience of God for yourself.

It is your knowing because of your direct experience and nothing more that gives you faith.

What is hope, but a feeling of optimism, a thought that says things will improve, you won't always be miserable, there's a way to rise above the present circumstances. Hope is an internal awareness that you do not have to suffer forever, and that somehow, somewhere, there is a remedy for despair that you will come upon if you can only maintain this expectancy in your heart.

Sometimes in the midst of all of our problems it's really hard to hold on to the feeling of hope. It's really hard to see that light at the end of the tunnel when day after day, one problem after another just keeps coming into your life. Sometimes I ask how much more you think you will be asking me to handle. I know it's my faith that keeps me sane through these problems. If I didn't have faith that the right thing will happen, I guess I'd just get a gun! Yes, some days the problems that we face feel as though they are destroying our world. But with faith you know that they are just lessons. Lessons that, for whatever reason, we must learn.

Sometimes when things have felt like they are just insurmountable, that seems like the time I will hear another song and find another message. It's like God knows just when to reach out and remind me that "I am a Lucky Man" (Woman). There are more reasons than I can count why I feel this way. Learn to count your blessings, not your problems.

♥

faith . **HOPE** . love . mind . **BODY** . *spirit* .

Despair is an attitude, experienced in the mind. It is a way of looking at a life situation and feeling hopeless. There is no despair in the world. You cannot bring home a bucket full of despair. There are only people thinking desperate thoughts. This is an important point to understand. There may be deplorable circumstances that exist in your life and in the lives of others, yet in and of themselves they are just plain circumstances, the facts of life. Despair itself is a mental process that sizes up and views a situation as awful. When you just recognize despair as being a mental attitude, you begin a process of bringing hope to the inner vision of despair and dissolving it.

Hope, too, is nothing more than a thought or a vision.

There is always someone else out there whose situation is worse than yours. We don't live in a perfect world. Not because God doesn't want our lives to be filled with joy and happiness, but because we have lessons to learn. There are always going to be people whose lives appear to be better than yours, and there will always be those whose lives are worse. But life is what you make it. You can choose to recognize the despair for what it is, or you can look for the lesson and move it out of your life. The choice will always be yours. Remember, when God closes one door he usually opens a window.

♥

Sadness is an attitude that is developed over a lifetime of focusing on what is wrong and missing in our lives.

Sadness is a habit of processing the world from the perspective of what you have and what is right. Joyful people rejoice in their strengths, talents, and powers and do not compare themselves to anyone else. They are not threatened by what someone else has or

faith . **HOPE** . love . mind . **BODY** . *spirit* .

does. Joy comes from rejoicing in all that you are, all that you have, all that you can be and from knowing that you are divine, a part of God.

Sadness comes from a scared consciousness that can be dissolved by tuning into the abundance that is yours for the taking. Quoted from the scriptures, "You are always with me, and everything I have is yours." (Luke 15:31) Now, what does everything I have leave out? Nothing! The antidote to sadness is to bring appreciation for the abundance of this world, in the form of your own joyfulgratitude for all that you have and all that you can have, to the presence of the mistaken belief that you are lacking something, and the illusion will dissolve.

The mistake of sad thinking is corrected when you bring joy to it. Remember, the world has no sadness in it, only people thinking sad thoughts. "God saw all that he had made, and it was very good". (Genesis 1:31).

Joy speeds up the illusion of time, while sadness appears to slow it down.

You obtain that attitude by becoming conscious of the many blessings life has already given you.

Count your blessings each and every day, "keep holding on till the heart ache is gone." Hold on to your faith; don't stop believing, for this too shall pass. Talk to your Father, talk to him everyday. Some days, I'm sure that people are looking at me while I am driving my car and think that I am either nuts or talking to myself. But I have found that it is during the really difficult times in life that when most people begin to get back on the path home. We all need someone to

faith . HOPE . love . mind . BODY . *spirit*.

Chapter 6 - Lessons from Mom

talk to in times of sadness or despair. When you feel the need to be alone, that you just want to walk away from this world; that is your Father calling you back to the right path. Start talking to him. Ask for forgiveness for all the wrongs that you have done, and then ask for HELP. God made us. We all have a Father, and sooner or later you will open up your eyes and realize you're going to have to start talking to him.

I suppose he might say something like:

"The first question I would like to ask you is where have you been? I haven't heard from you in quite some time! I have missed you. You are my child. Why did you stay away so long? You know that I love you no matter what, so why did you not ask sooner? Well, let's talk now; tell me everything that is weighing down your heart. Feel free to pour out your soul to me, and let's see what we can do to make your world a better place.

And my child, please learn this one important lesson. I am your Father, your parent; I brought you into this world. You are a very special part of me. Would you mind keeping that in your heart forever? I will always love you." That is what I would expect him to say.

♥

There are four unique human endowments, which all people have:
1. Self-awareness – the ability to examine your own life, to stand apart from it and study the scripting inside you.
2. Your power of imagination, your vision of how you can create a better situation for people, for yourself and society.
3. Your conscience, a deep moral sense of what is right and wrong.
4. You have independent will, which you can exercise to act on the other three endowments.

faith . **HOPE** . love . mind . **BODY** . *spirit* .

Grandma's Shoebox

♥

Emotions focus you in time and space. Your emotions are the fuel that propels your thoughts into expression or demonstration. Your feelings of wanting something make it easier to bring it into your life. Although you need to have a feeling about something before you can create it, you can create more things from positive, harmonious emotions rather than from negative, disharmonious ones.

♥

Absolute faith is a necessity for success in anything you do. You must believe in order for it to be true.

Stop doubting and start believing, for skepticism will get you nowhere. Your doubt is a lack of trust in your beliefs. It may cause you to hesitate to take the proper action.

♥

Anytime you catch yourself feeling powerless or victimized, strengthen your belief that you are the creator of your reality by saying to yourself, "I can choose whatever reality I need in my life." No matter what is happening, how you are being treated, or how powerless you feel to change your relationship, start by telling yourself that you do have a choice and this is what you are choosing. You do not need anyone to give you what you want; you and your soul can create any life you can imagine for yourself.

♥

The search for self-knowledge is a part of everyone's life. We are all searching.

Your soul, as all others, was sent here with a purpose. Start today to live your purpose.

. *faith* . **HOPE**. love . mind . **BODY** . *spirit* .

The Implicate Order, (from the Latin "to be enfolded") is a level of reality beyond our normal everyday thoughts and perceptions, as well as beyond any picture of reality offered by a given scientific theory. These, according to Bohm, belong to "the explicit order."

In the Implicate Order, the totality of existence is enfolded within each "fragment" of space and time - whether it is a single object, thought or event. Thus everything in the universe affects everything else because they are all part of the same unbroken whole.
What you do in this life always has and always will affect others.
You have a purpose. We all have a purpose. We were sent here to be loving, kind, generous, and most of all to learn.

♥

Rejoice, knowing you are being freed, cleansed and healed, and that divine adjustment is taking place. Greater good always comes to you after these severe periods, if you dare to expect it. When your life is going through difficult times it is vitally important that you know something better is coming your way. It is simply time for a change. Keep talking to our Father and asking for guidance, and soon something better will happen for you.

♥

If you feel that you have been going without all of your life, then it is time that you realize that you never had to do this. There is nothing you cannot be, there is nothing you cannot do. There is nothing you cannot have.
You just have to follow the right path; it will take you to the end of the rainbow.

♥

There is always someone else out there whose situation is worse than yours. We don't live in a perfect world. This is not because God doesn't want our lives to be filled with joy and happiness, but

. *faith* . **HOPE** . love . mind . **BODY** . *spirit* .

because we have lessons to learn. There are always going to be people whose lives appear to be better than yours, and there will always be those whose lives are worse. But life is what you make it. You can choose to recognize despair for what it is, or you can look for the lesson and move it out of your life. The choice will always be yours. Remember when God closes one door he usually opens a window. There is always a way.

In this life here on earth, you don't want to count your heartaches, you need to count your blessings.

♥

Right use of will is when you love doing something so much that you do it without having to will it or push yourself.

Will is a clear focus that is directed toward something you love.

♥

faith . HOPE . love . mind . BODY . *spirit* .

Chapter 6 - Lessons from Mom

. *faith* . **HOPE** . love . mind . **BODY** . *spirit* .

Chapter 7

Angels

"Ask, and it shall be given you, seek and ye shall find, knock and the door shall be opened unto you."

♥

True forgiveness…must heal the mind that gives, for giving is receiving.

♥

I believe that God sends his Angels to teach us many lessons. "Take every breath that God gives you for what it is worth." Aren't those beautiful words? That's the power of God talking through the airways again. He's always sending us messages to try and make us think.

♥

Coincidences, synchronicity, and serendipity are all examples of our Guardian Angels at work.
If we fall too far off the path, our guardian angel will usually help us find our way back. There are angels in heaven and on earth. (On earth as it is in heaven) It's like someone whispering the answer in your ear.

♥

The following is a poem that was sent to me in my email. I was so touched by this poem that I sent it out by mail for Mother's Day one year to every woman that I know: my friends, my family and all of my customers. I believe that at some point in all of our lives we are all an angel for someone.

A CHILD'S ANGEL

Once upon a time there was a child ready to be born. So one day he asked God
"They tell me you are sending me to earth tomorrow but how am I

going to live there being so small and helpless?"

"Among the many angels, I chose one for you. She will be waiting for you and will take care of you."

"But tell me, here in Heaven, I don't do anything else but sing and smile, that's enough for me to be happy."

"Your angel will sing for you and will also smile for you every day. And you will feel your angel's love and be happy."

"And how am I going to be able to understand when people talk to me, if I don't know the language that men talk?"

"Your angel will tell you the most beautiful and sweet words you will ever hear, and with much patience and care, your angel will teach you how to speak."

"And what am I going to do when I want to talk to you?"

"Your angel will place your hands together and will teach you how to pray."

"I've heard that on earth there are bad men. Who will protect me?"

"Your angel will defend you even if it means risking its life."

"But I will always be sad because I will not see you anymore."

"Your angel will always talk to you about me and will teach you the way for you to come back to me, even though I will always be next to you."

At that moment there was much peace in Heaven, but voices from earth could already be heard, and the child in a hurry asked softly: "Oh God, if I am about to leave now, please tell me my angel's name."

"Your angel's name is of no importance, you will call your angel, 'Mommy.'"

~ Author Unknown ~

faith . **HOPE** . love . mind . **BODY** . *spirit* .

Chapter 7 - Angels

♥

An angel sees something, for example, and we do not. The difference is a barrier. An angel does not have barriers, and so it cannot create the karma that we do. It has a level of sight and knowledge that prevents certain actions from happening simply because of the depth of knowledge that is of its rank in creation.

♥

The great law of karma works because an angel still has will, but an angel is armed with a great deal more than the limitation that characterizes the human experience. An angel does not fear death. It has no physicality. It is only that it is immortal. It is with all that is. It has no doubt. It sees and lives in the Light, so the ingredients that create karma for the human experience are not part of its personal reality. Although an angel has will, an angel can be considered to have evolved beyond the need to be tested, and, therefore, for it, there is no karma.

♥

God's purpose is to glorify the creative energy. Should the Maker use a gnome, a fairy, an angel, a developing entity for a guide, all right for a specific direction; for He hath given His angels concerning thee, and thy god, thy face, is ever before the Throne of the Infinite.

♥

The following is a list of many passages in the Bible that talk about Angels:
1. Genesis 19:1 And there came two angels to Sodom at even; and Lot sat in the gate of Sodom: and Lot seeing them rose up to meet them; and he bowed himself with his face toward the ground;
2. Genesis 19:15 And when the morning arose, then the angels hastened Lot, saying, Arise, take thy wife, and thy two daughters, which are here; lest thou be consumed in the iniquity of the city.

.faith. HOPE. love. mind. BODY. spirit.

3. Genesis 28:12 And he dreamed, and behold a ladder set up on the earth, and the top of it reached to heaven: and behold the angels of God ascending and descending on it.

4. Genesis 32:1 And Jacob went on his way, and the angels of God met him.

5. Job 4:18 Behold, he put no trust in his servants; and his angels he charged with folly:

6. Psalm 8:5 For thou hast made him a little lower than the angels, and hast crowned him with glory and honour.

7. Psalm 68:17 The chariots of God are twenty thousand, even thousands of angels: the Lord is among them, as in Sinai, in the holy place.

8. Psalm 78:25 Man did eat angels' food: he sent them meat to the full.

9. Psalm 78:49 He cast upon them the fierceness of his anger, wrath, and indignation, and trouble, by sending evil angels among them.

10. Psalm 91:11 For he shall give his angels charge over thee, to keep thee in all thy ways.

11. Psalm 103:20 Bless the LORD, ye his angels, that excel in strength, that do his commandments, hearkening unto the voice of his word.

12. Psalm 104:4 Who maketh his angels spirits; his ministers a flaming fire:

13. Psalm 148:2 Praise ye him, all his angels: praise ye him, all his hosts.

14. Matthew 4:6 And saith unto him, If thou be the Son of God, cast thyself down: for it is written, He shall give his angels charge concerning thee: and in their hands they shall bear thee up, lest at any time thou dash thy foot against a stone.

15. Matthew 4:11 Then the devil leaveth him, and, behold, angels came and ministered unto him.

faith . HOPE . love . mind . **BODY** . *spirit* .

Chapter 7 - Angels

16. Matthew 13:39 The enemy that sowed them is the devil; the harvest is the end of the world; and the reapers are the angels.
17. Matthew 13:41 The Son of man shall send forth his angels, and they shall gather out of his kingdom all things that offend, and them which do iniquity;
18. Matthew 13:49 So shall it be at the end of the world: the angels shall come forth, and sever the wicked from among the just,
19. Matthew 16:27 For the Son of man shall come in the glory of his Father with his angels; and then he shall reward every man according to his works.
20. Matthew 18:10 Take heed that ye despise not one of these little ones; for I say unto you, That in heaven their angels do always behold the face of my Father which is in heaven.
21. Matthew 22:30 For in the resurrection they neither marry, nor are given in marriage, but are as the angels of God in heaven.
22. Matthew 24:31 And he shall send his angels with a great sound of a trumpet, and they shall gather together his elect from the four winds, from one end of heaven to the other.
23. Matthew 24:36 But of that day and hour knoweth no man, no, not the angels of heaven, but my Father only.
24. Matthew 25:31 When the Son of man shall come in his glory, and all the holy angels with him, then shall he sit upon the throne of his glory.
25. Matthew 25:41 Then shall he say also unto them on the left hand, Depart from me, ye cursed, into everlasting fire, prepared for the devil and his angels:
26. Matthew 26:53 Thinkest thou that I cannot now pray to my Father, and he shall presently give me more than twelve legions of angels?
27. Mark 1:13 And he was there in the wilderness forty days, tempted of Satan; and was with the wild beasts; and the angels ministered unto him.

faith . **HOPE** . love . mind . **BODY** . *spirit* .

28. Mark 8:38 Whosoever therefore shall be ashamed of me and of my words in this adulterous and sinful generation; of him also shall the Son of man be ashamed, when he cometh in the glory of his Father with the holy angels.
29. Mark 12:25 For when they shall rise from the dead, they neither marry, nor are given in marriage; but are as the angels which are in heaven.
30. Mark 13:27 And then shall he send his angels, and shall gather together his elect from the four winds, from the uttermost part of the earth to the uttermost part of heaven.
31. Mark 13:32 But of that day and that hour knoweth no man, no, not the angels which are in heaven, neither the Son, but the Father.
32. Luke 2:15 And it came to pass, as the angels were gone away from them into heaven, the shepherds said one to another, Let us now go even unto Bethlehem, and see this thing which is come to pass, which the Lord hath made known unto us.
33. Luke 4:10 For it is written, He shall give his angels charge over thee, to keep thee:
34. Luke 9:26 For whosoever shall be ashamed of me and of my words, of him shall the Son of man be ashamed, when he shall come in his own glory, and in his Father's, and of the holy angels.
35. Luke 12:8 Also I say unto you, Whosoever shall confess me before men, him shall the Son of man also confess before the angels of God:
36. Luke 12:9 But he that denieth me before men shall be denied before the angels of God.
37. Luke 15:10 Likewise, I say unto you, there is joy in the presence of the angels of God over one sinner that repenteth.
38. Luke 16:22 And it came to pass, that the beggar died, and was carried by the angels into Abraham's bosom: the rich man also died, and was buried;

faith . **HOPE** . love . mind . **BODY** . _spirit_ .

Chapter 7 - Angels

39. Luke 20:36 Neither can they die any more: for they are equal unto the angels; and are the children of God, being the children of the resurrection.

40. Luke 24:23 And when they found not his body, they came, saying, that they had also seen a vision of angels, which said that he was alive.

41. John 1:51 And he saith unto him, Verily, verily, I say unto you, Hereafter ye shall see heaven open, and the angels of God ascending and descending upon the Son of man.

42. John 20:12 And seeth two angels in white sitting, the one at the head, and the other at the feet, where the body of Jesus had lain.

43. Acts 7:53 Who have received the law by the disposition of angels, and have not kept it.

44. Romans 8:38 For I am persuaded, that neither death, nor life, nor angels, nor principalities, nor powers, nor things present, nor things to come,

45. 1 Corinthians 4:9 For I think that God hath set forth us the apostles last, as it were appointed to death: for we are made a spectacle unto the world, and to angels, and to men.

46. 1 Corinthians 6:3 Know ye not that we shall judge angels? how much more things that pertain to this life?

47. 1 Corinthians 11:10 For this cause ought the woman to have power on her head because of the angels.

48. 1 Corinthians 13:1 Though I speak with the tongues of men and of angels, and have not charity, I am become as sounding brass, or a tinkling cymbal.

49. Galatians 3:19 Wherefore then serveth the law? It was added because of transgressions, till the seed should come to whom the promise was made; and it was ordained by angels in the hand of a mediator.

50. Colossians 2:18 Let no man beguile you of your reward in a voluntary humility and worshipping of angels, intruding into those things which he hath not seen, vainly puffed up by his fleshly mind,

51. 2 Thessalonians 1:7 And to you who are troubled rest with us, when the Lord Jesus shall be revealed from heaven with his mighty angels,

52. 1 Timothy 3:16 And without controversy great is the mystery of godliness: God was manifest in the flesh, justified in the Spirit, seen of angels, preached unto the Gentiles, believed on in the world, received up into glory.

53. 1 Timothy 5:21 I charge thee before God, and the Lord Jesus Christ, and the elect angels, that thou observe these things without preferring one before another, doing nothing by partiality.

54. Hebrews 1:4 Being made so much better than the angels, as he hath by inheritance obtained a more excellent name than they.

55. Hebrews 1:5 For unto which of the angels said he at any time, Thou art my Son, this day have I begotten thee? And again, I will be to him a Father, and he shall be to me a Son?

56. Hebrews 1:6 And again, when he bringeth in the firstbegotten into the world, he saith, And let all the angels of God worship him.

57. Hebrews 1:7 And of the angels he saith, Who maketh his angels spirits, and his ministers a flame of fire.

58. Hebrews 1:13 But to which of the angels said he at any time, Sit on my right hand, until I make thine enemies thy footstool?

59. Hebrews 2:2 For if the word spoken by angels was stedfast, and every transgression and disobedience received a just recompence of reward;

60. Hebrews 2:5 For unto the angels hath he not put in subjection the world to come, whereof we speak.

61. Hebrews 2:7 Thou madest him a little lower than the angels; thou crownedst him with glory and honour, and didst set him over the works of thy hands.

. *faith* . **HOPE** . love . mind . **BODY** . *spirit* .

62. Hebrews 2:9 But we see Jesus, who was made a little lower than the angels for the suffering of death, crowned with glory and honour; that he by the grace of God should taste death for every man.

63. Hebrews 2:16 For verily he took not on him the nature of angels; but he took on him the seed of Abraham.

64. Hebrews 12:22 But ye are come unto mount Sion, and unto the city of the living God, the heavenly Jerusalem, and to an innumerable company of angels,

65. Hebrews 13:2 Be not forgetful to entertain strangers: for thereby some have entertained angels unawares.

66. 1 Peter 1:12 Unto whom it was revealed, that not unto themselves, but unto us they did minister the things, which are now reported unto you by them that have preached the gospel unto you with the Holy Ghost sent down from heaven; which things the angels desire to look into.

67. 1 Peter 3:22 Who is gone into heaven, and is on the right hand of God; angels and authorities and powers being made subject unto him.

68. 2 Peter 2:4 For if God spared not the angels that sinned, but cast them down to hell, and delivered them into chains of darkness, to be reserved unto judgment;

69. 2 Peter 2:11 Whereas angels, which are greater in power and might, bring not railing accusation against them before the Lord.

70. Jude 1:6 And the angels which kept not their first estate, but left their own habitation, he hath reserved in everlasting chains under darkness unto the judgment of the great day.

71. Revelation 1:20 The mystery of the seven stars which thou sawest in my right hand, and the seven golden candlesticks. The seven stars are the angels of the seven churches: and the seven candlesticks which thou sawest are the seven churches.

72. Revelation 3:5 He that overcometh, the same shall be clothed in white raiment; and I will not blot out his name out of the book of life, but I will confess his name before my Father, and before his angels.

faith . **HOPE** . love . mind . **BODY** . *spirit* .

73. Revelation 5:11 And I beheld, and I heard the voice of many angels round about the throne and the beasts and the elders: and the number of them was ten thousand times ten thousand, and thousands of thousands;
74. Revelation 7:1 And after these things I saw four angels standing on the four corners of the earth, holding the four winds of the earth, that the wind should not blow on the earth, nor on the sea, nor on any tree.
75. Revelation 7:2 And I saw another angel ascending from the east, having the seal of the living God: and he cried with a loud voice to the four angels, to whom it was given to hurt the earth and the sea,
76. Revelation 7:11 And all the angels stood round about the throne, and about the elders and the four beasts, and fell before the throne on their faces, and worshipped God,
77. Revelation 8:2 And I saw the seven angels which stood before God; and to them were given seven trumpets.
78. Revelation 8:4 And the smoke of the incense, which came with the prayers of the saints, ascended up before God out of the angel's hand.
79. Revelation 8:6 And the seven angels which had the seven trumpets prepared themselves to sound.
80. Revelation 8:13 And I beheld, and heard an angel flying through the midst of heaven, saying with a loud voice, Woe, woe, woe, to the inhabiters of the earth by reason of the other voices of the trumpet of the three angels, which are yet to sound!
81. Revelation 8:13 And I beheld, and heard an angel flying through the midst of heaven, saying with a loud voice, Woe, woe, woe, to the inhabiters of the earth by reason of the other voices of the trumpet of the three angels, which are yet to sound!
82. Revelation 9:14 Saying to the sixth angel which had the trumpet, Loose the four angels which are bound in the great river Euphrates.

faith . HOPE . love . mind . **BODY** . *spirit* .

Chapter 7 - Angels

83. Revelation 9:15 And the four angels were loosed, which were prepared for an hour, and a day, and a month, and a year, for to slay the third part of men.

84. Revelation 10:10 And I took the little book out of the angel's hand, and ate it up; and it was in my mouth sweet as honey: and as soon as I had eaten it, my belly was bitter.

85. Revelation 12:7 And there was war in heaven: Michael and his angels fought against the dragon; and the dragon fought and his angels,

86. Revelation 12:9 And the great dragon was cast out, that old serpent, called the Devil, and Satan, which deceiveth the whole world: he was cast out into the earth, and his angels were cast out with him.

87. Revelation 14:10 The same shall drink of the wine of the wrath of God, which is poured out without mixture into the cup of his indignation; and he shall be tormented with fire and brimstone in the presence of the holy angels, and in the presence of the Lamb:

88. Revelation 15:1 And I saw another sign in heaven, great and marvellous, seven angels having the seven last plagues; for in them is filled up the wrath of God.

89. Revelation 15:6 And the seven angels came out of the temple, having the seven plagues, clothed in pure and white linen, and having their breasts girded with golden girdles.

90. Revelation 15:7 And one of the four beasts gave unto the seven angels seven golden vials full of the wrath of God, who liveth for ever and ever.

91. Revelation 15:8 And the temple was filled with smoke from the glory of God, and from his power; and no man was able to enter into the temple, till the seven plagues of the seven angels were fulfilled.

92. Revelation 16:1 And I heard a great voice out of the temple saying to the seven angels, Go your ways, and pour out the vials of the wrath of God upon the earth.

faith . HOPE . love . mind . BODY . *spirit*

93. Revelation 17:1 And there came one of the seven angels which had the seven vials, and talked with me, saying unto me, Come hither; I will shew unto thee the judgment of the great whore that sitteth upon many waters:

94. Revelation 21:9 And there came unto me one of the seven angels which had the seven vials full of the seven last plagues, and talked with me, saying, Come hither, I will shew thee the bride, the Lamb's wife.

95. Revelation 21:12 And had a wall great and high, and had twelve gates, and at the gates twelve angels, and names written thereon, which are the names of the twelve tribes of the children of Israel:

♥

The spirits of those who come to us to give messages through meditation or appear in dreams are guiding influences that come to help us increase our awareness of our unity and closeness with the Creator. Our deceased loved ones, according to the Cayce readings, can offer positive guidance in our journey through the earth and help direct us toward greater spiritual enfoldment.

♥

It isn't by chance then that each soul is in its current life experience. "All the world's a stage," Shakespeare said, and we are not only the actors, but we are writing the script, directing, producing, and creating our storylines and plot. The earth is a dimension where, according to Cayce, all Universal Forces may be applied in three dimensions. Life is an unseen essence that flows through us and through the material world; it does not have its source in physical terms. The lessons or challenges each faces during its lifetime are opportunities to manifest its spiritual expression in a material world. When a soul departs the material world's stage, it moves into a dimension where it can review the life just lived - every thought, every deed, every event - and the life is measured by how much love the soul imprinted upon

. faith . HOPE . love . mind . BODY . spirit .

the world of three dimensions. All along the way, we can be reassured that we do not travel this road alone. We are, and will eventually become aware that we are, in the loving companionship of many guides, spirits, and other messengers sent by the Creator.

♥

The ancients believed that the angel of God's presence is a miracle-working presence that is available to every man; that there are angel-protectors all around us who are only too glad to guide and protect us, when called upon to do so. They felt that every person has an angel or higher self. When challenges arise, say to yourself," I HAVE NOTHING TO FEAR. MY GUARDIAN ANGEL GOES BEFORE ME, MAKING RIGHT MY WAY." Decree this often for others, too.

♥

The Hebrews of old felt that Rapheal was the angel of healing. At times you may wish to decree: "ANGEL OF HEALING, COME FORTH HERE AND NOW." Or you may wish to call on the Angel of Prosperity, or the Angel of Love, Harmony and Marriage, in the same way.

♥

The prophet Malachi might have been speaking of his angel-protector when he said, "Behold, I send my messenger, and he shall prepare the way before me" (Malachi 3:1).

♥

Divine protection is promised mankind.

♥

"Psalm of Protection": "There shall no evil befall thee. Neither shall any plague come nigh thy dwelling. For he will give his angels charge over thee, to keep thee in all thy ways" (91st Psalm)

♥

If the universe cannot reach you with its messages about those close

faith . **HOPE** . love . mind . **BODY** . *spirit* .

relationships, it will send a stranger to you to catch your attention. It is only a reminder that there is some area in your life in which you are undervaluing yourself. Thank the person for that reminder, and then begin to look more closely at your relationships. Ask, "Where am I giving out my energy and not having it returned?"

If you ask for guidance, trust the messages that come into your mind.

You can also call upon the guides and masters, for whoever calls is always heard and sent love and guidance. All you need do is ask for the help, and it will be there.

♥

There are many different ways in which your guide can send you information. Any answers you seek, any information you want, is always there. Information is always being sent to you. Guides wish to help you become aware of your ability to reach higher planes of knowledge and experience, to help you discover your own wisdom and your soul's constant guidance. They will never take away your lessons, but they will help you see what you are learning so that you may move through your growth lessons more quickly.

All you need to do to receive guidance is to ask for it and then listen!

♥

If you want to connect with your spirit guide, for instance, all you need to do is decide you will, and ask the universe to lead you to that experience. It will come to you if that is where you put your will, intent, and determination. The degree to which you are sure you want to attract a guide will determine the speed with which you attract one into your life. You may be led to certain books, people, and so forth, to help show you the way.

♥

faith . HOPE . love . mind . BODY . *spirit* .

Chapter 7 - Angels

You first become aware of it through your thoughts and your inner seeing. The first indication most of you have that you have received the broadcast is a change of heart. As this guidance comes into your emotional self, you soon find that old situations no longer trigger the emotional response they used to. As you bring the broadcast into your heart, you find yourself expanding and able to feel love and forgiveness where you didn't before.

The information is always there; the only block is your lack of will and intent to receive the broadcast. If you wish to receive more knowledge, all you need to do is make the decision to do so and focus upon it.

♥

It is easy to receive from the universal mind; all you need to do is want to receive. The information may come to you through a friend or book. You may hear it or see it. It may come in the form of a new thought. You can direct it better by becoming silent, going into a relaxed state, and quieting your mind. It is important to acknowledge that it has come. By connecting it with your will and intent you strengthen your belief in your ability to create.

You are independent individuals who determine your own lives and destiny by your will and intent. The more aware you are of the connection between what you want and its arrival, the more you will find your ability to create what you want to increase. Whenever you have a new idea or a new thought and acknowledge it, you're open to receiving more.

♥

Another way is to affirm yourself when you are in a quiet space that you would like new insights about your work. Be willing to recognize new insights, and then let go of the request.

. *faith* . HOPE . love . mind . **BODY** . *spirit* .

Grandma's Shoebox

These states are associated with the right brain, your creative nature, and are the states that most contribute to receiving higher guidance. Whenever you get quiet, you are in a more receptive state.

As you sit quietly, ask for guidance. Then, be willing to listen.

If you can focus for even five minutes on what you want guidance on, you will receive a new way of thinking, a higher outlook in that short space. Your call is always heard; the only problem comes in your ability to listen.

The guidance that is available to you is unlimited in whatever form you choose and whatever field you choose, be it business, the healing arts, performing arts, science, education, or others. The will to do anything magnetizes you to the information and guidance you need in that area. The main function of the higher centers of telepathy is to attune you with your higher purpose, help you discover what you came to earth to do, and bring to you the information you need to do it. As you experience working in these higher levels, you will increase your ability to be a loving influence on those around you, and increase your ability to see with your inner eyes. The intent to do so is all that is necessary to attune yourself to the higher realms of guidance.

♥

Writing to Angels

It is good in the face of adverse appearances to secretly write out each day how you wish your affairs might be, in contrast to how they appear. Not only does that help your mind to accept the improvement you desire; but it is as though your written-out desire goes out into the ethers and is subconsciously tuned in, so that everyone concerned begins to cooperate and help.

faith . **HOPE** . love . mind . **BODY** . *spirit* .

Chapter 7 - Angels

Just the process of reflecting, or spontaneously putting down on paper the feelings that were overwhelming me has helped me many times. This process helped to bring order to my life and my mind. It also helped me to focus on what was important and it brought clarity to my thoughts so that I could concentrate on my solution and not my problem. Writing out my problems, sending a message to my Angel also helped me to gain a certain amount of peacefulness that I needed in order to find my solution.

I also realized that in those moments of silent dialogue I was able to gain important insights that later helped me and guided me as I made certain choices concerning my life.

In addition to writing, I also found that during these experiences I would have a deeper awareness of how I was living my life, where I was headed, and thoughts about what I really wanted to do with my life. I was also reading, studying and searching for my answers. I believe that if God wants you to have information he will get it to you one way or another.

When I was in my late twenties my husband and I were going through some really difficult times. One of my neighbors brought me the book _Foundations of Truth_ by Mary Elizabeth Fields. That book opened my eyes to many things. I still tell people that it is one of the best books that I have ever read. I believe that she brought it to me for a reason.

♥

There is a special method for getting your thinking into divine order, promptly and surely. It is a mystical prayer method that can add years to your life. It can work wonders in your relationship with others. This special method is done with love, secretly with your words. True words of love are angels. When your words are alive with good and love, then they produce good from them. The method by which you can use your words and produce angelic results is by

faith . **HOPE** . love . mind . **BODY** . _spirit_ .

thinking of the person you are concerned about, and writing to their angel. By writing to a person's angel, you establish a harmonious belief about this person and you then radiate your harmonious feelings to that person subconsciously.

There is a special power when you write to the angel of a person that you are struggling with. There is just something about written words of truth that will reach to the judgment seat of a person, bypassing any of your past emotional issues or blocks and penetrating straight to the "God self." Emma Curtis Hopkins taught this secret method of prayer in her master teaching classes.

The Bible also contains numerous passages for invoking angel-powers in times of need. Abraham promised: "Jehovah before whom I walk will send his angel with thee, and prosper thy ways." (Genesis 24:40)

Many religious cultures have taught that a man's word is his power, and many teachings have realized the special power in the written word.

John, in his Revelation, speaks of writing to the angels of the seven churches. (Revelation 1:19,20) The word "church" most often symbolizes spiritual consciousness. The seven churches are symbolic of the seven types of people whom we can best reach spiritually by writing to their angels or higher selves in specific ways. These may be people we have seemed unable to reach in other ways.

When writing many mystics believed that 15 is the number that dissolves adversity and hard conditions, so they would write 15 letters to the angels of the person they were focusing on in order to assure that their message was being received.

It is also important to take the time to write to your own angel. When writing to another's angel, it may appear that nothing is being accomplished. Then suddenly everything will shift, changes will

.faith . HOPE . love . mind . BODY . spirit.

come, and matters that seem destined for failure will clear up very quickly; but sometimes one must practice patience before this happens.

The word angel means "messenger of God." Do not fail to write to your own angel when it seems that your life is filled with defeat or when you are tempted to criticize or condemn yourself. The Metaphysical Bible Dictionary explains: "The office of the angels is to guard and guide, as well as direct the natural forces of mind and body which have in them the future of the whole man."

One thing that you can know for sure is that writing to your angel or the angel of another will in no way produce any hurt or harm to anyone.

♥

Ella Wheeler Wilcox once said that God measures souls by their capacity for entertaining His best angel, love. Truly, love never fails.

♥

The story of Jacob wrestling with the angel until the break of day shows the power of persistence in producing success. He vowed to the angel, "I will not let thee go, except thou bless me." (Genesis 32:26) The angel renamed him "Israel," which means "Prince of God." You can, like Jacob, become a "Prince of God" through persistence.

♥

The Book of Isaiah says: "Before they call, I will answer; and while they are yet speaking, I will hear" (Chapter 65, verse 24)

♥

Once the world was created, angels were given the task of looking after and protecting people. In the Psalms (91:11-12) we are told:
For he shall give his angels charge over thee, to keep thee
In all ways. They shall bear thee up in their hand,
Lest thou dash thy foot against a stone.

♥

. *faith* . HOPE . love . mind . BODY . *spirit* .

In the Catholic Church it is believed that at birth everyone is given at least one guardian angel.

♥

When you are asking for help from your angel you will find the freedom to follow your life's purpose with more commitment than you alone could muster. At the same time, if you allow life's creative forces to move through you, without trying to make it happen, this is by far a much more powerful way of finding your solutions. It is about lifting yourself out of ignorance and finding the creative excellence that is available to everyone. It is about discovering your higher purpose in life.

It is a capacity for a new way of knowing and being. It's about visualizing, and the process of seeing ourselves as a part of our ultimate state. It is most assuredly about overcoming the fear of learning and the fear of seeing the godlike in ourselves.

This state of being is there for anyone who wants to discover it. You first must change your level of consciousness, change the way that you think about yourself. Once you discover this within yourself, once you taste it and experience it, then you will find that unlimited being within.

♥

Adventure has always been an important step toward any significant learning. It is extremely important to see the world as full of possibilities. If you are to participate in the unfolding process in this universe, then you must let life flow through you, rather than attempt to control it. When I began to explore, study, research all these possibilities I knew that there was a new awareness that was growing within me. I also knew that if I continued on my quest for spiritual knowledge there would be more to come.

♥

. faith . HOPE . love . mind . BODY . spirit .

Chapter 7 - Angels

Fromm explains that Being is a fundamental mode of existence or orientation to the world, one of aliveness and authentic relatedness. It has to do with our character, our total orientation to life; it is to state inner activity. For the first time in history, he argues, the physical survival of the human race depends on a radical change of the human heart. This is a call to service that will take great courage - to leave what we have and move out, not without fear, but without succumbing to that fear. It is a call to redefine what is possible, to see a vision of a new world and to be willing to undertake, step by step, what is necessary in concrete terms to achieve that vision.

♥

In your search for self-knowledge, somewhere deep down you must know that to cooperate with destiny would bring you greater responsibility, and you must not fear accepting this responsibility. You must realize that you are being called to engage in your own destiny plans. You are yielding to the design of the universe. When you begin to realize this, it will no longer be a choice of what you ought to do, but more a matter of what you could not otherwise do. Take one day at a time, one step at a time, and you will gain an inner confidence that things will work out in just the right way.

Looking back on my own life, when I realized what I was longing to do, I developed a very strong certainty that I would be able to accomplish my dreams, and that nothing in this world was going to stop me from doing so. I think that my convictions became so strong that my family had a hard time understanding me and dealing with me. I tried desperately to explain my situation to them, but until someone experiences this for themselves, they have a real hard time understanding someone who is filled with desire and a strong passion to succeed. I was highly focused and extremely committed to proceed. Some might have even seen me as a bit irrational. But, I had a

faith . **HOPE** . love . mind . **BODY** . *spirit* .

Grandma's Shoebox

mysterious quality of life within me, and things began to fall in place right before my very eyes. There were incidents and meetings with people that were almost remarkable, and all these people provided me with crucial information and assistance that I needed.

So, I believe in angels. I believe that is how the universe holds things together. Believing provides us with a world view that helps us to understand the physical phenomena that happen in our lives. It strongly suggest that the material world and consciousness are actually part of a single unbroken totality of movement. In this world everything is connected to everything else. You may not be sure of just how this works, but there is separation without separateness. That is just the way our universe has been constructed.

♥

There is the idea of implicate order, that everything is enfolded in everything. The entire past is enfolded in each one of us in a very subtle way. When you reach deeply into yourself, you are reaching into the very essence of mankind. When you learn to become sensitive to that, you realize that is the key to change all of mankind. We are all connected.

♥

The seven archangels of Christianity are derived from these.

The archangel Raphael appeared before Muhammad and this led to the creation of Islam. Likewise, the appearance of the angel Moroni before Joseph Smith on September 21, 1823, led to the creation of the Church of Jesus Christ of Latter-Day Saints.

The church became extremely popular, as it encouraged people to consider angels their own personal shepherds of God.

Thomas Aquinas's most famous book, _Summa Theologiae_,

faith . HOPE . love . mind . BODY . *spirit* .

Chapter 7 - Angels

contains fifteen of his lectures on angels.

"Soulless beings who represent nothing but the thoughts and intuitions of their Lord."

♥

Coincidences, synchronicity, and serendipity are all examples of our guardian angels at work.

♥

A particularly powerful way of making contact with your guardian angel is to write a letter, "Dear Guardian Angel."
Speak to your guardian angel. Ask for whatever you need. Make your request as clear as possible. Getting into the habit of making your requests clear and concise is a valuable one.
It can be useful to have regular conversations with your guardian angel.

It is a good habit to thank your angel every night for looking after you and helping you.

♥

The angel is part of you.

Angels personify "the coming into consciousness of something new arising from the deep unconscious."

"When man opens his heart, even for an instant, the figure he perceives (or the intuition he receives) is his Guardian Angel." - not to place faith in the outer world, but always to turn within and become better acquainted with our guardian angel, the angel of the Lord…which has been planted in the midst of us since the beginning of all time."

♥

. *faith* . **HOPE** . love . mind . **BODY** . *spirit* .

Your angel guardian is with you all the time to help and protect you.

If you need extra power or extra protection, summon the correct archangel to your aid.
Each archangel - Michael, Gabriel, Raphael, and Uriel has special responsibilities.

We can summon an archangel in many different ways.

♥

Your angel can help you heal your mind, body, and spirit. As this happens you will also improve the life of everyone else whose life touches yours.

You can also help other people. There is an old prayer that says,
May the healing power of Jesus Christ descend upon
(your friend's name) and may the holy angels encompass him (or her)

♥

Angels have been seen in a wide range of healing places.

Raphael provided a formula for healing. The story is fascinating.

"All you need to do is open up your heart, and your guardian angel will be with you."

faith . **HOPE** . love . mind . **BODY** . *spirit* .

♥

People discover their talents by accident. Some people go through their entire lives never finding out what their talents are. All we need to do is ask our guardian angels for help in finding our talents. Our guardian angels will also help us to develop our talents once we've found them.

♥

One in every ten popular songs mentions angels.

♥

Next time you want to write a letter, bake a cake, plant something in the garden, or do anything that you consider in any way creative, call on your guardian angel for assistance. It will be given willingly, and you will be amazed to discover how creative you really are.

♥

Even though our guardian angels sometimes work in mysterious ways, they have our best interests at heart.

♥

No matter what happens in your life, remember, you can always open up your heart and allow your guardian angel in to bathe you in the healing energy.

Your guardian angel is there to help protect you.

♥

Your guardian angel will not only help you find your life's purpose, but will also provide ongoing assistance. Your angels will guide and direct you, encourage you when necessary, and provide continual support.

♥

faith . **HOPE** . love . mind . **BODY** . *spirit* .

The Wings of an Angel
So Pure and So White,
The Wings of an Angel
Holding You Tight,
The Wings of an Angel
Caressing Your Skin,

The Wings of an Angel
Keeping The Love Within.
These Wings from an Angel
Are My Gift to You,
These Wings from an Angel
Will Help See You Through.
♥

. *faith* . **HOPE** . love . mind . **BODY** . *spirit* .

Chapter 7 - Angels

.faith. HOPE. love. mind. BODY. spirit.

Grandma's Shoebox

Chapter 8

Prayer

If there was one thing that I could say that I learned from my Grandma and the secrets in her shoebox, it was the "power of prayer, and that this power is really no secret."

♥

"What you want wants you." This statement is so much more profoundly and overwhelmingly true than most people will ever realize. It doesn't matter what you want, first you must ask for it. Did you know that God answers your prayers in one of four ways? Sometimes he says yes, sometimes no, sometimes the answer is wait, and then often the answer is "Here is something better for you." If what you want is really for the good of others and yourself then our loving Father will not fail to answer the soul that sincerely asks, anytime, anywhere. Everyone who seeks and everyone who asks will be given something in answer to their prayer. They are always answered!

♥

The purpose of prayer is not to get what you want, but to become what you should be.
Try to remember this while you are praying.

Know in your heart that what you are asking for must be for the better of all involved. Listen to that still, small voice.
Know in your heart what you will do with the blessings you are asking for. God has placed every good thing in the world for your prosperity and success. He has placed the power to gain them and the power to use them in your heart also.
With faith in God, good fortune can come to you in ways you know not.
If what you are asking for is pure and from your heart, then God has seen you, He is watching you. He is guiding friends/souls and conditions to your prosperity, your success in life and good fortune.

. *faith* . **HOPE** . love . mind . **BODY** . *spirit* .

He will bring you success in your undertakings just as soon as he finds a person or condition through which to work.

Along the way you must be helping others to find success and happiness.

Take the time to count your blessings while you pray and they will be magnified and multiplied.

Love is the start of all worthwhile actions; are you asking out of Love? Loving is the most important step in gaining your prosperity. Are you loving all the blessings you have at this moment? Right where you are your loving Father has provided you with everything you need for your success.

Do you know where it is? Do you know what you are looking for? Believe and you will be justified in saying, "with God all things really are possible."

After all, God helps those who help themselves. What are you doing?

"What so ever thy hand findeth to do, do it with all thy might." (Ecclesiates 9:10)

Nothing but your own thoughts can hamper your progress.

Anything that you want deeply enough can be yours.

We never really know what we can do until we believe we can do it and try.

If you just pray and do not work you will accomplish nothing. If you work and do not pray you will also accomplish nothing. It is when you pray and work that you will move ahead because that is when God is helping us.

When I was in my 30s I learned that if you really want it, and God wants you to have it, he is going to give it to you. Just keep asking

faith . **HOPE** . love . mind . **BODY** . *spirit* .

Chapter 8 - Prayer

him for what you want and be clear in your mind what you are asking for. Hopefully it's a better life, because that is really what every father wants for their child, a better life.

As I move into the next phase, I find myself asking for a lot these days. But figuring out just what you want out of life does seem to take about 50 years or so! (Ha-ha) Sometimes, you know what you wanted; you just let others stop you from doing it. You have to believe in yourself in order to believe in God, because the 2 are 1. So you might be asking God for something, but you have to believe you are ready for the blessing to take it. This world needs to start believing, and the best place to start is in your own thoughts!

♥

Trust is opening your heart, believing in yourself and in the abundance of the universe. It is knowing that the universe is loving and friendly and supports your higher good. Trust is knowing that you are part of the process of creating, and believing in your ability to draw to you what you want.

So what do you want? Ask and ye shall receive. Just remember you must be asking for the right reasons.

I can tell you from years of experience that it really does feel the darkest right before the dawn. When the dawn begins to shine and you start receiving the answers to your prayers, your mind will fill with new ideas and all the different ways that are available to solve any problem you may be facing. When that happens you are on the path once again.

♥

Never ask for more than you need. A gift or blessing should never be wasted.

♥

faith . **HOPE**. love . mind . **BODY** . *spirit*.

Grandma's Shoebox

While it is fine to seek outside guidance, make the final decision from your own heart and follow your intuition. No matter what you are doing, take the time to think about your life and look for creative ways to solve some of your problems. Discover your own answers.

Always remember you can listen to anyone, but the best advice is going to come from within you. When you are giving your problems to your Father and then asking him for the solution, ask to be shown how to get the solution, ask what he should have you do. Then do it!

♥

In order to solve your problems you must go within; you must listen to what your heart and soul are telling you to do. You will always discover your answers there.

♥

Appreciation is the highest form of prayer, for it acknowledges the presence of good wherever you shine the light of your thankful thoughts. Gratitude incorporates both the heart and mind and instantly paves the shortest road to happiness.

When you give thanks for something, you are focusing attention on what moves your soul, and the Law of Attraction will draw more of the same into your experience. By the same gesture, when you complain about what you don't want, you draw more of that into your life experience. Curse what you see and you will live in a world of pain; give thanks, and you will find more to be thankful about. The choice is always yours.
After you have laid down your burdens, then count your blessings. Then give Him thanks for all those blessings and remember to always praise Him.

♥

faith . **HOPE** . love . mind . **BODY** . _spirit_.

Chapter 8 - Prayer

Every person should take time daily for quiet and meditation. In daily meditation lies the secret power. No one can grow in either spiritual knowledge or power without it.

Dr. Emmett Fox once explained in his booklet The Mental Equivalent: "The great enemy of prayer is the sense of tension. Tension in prayer is probably the greatest cause of failure. The mind always works inefficiently when you are tense. You must relax to go within and get there."

The Buddha taught that, through using this current, a man could become so peaceful that nothing could ever hurt him again. Confucius taught that by using this God-force, man would no longer say unkind words to, or perform unkind deeds upon, his neighbor. Job spoke of this magnetic current as a "spirit in man "(Job 32:8). Jesus described it as the Kingdom of God within you (Luke 17:21). Paul thought of that as "Christ in you, the hope of glory" (Colossians 1:27).

♥

If you can get quiet and still and remain in a peaceful state of mind, you become a receptive channel for every other rich blessing in life. This is true because peace releases a stronger vibratory force, which is teaming with life and recharges one quickly. Establishing peace internally has been known to heal diseases.

♥

Speech is the very breath of God because it creates. Nothing is more alive with power; nothing has more creative power than affirmative words. This is true because words of truth have life, intelligence and substance within them, which are released through decree.

Faith can be developed as the result of many affirmations.

faith . HOPE . love . mind . **BODY** . *spirit* .

Grandma's Shoebox

Practice makes perfect, and repetition is the mother of wisdom. It is through repeated affirmations of the Christ consciousness that miracle power is released. When you keep calling on the Christ consciousness to help you, the Christ power goes to work for you, helping you break out of the negative thoughts that have bound you.

The word "concentrate" means "the act of drawing to a center." To concentrate is to rest the mind on an idea. You are concentrating all the time. The normal action of the mind is to concentrate as it dwells upon and feeds upon ideas. Every time you think about all that is wrong in your life and dwell upon your problems, you are concentrating. Every time you think about all that is good and right in your life, you are also concentrating.

The importance of concentration is an ancient teaching. The people of Rome, Greece, Persia, Egypt, and India all knew that in order to experience anything worthwhile in life, they had to concentrate upon it.

Among the spiritual giants of the Old Testament, the prophet Elijah was among the more obvious in his use of concentration; by the power of his thought, Elijah penetrated the atoms and precipitated an abundance of rain. By the same power, he increased the widow's oil and meal.

The Hindus regarded concentration as being "one pointed." They felt that concentration was the basis of all success in life. The masters of the East have long felt that the man who was truly "one-pointed" was destiny's darling and was bound to succeed.

Hindu devotees have spent whole lifetimes in the study and practice of concentration because they felt that, through constructive concentration, every good thing would come to them in life: power, knowledge, bliss. They also felt through the practice of concentration they would be delivered from every ill.

♥

Faith can be developed as the result of many affirmations.

To change your reality, simply stop thinking like that. In this case, instead of thinking "I want success," think" I have success."

Affirmations work only when they are statements of something you already know to be true. The best so-called affirmation is a statement of gratitude and appreciation. "Thank you, God, for bringing me success in my life."

♥

NEVER UNDERESTIMATE THE POWER OF QUIETNESS

Quiet times, reflective times, peaceful times, when you are relaxed and somewhat idle, are the times when inner powers are best able to gain your attention and release true genius through you.
Get quiet, know God, find him within; then the world is really there at your fingertips.

♥

Asking out loud is even more powerful.
Your conversations, your prayers, don't always have to be within your mind. It's Ok to talk aloud; sometimes there is a little more power in the spoken word.
If your words are getting you into trouble, then maybe it's time for silence…

♥

faith . **HOPE** . love . mind . **BODY** . *spirit* .

Grandma's Shoebox

Words are filled with immense cosmic power; One really can do anything with words, build or destroy.

Praise is one of the strongest forms of love. Praise expands your good. Praise is resurrecting power because it brings back into notice and use, back to life, the good in yourself and in others.
Praise is an impassioned exaltation of God the Supreme Being.

The word "praise" means to express approval, to glorify, to appraise as good. When you express approval of yourself or others, you are glorifying the divine in yourself and others. Always you can resurrect or bring back to notice the good, the divinity in people and situations through praise.
Praise is an integral part of spirituality; it holds God as a Supreme Being who is worthy of praise. The Book of Psalms is a collection of hymns and poems that give praise to Yahweh…God.

When you pray, you end your prayer with the word "Amen" The word "amen" means "Be it unto me." So when you are focusing on your prayers be sure you end them with a positive "AMEN."
We should all know the value of a good prayer. It's important that we stay strong in love and the Lord up above.

When you pray, know first that in your heart what you are asking for is genuine, for the good of your family and others. You must be prepared to share your blessings, for the good of God and all his Church! I learned this lesson many years ago from my Grandma. I also took the lesson one step further and I tested it myself to see if it worked, and it did. Offer up your mistakes to God. Yes, he already knows what you have done wrong, but you still must account for it, and seek his forgiveness if you want to move on in your life. Go

faith . **HOPE** . love . mind . **BODY** . *spirit* .

back and fix any mistakes that you can. Once you are "right with the Lord," then you will find true happiness and success in your life.

♥

Inside all of us is the heart of the child that will always seek approval from its Father. When you pray, draw from your heart, be sure you let it all out, put all your cards on the table.

When you pray be sure you are thanking God for all the blessings you have gotten from him along your way. Ask forgiveness for the wrongs that you have done each day, and try not to ask for the same wrong everyday. Learn from your lessons. If you find that you need a little help in knowing how to pray, go visit with a loving elderly person in your family. They just might surprise you. Most of them are filled with words of wisdom.

We are supposed to be on a path of righteousness, a right way of thinking and doing. If you use your mind to think "Right," you will usually do the right thing. Our world desperately needs a right way of thinking. If we each just tried to develop this technique there would be a lot less crime. Teach your family what you know. Teach them right from wrong; remind them of it day after day. If you do more wrong than right, you will not be feeling God's love. Your path will get harder until you figure out the difference between what you know is really right and how you are living your life. Think back to a time when your parents were at their wits end with your behavior. Your life was not easy, and it did not get easy again until you found your way back to the "right path."

We don't all take the same path. We don't all follow the same road. But all of the roads lead to one final destination. I hope that in time you will find the love that is written in the stars for you and pass on your knowledge to the ones you love so that they become a greater person than you or I.

♥

faith . **HOPE** . love . mind . **BODY** . *spirit* .

Grandma's Shoebox

Sometimes your prayers are not answered because you have not done your part. "God helps those who help themselves" and He answers your prayers only after you have tried all that you can do to help yourself. If you know that there are things that you can do to make your life better, He expects you to be doing those things. Prayer is not magic. Often when prayers are answered they are "miraculous."

♥

When you pray, you should always be giving thanks. Keep a journal of all the things in your life that you are thankful for. Add something to it everyday. Before you know it, you have left a very special message behind for your loved ones. It's never too late to show thanks and praise, and it's never too late to show your children how to do the same.

♥

Our capacity to recognize universal values in life's experiences is what we call wisdom. Wisdom also lies in the selectivity of the discriminating intelligence. You choose and follow that which you determine as truth in the countless circumstances of everyday living. In fact, wisdom is the mastership of knowledge.

♥

It's no secret to the people who know me that I believe in the power of prayer. I have spent years researching the topic of prayer. I have tested many different methods, and I have noted the ones that seem to work the best for me. There are many people who will call me just to ask me to pray for something for them. I always add them to my prayers, but I also remind them that there is power in prayer, and when 2 or more people start asking for the same thing, somehow that lets the Lord know that there is an urgency in the message. Remember that the next time you feel like you are in the middle of a crisis. There is surely power in prayer.

♥

. faith . HOPE . love . mind . BODY . spirit .

Chapter 8 - Prayer

It is often in meditation and silent, contemplative prayer that you feel the presence of God's goodness very strongly. In this type of prayer, you take a few meaningful words and think about them and feed upon them silently. As you think about them and contemplate them, they grow in your mind as expanded ideas that move you to right action, or perhaps as peaceful assurance that all is well and no action is needed. If nothing seems to happen in meditation, you have nevertheless made the mind receptive to God's good and, at the right time, ideas and opportunities will be revealed as a result of your spiritual exercise in meditation.

Perhaps you are thinking, "This is all pretty good spiritual theory, but how do I know that meditation and silent prayer will produce tangible, satisfying results in my workaday world?" Moses, Elijah and Jesus, among others, proved the practical, result-getting power of silent meditation.

Perhaps you are thinking, "But I'm no Moses, Elijah or Jesus, and I frankly am not sure how to practice meditation and silent prayer." The truth is that you meditate whether you've been aware of it or not. Everyone does. The word "meditate" means "to think about, contemplate, to consider deeply and continuously."
Whatever you think about constantly is the subject of your meditation. In silent prayer it is good to meditate upon the divine solution of any problem. You can begin by taking the term "divine solution" and letting the thought grow in your mind. You can take some spiritual word or phrase, think about it, and let it unfold to you. Or you can simply clear your mind, close your eyes, turn your attention within your own being and think of "God," "love," "God is love," "peace," or any such idea that gives you a feeling of oneness with God in a relaxed way.

. *faith* . **HOPE**. love . mind . **BODY** . *spirit* .

Grandma's Shoebox

Everyone should take time daily for quiet and meditation. In daily meditation lies your secret power. You may be so busy with many activities and demands that you feel you have no time to "go apart." But the invitation is "Come ye yourselves apart and rest awhile." (Mark 6:31) It is the only way in which you will ever gain definite knowledge, newness of experience, steadiness of purpose or power to meet the unknown in daily living victoriously.

"I and the Father are one," "Thy will be done in me," "I love you, God," "Thank you, Father," I am in thy presence, Lord," "this is the day which the Lord hath made, I will rejoice and be glad in it," "Peace, be still."
Until you have practiced the presence of God in this simple way, you can have no idea how it quiets all physical nervousness, all fear, all over-sensitivity, all the little raspings of everyday life. A time of calm, quiet waiting alone with God is one of restfulness and renewal. This is the "secret place of the Most High" of which the Psalmist speaks. (Psalms 91:1) This is going into the closet and shutting the door, which Jesus recommended. (Matthew 6:6)
♥
All the words and thoughts we use in prayer or meditation ultimately lead to the place beyond words and thoughts. When you have heard the voice of peace sing its silent song within your heart, you will never again place your faith in language.
Many spiritual masters teach through silence…
Jesus taught, "Do not be like the Publicans who utter long prayers in front of others to impress them with false piety. Instead, go into the closet and pray in secret; your Heavenly Father will hear your private prayers and reward you openly." If your prayer comes from the heart, your communication is sent and received in one holy instant, and your answer will be manifested quickly.

faith . **HOPE** . love . mind . **BODY** . *spirit* .

Chapter 8 - Prayer

Prayer and meditation are our ways of tapping into the deepest ground of our being and drawing sustenance from the light that we are. Look not to the outside world to give you what only Spirit can provide. And Spirit will provide.

♥

Somewhere in your home you should have your own special altar. Not like the altar at church. Just a special area of your home that you can go to pray. My Grandma had a little kneeler in front of her kitchen window, behind her rocking chair. On the window sill there were 2 African violets, a statue of Mary, and a rosary. Whenever she was praying for something specific or doing one of her novenas that is where you would find her.

The purpose of your altar is to have an area in your home that simply reminds you of God, and that area should bring you peace. It should be somewhere that you enjoy being. That's why my Grandma had hers in her kitchen. She loved sitting in her rocking chair and looking out her window. Out her window was always a yard filled with kids. Then, when we all grew up, she planted her garden outside of her window.

My altar is in my bedroom. I have a beautiful hand-painted picture of my Grandma's church, one of her rosaries and one of her statues sitting there for me to see. When I look at those things I am not only closer to God, but I feel her heart within me.

Life is funny. As time goes by, the simple things in life are really the best pleasures of your life.

You realize that more and more as each day goes by.

♥

We all need to take a little time each day for quiet reflection/meditation. It's what keeps us grounded. It's what shows us there is always hope in this world. When God enters your heart during prayer I assure you that you will know he is there.

. *faith* . **HOPE** . love . mind . **BODY** . *spirit* .

Grandma's Shoebox

He who meditates upon Jesus's words, turning them over and over in his mind, using them as his own, studying the very essence and spirit of them, will receive new thoughts, new revelations and inspirations each day of untold value. This method leads to a life of infinite satisfaction. Eat and drink the words of Jesus!

♥

There is no great world religion that does not have its method of concentration. What the Hindu calls "yoga" or the prayer of concentration, the Christian simply calls prayer.

The great teachers of the Bible emphasized the importance of prayers of concentration. Jesus referred to the prayer of concentration in healing when he said: "If thine eye be single, thy whole body shall be full of light" (Matthew 6:22). Concentration played a big part in many of His healings as well as in His prosperity miracles. Paul's powers of concentration had much to do with the successful establishment of early Christianity in a hostile world.

♥

If my Grandma had been alive when the movie <u>The Passion of the Christ</u> was released I am sure that I would have taken her there, and then bought the movie for her to own and watch again and again. Throughout the year there are definitely things that we should be acknowledging in our spiritual paths. I have always known that there was a reason behind every ritual. Sometimes it is just as important to know what those reasons are.

♥

It's not hard to meditate. I have had people tell me that they have tried to meditate and were never able to do so. I feel obligated to explain to them that meditation is not a special art. It's more like reflective thinking. Whatever you are thinking about constantly will be the subject of your meditation/prayer. Meditation is basically a silent form of prayer. It's nothing more than thinking out loud in your mind.

faith . HOPE . love . mind . BODY . *spirit* .

Chapter 8 - Prayer

If you have a specific issue that you are trying to work through, it is absolutely necessary to meditate on this issue. Simply put the thought in your mind that you are looking for a solution to your problem. You can sit quietly in a chair and run the thought through your mind, "I need a solution to this problem: _____?_____. How can I solve this problem? What can I do to fix this situation? How can I make things better? Focus your mind on your issue. Then begin your prayer request.

Almost all people of all religions pray, and all of our prayers are headed to the exact same destination. All the words and thoughts that we use in prayer are all leading to the place beyond words and thoughts. Ask for guidance to find a way to solve the problem that you are dealing with. God doesn't just take away our issues. These issues are teaching us a lesson. God wants us to do the right thing. He will bring people and situations into your life to help you correct any issue that you are dealing with, but if you are simply asking him to make it go away, you might want to re-phrase your request. Our problems never just go away.

While you are meditating/praying, it helps if you put the thought in your mind that you are looking for a divine solution. As you are sitting quietly thinking, be thinking on the subject of a solution. There are many times that I say over and over in my mind, "Lord, Father, I need a little help. Please help me to find the solution to my problem. I just can't seem to figure this out on my own. Please, guide me and guide others to help me so that I can move on from this issue." Meditating and prayer are really just a way for you to have a conversation with the Lord. If you could take your issues home and ask your father for help, asking God is no different. He hears your prayers.

faith . **HOPE** . love . mind . **BODY** . *spirit* .

You can add a special spiritual word or phrase and just let it unfold in you mind as you are meditating. Just think about it, clear your mind from distractions. You really don't want to be in a room with the phone ringing and the TV blaring while you are trying to focus your prayers and thoughts.

God loves you, he wants the best for you, and he is there to help you see and find your way through this world, so that you may go on to the next.

He did not put us here to fail, however; we are here to learn, love and grow in love.

♥

The Catholic religion is a beautiful act of spirituality. It is obvious by the prayers, novenas, and litanies inside Grandma's shoebox that she adored her faith. She was proud to be a Catholic woman. She prayed often to Mary the Blessed Mother.

A few months after I was married in 1978 I became pregnant. A few months later I lost the baby. My heart was just simply broken to pieces. Just the thought of losing a baby seemed to devastate me. I was sitting in my Grandma's kitchen when she brought out the shoebox. She gave me a pencil and she told me she was going to give me a list of prayers, novenas and litanies to say and I should write them down and start saying them immediately. She told me to pray to Mary. Ask the Blessed Mother to help you keep the next baby. I prayed those novenas everyday. On August 11, 1980, my daughter was born. She was the most beautiful child I had ever seen. (And she still is). A few weeks later, when we were making plans for her baptism, I made a banner for the Church thanking the Blessed Mother for hearing my prayers and answering them.

I know that other faiths don't understand why we pray to Mary, but when I look at my daughter, now 28 years later, a graduate of

faith . HOPE . love . mind . BODY . *spirit*.

Chapter 8 - Prayer

Washington University Law School, I know why I prayed to her. I know why my Grandma called me down to her home to give me the prayers. My Grandma had also lost a child. She knew exactly how my heart was feeling. She knew just what to do to make it better. Maybe it takes a while for people to realize that their prayers really have been answered. I don't know, I was blessed to have been born in my Grandma's family. Faith was an open book in her home, as it should be in all of our homes.

When I say my prayers at night I thank God for my Grandma. She's been dead for 10 years now. But she's been alive in my heart for 50 years and she will always, always be there.

♥

There are many, many books for sale that cover the topic of prayer. You don't need to buy a book to know that your prayers will be heard. You don't need to buy a book to know how to pray, although reading many books on the topic of prayer will help you focus while praying. Books are all out there for the world to read and learn from. There has never been a book that I have read that I did not learn something from.

However, praying is as simple as having a conversation with your father. Open up your heart and let him in. I promise you he will guide you through any issues that you are facing. Just remember, there is a reason for everything. Prayers are not always answered how you would like them to be. When you realize this it really helps you see the answer to your prayer. You might not get what you asked for, but if you are asking for help - for a solution - for guidance - that you will get.

♥

When you discover that God is hearing your prayers and answering them, it will be one of the most thrilling moments in your life. That is why everyone really should take time every day of their life to pray.

. *faith* . **HOPE** . love . mind . **BODY** . *spirit* .

Grandma's Shoebox

So many people only pray when they are in need, but it is very clear that God wants us to give him thanks and praise everyday.

Think about a time when you know that your prayers were answered. Sometimes when we are desperate, we will try to bargain with the Lord. We might say things like, "If you just help me get through this, I promise you that I will never ever miss mass again the rest of my life." Really, honestly, we should not make promises that we are not going to keep. However, if someone told you I will take away your worst nightmare, but in return you must spend 15 minutes a day with me for the rest of your life what would you do?

You will learn that in daily prayer/meditation lies a secret power. "Come ye yourselves apart and rest awhile." (Mark 6:31) This is how you gain knowledge, experience; this is how you steady yourself to meet the challenges of each new day. It is also how you help keep your life on track and it really helps you to stay focused on living your life with a purpose.

"This is the day that the Lord hath made, I will rejoice and be glad in it." The Lord has given us each and everyday. He wants us to rejoice (be thankful) and be happy (feel good about our day and ourselves). We need to be able to say at the end of each day a prayer of thanksgiving and know that what we did that day was in the best interest of all those whom we encountered. "Thy will be done on earth as it is in Heaven." We should not be doing things that are not of his will. When you say the words of our Lord's prayer you need to meditate on them. "Our Father" : He is our Father, he is "everyone's Father, not just yours or mine but everyone. This means that he loves us all, every single person the same. "Who art in Heaven," : Heaven is our final destination. Once we have learned all that we can, and we have mastered our lessons, we will go home to Heaven.

faith . **HOPE** . love . mind . **BODY** . *spirit* .

"Hallowed be thy name" : There is no other name, person, place or thing that we should love more than the Lord. "Thy will be done" : live your life as Jesus did, live your life doing what you think will please the Lord. "On Earth as it is in Heaven" : Live your life here on earth just as you would expect to be living if you were in heaven. You can't be a different person on earth than you will be in heaven. Right is always right, and wrong will always be wrong. Love reaches through out eternity.

♥

(Matthew 6:6) "But thou, when thou prayest, enter into thy closet, and when thou hast shut thy door, pray to thy Father which is in secret; and thy Father which seeth in secret shall reward thee openly." When you read this from the Bible this tells you to meditate/pray in silence. Close the door, shut out all noise and pray. The Lord our Father will hear your prayers.

Once you get into the routine of meditating/praying in this manner, you will soon find that it will help you calm down any fears or anxiety that you may be feeling. You will not be worrying over all of your day to day issues of everyday life.
(Psalms 91:1) "He that dwelleth in the secret place of the most High shall abide under the shadow of the Almighty."
Throughout this book I have been telling you the things that I have found to be true based on my study of the Bible and life.

♥

Jesus taught, "Do not be like the Publicans who utter long prayers in front of others to impress them with false piety. Instead, go into the closet and pray in secret; your Heavenly Father will hear your private prayers and reward you openly." If your prayer comes from the heart, your communication is sent and received in one holy instant, and your answer will be manifested quickly.

♥

. *faith* . **HOPE** . love . mind . **BODY** . *spirit* .

Jesus taught us that we should pray without ceasing. This means that we must keep a positive healing consciousness, and we must keep this level of consciousness every day.

♥

When we pray/meditate, we are tapping into our deepest being and drawing on that sustenance from our light within. Never look to the outside world to give you what only the Lord can provide, and he will provide.

Today I see with the eyes of God. I lift my vision from the mortal, the frail, and the false, and focus on the truth of eternal love. I am not deluded by the shadows of earth; I look upward and inward, and with my spiritual eye I behold a universe of infinite good. I release my loved ones to the hands of God and I trust. I know that all my prayers reach heaven because heaven is my birthright and my God welcomes me home.

So build your altar in your home, spend time there every day, and give thanks for the blessings that have come your way. You won't know how much better your life can be until you begin to give thanks and worship every day.

♥

"Silence is a constant source of restoration. Yet its healing power does not come cheaply. It depends on our willingness to face all that is within us, light and dark, and to heed all the inner voices that make themselves heard in silence."

When reading the Gospels you will notice that Jesus often went off to be alone and to be quiet. Jesus left the crowds on a regular basis to pray in solitude and silence.

faith . HOPE . love . mind . **BODY** . *spirit* .

Chapter 8 - Prayer

Passage Matthew 14:23:

23And when he had sent the multitudes away, he went up into a mountain apart to pray: and when the evening was come, he was there alone.

Passage Mark 1:35:

35And in the morning, rising up a great while before day, he went out, and departed into a solitary place, and there prayed.

Passage Mark 6:45-46:

45And straightway he constrained his disciples to get into the ship, and to go to the other side before unto Bethsaida, while he sent away the people.

46And when he had sent them away, he departed into a mountain to pray.

Passage Luke 4:42:

42And when it was day, he departed and went into a desert place: and the people sought him, and came unto him, and stayed him, that he should not depart from them.

Passage John 6:15:

15When Jesus therefore perceived that they would come and take him by force, to make him a king, he departed again into a mountain himself alone.

There are 5 passages above that tell you Jesus prayed in silence as often as he prayed out loud.   When you pray/meditate in silence it will help you in the sense that you will be calm, there will be peace within you, if only for a short while.

.*faith*. **HOPE**. love. mind. **BODY**. *spirit*.

Grandma's Shoebox

I know how hard life can be, I know that there are people out there with problems more serious than mine, but I also know that there are people out there with problems less serious than mine. But when the problems are yours, then they have a tendency to weigh on your mind as well as your shoulders. Just try to remember, the bigger the problem, the bigger the lesson you are learning. And most of all remember, "This too shall pass." But it won't pass if you don't get right with yourself and your God.

♥

Prayer and meditation nourish your soul, prayer/meditation is your access to divine assistance. If you can let go, and let God help you, you can right the wrongs of your life and begin again. But you have to let go of all of the "who did it, what happened" stuff and "who's fault was it." There is no need to try to place blame anywhere. First just ask God for help, ask for forgiveness and move on to the next lesson. There will always be another lesson just around the bend. We are here to learn.

♥

It is one thing to "know God" and a completely different thing just to "know about God." We all need to know God. When you experience "knowing God," you develop a level of faith that removes fears and doubts from your mind and brings you a certain level of peace in your life no matter what you are going through. Faith involves going beyond our senses of touch, taste or smell. It takes you to a place of connections with your soul and your spirit.

There is a line in the Old Testament that says, "Be still and know that I am God." There are two key words here: still and know. To know is to make a conscious contact and still refers to silent meditation/prayer. I promise you, when you do this on a regular daily basis you will, in fact, know God.

♥

faith . HOPE . love . mind . BODY . *spirit* .

Chapter 8 - Prayer

In the stillness, you will find your true being. In the silence you will hear the breathing of your soul - and of God.

In that moment of communion, you will know that unity is the truth of your being. And when you come out of your meditation, you will understand, and see from your experience, that it is the denial of this truth that perpetuates the negative effects of the illusion.

Some have said that prayer is asking God, and meditation is listening to his answer.
Practicing the presence of God is a skill, a habit you can develop. Just as musicians practice scales every day in order to play beautiful music with ease, you must force yourself to think about God at different times in your day. You must train your mind to remember God through continual meditation. A second way to establish a friendship with God is by thinking about his Word throughout your day. This is called meditation on who God is, what he has done, and what he has said.
Prayer lets you speak to God; meditation lets God speak to you. Both are essential to becoming a friend of God.

♥

Passage 1 Corinthians 3:21:
    21Therefore let no man glory in men. For all things are yours. When you bring God your Father into all of your affairs each and every day, when you ask him for guidance and help, you will soon see that every phase of your life will become easier to deal with. God wants us to have what we truly want.

♥

In all of my studies and my quest for soul knowledge, I created a folder on "How to" prayers. I was always curious as to whether or not there was a certain way to ask for what you needed, or whether

God wanted us to pray in a specific manner before he actually heard our prayers. What I learned throughout my research is that first of all it is extremely important that you pray. You should not be afraid to ask for anything that you really desire. In Matthew 7:7 7Ask, and it shall be given you; seek, and ye shall find; knock, and it shall be opened unto you:

This is a promise made by the Lord.

Research further shows:

Job 36:11

11 If they obey and serve him, they shall spend their days in prosperity, and their years in pleasures.

It is very important that you understand that God is the source of your supply. It is OK to expect great things from God, because when you do, then great things you will have.

The following information is what I discovered when I was researching my "HOW TO" prayers.

* The number fifteen was believed to have the power to dissolve affliction and adversity.

* Deep spiritual power is contacted and brought alive when one repeats the Lord's Prayer over and over, either silently or audibly.

* Declare the name Jehovah over and over again.

* As for the power of calling on the name "Jesus Christ," Charles Fillmore has written:

Jesus Christ still lives in the spiritual ethers of this world and is in constant contact with those who raise their thoughts to Him in prayer...The mightiest vibration is set up by the speaking of the name Jesus Christ. This is the name that is named far above all rule, and authority, the name above all names, holding in itself all power in heaven and in earth. It is the name that has power to mold the

faith . **HOPE** . love . mind . **BODY** . *spirit* .

universal substance. And when spoken it sets forces into activity that bring results, as Jesus promised when He said, "Whatsoever ye shall ask of the Father in my name, He may give it you." "If you shall ask anything in my name, that will I do."

I can honestly tell you that my prayers have been answered in this fashion. The Catholic religion has taught me that it is through Jesus Christ that all things will happen.
* Prayers of denial - Many caring people cringe at the word "denial," believing that its only meaning is "to take away or withhold." But the word "deny" also means "to dissolve, to erase or be free from, to refuse to accept as true or right that which is reported to be true." Prayers of denial are for the latter purpose—to refuse to accept as necessary, true, lasting or right anything that is not satisfying or good.

Prayers of denial are your "no" prayers. They help you to reject things as they are and to dissolve your negative thoughts about them. They help you to make way for something better. Prayers of denial help you to erase, to be free from less than the best in your life. Prayers of denial are expressed in those attitudes that think, "I will not put up with or tolerate this experience as necessary, lasting or right. I refuse to accept things as they are. I am God's child and I will accept nothing but His complete goodness for me."
It is good to follow up thoughts of what you don't want with what you do want. After claiming "No, I will not accept this," you should add, "Yes, I will accept this or something better."
　　　　Jesus was speaking of your "no" and "yes" powers when He said "Let your speech be yea, yea and nay, nay." (Matthew 5:37) The prophet Hosea went into more detail to show you how to use your "no" and "yes" powers when he advised, "Take with you words and return unto Jehovah; say unto Him, take away all iniquity, and

faith . HOPE . love . mind . BODY . *spirit*.

accept that which is good." (Hosea 14:2) This passage is a dynamic "no" and "yes" prayer formula. To any situation that is dissatisfying, you can deny it by declaring to a loving Father, "TAKE AWAY ALL INIQUITY." Then follow it up with the affirmation, "I WILL ACCEPT ONLY THAT WHICH IS GOOD."

♥

Long before the time of Jesus, the Egyptians followed the command to take away all iniquity through the power of denial. The Egyptians used the sign of the cross to indicate a crossing out or blotting out of evil, a form of denial that still is used by some churches.

♥

So many people get the erroneous idea that somebody else can keep their good from them, and so they unhappily go through life believing it. Prayers of denial can dissolve such false beliefs. When you catch yourself thinking in such a limited vein, change the thought and declare, "NOTHING CAN OPPOSE MY GOOD." As you do, you will find that where people and affairs seemed to work against you, everything will shift and begin working for you.

♥

The Hebrews were warned repeatedly not to bow down and worship false idols or gods. The gods of unhappiness, lack and limitation are "heathen gods" which are still with us. They cause us as much havoc as did the early Hebrews' worship of false gods.

♥

PRAYERS OF AFFIRMATION. Affirmations should be used with denials. When you use denials, you erase, dissolve, liquidate. You then wish to make firm new good, which is done through affirmative prayers.

♥

The prayer of meditation and silence. It is often in meditation and

faith . HOPE . love . mind . BODY . *spirit* .

Chapter 8 - Prayer

silent, contemplative prayer that you feel the presence of God's goodness most strongly. In this type of prayer, you take a few meaningful words and think about them and feed upon them silently. As you think about them and contemplate them, they grow in your mind as expanded ideas that move you to right action, or perhaps as peaceful assurance that all is well and no action is needed. If nothing seems to happen in meditation, you have nevertheless made the mind receptive to God's good and, at the right time, ideas and opportunities will be revealed as a result of your spiritual exercise in meditation.

♥

THE LORD'S PRAYER HAS HEALING POWER

The Lord's Prayer is a powerful healing treatment because it is basically a series of strong, powerful, affirmative statements in which one claims the power, substance, guidance, and goodness of God. Affirmation is not only ancient healing art, but also a modern, scientific healing technique. Scientists now declare that the body as well as the universe is filled with innate intelligence.

♥

By taking a statement filled with good words and declaring it over and over, man gains conscious attention of the innate intelligence ever active in the subconscious functions of the body. As man continues to speak good words, that innate intelligence is stepped up in its power to respond with conscious as well as subconscious positive results. The body, including our physical affairs, is the obedient servant of the mind and is plastic to our thoughts and words. When our thoughts and words are uplifting, they are life-giving to our physical world.

♥

YOUR PRAYERS FOR ANOTHER'S HEALING HAVE POWER

Perhaps you know someone you would like to assist in solving a healing need, but you hesitate to mention it to them,

. faith . HOPE . love . mind . BODY . spirit .

Grandma's Shoebox

because you feel they might not agree. In that event, begin declaring affirmations for them or ask some prayer group or trusted friend to join you in praying for them.

Mentally picture yourself or the one who seeks healing as completely strong and well.

Imaging is particularly powerful for healing. By forming pictures in your mind of the results you desire, and by holding to that mental picture, you are releasing your faith to go to work in a simple but supreme way to produce wondrous results.

♥

A number of great healers in the Bible wisely used the imaging power of the mind to produce healing. An interesting case is noted in Jesus's healing of the man blind from birth. When his disciples asked Jesus who had sinned to produce this blindness, instead of giving such an analysis Jesus turned to healing him. His method was clear enough to one who understands mental processes. First, Jesus spat on the ground and made clay of the spittle. He then anointed the man's eyes with that clay and instructed him to "go, wash in the pool of Siloam." This statement set up the mental image of an expected healing in the man's thinking, and it motivated him to then act upon the image. Thus, he followed through on that mental image of healing: he "went, washed, and came away seeing." (John 9:7)
Passage John 9:7:
　　7And said unto him, Go, wash in the pool of Siloam, (which is by interpretation, Sent.) He went his way therefore, and washed, and came seeing.

♥

The early Christians undoubtedly realized the healing power of the imagination. When Peter and John were going up into the temple,

faith . HOPE . love . mind . BODY . *spirit*.

they encountered a beggar at the temple door who had been lame from birth. In response to the beggar's request for alms, Peter fastened his eyes (imaging power) upon the beggar and along with John said "Look on us!" The beggar did so, expecting to receive a donation from them.

It was then that Peter declared a strong affirmation which instilled the image of healing within the beggar's mind: "Silver and gold have I none, but what I have, that give I thee. In the name of Jesus Christ of Nazareth, walk!" To help the beggar accept that mental image of healing, Peter then took him by the hand, raised him up, and immediately he did walk and was healed. (Acts 3)

Passage Acts 3 :
Acts 3

1Now Peter and John went up together into the temple at the hour of prayer, being the ninth hour.

2And a certain man lame from his mother's womb was carried, whom they laid daily at the gate of the temple which is called Beautiful, to ask alms of them that entered into the temple;

3Who seeing Peter and John about to go into the temple asked an alms.

4And Peter, fastening his eyes upon him with John, said, Look on us.

5And he gave heed unto them, expecting to receive something of them.

6Then Peter said, Silver and gold have I none; but such as I have give I thee: In the name of Jesus Christ of Nazareth rise up and walk.

7And he took him by the right hand, and lifted him up: and immediately his feet and ankle bones received strength.

faith . **HOPE** . love . mind . **BODY** . *spirit* .

Grandma's Shoebox

8And he leaping up stood, and walked, and entered with them into the temple, walking, and leaping, and praising God.

9And all the people saw him walking and praising God:

10And they knew that it was he which sat for alms at the Beautiful gate of the temple: and they were filled with wonder and amazement at that which had happened unto him.

♥

Jesus was teaching us to lift our consciousness to the place where what we want is already real and given. In this way, we are proceeding from the result, not from the need.

Jesus acted with the confidence that his prayer had already been answered, and so it was.

When confronted with a situation that appears fragmented or impossible, step back for a moment, close your eyes, and mentally envision perfection behind the situation. Go to the inner place where there is no problem, and abide in that consciousness. Then step into the vision of how different things would (and will) be when the problem has been handled, and it will. "This, too, shall pass." To live in a heavenly world, we must see through heavenly vision.

♥

Because God is the source of all manifestation, our best approach in prayer is an attitude of calm and confident receptivity.

Tell God the "what," and leave the "how" up to Spirit.

God promised you that you could have all that you want, as long as you do not try to control the way it will come. Would you give up your attempts to engineer your good? That is precisely the offer on the table before you now. Jesus promised, "Ask and ye shall receive"; "Take no care for what you shall eat or how you shall be clothed; God cares for the lilies of the field, and He shall take even greater care of you.

faith . **HOPE** . love . mind . **BODY** . *spirit* .

Chapter 8 - Prayer

When we pray for things, we are really seeking the attribute of life
the object represents to us.
When you begin to know who you are and what you deserve, then
you will begin to attract all that your life will require.

Jesus aptly taught, "Wherever two or more are gathered in my name,
there I am." This fundamentally important principle applies to
agreements of all kinds for all purposes: When two people agree on
any thoughts, that idea is given reality.

It is not a sign of weakness to ask for support in prayer, but a sign of
great faith and strength. To invite another to pray on your behalf is to
honor that person and yourself. If you truly wish to manifest your
dreams, allow them to be delivered through whatever channels Spirit
chooses. Sometimes you need help. Developing prayer partnerships
will not only increase your material manifestation, but will open your
heart and deepen your bond with your brothers and sisters.

Be strong enough to ask for help, and be humble enough to give it. If
other individuals ask you to support them in prayer, assume that
Spirit has sent them to you for a reason. If they believe you can help
them, you can.

Pray for whatever you feel moved to pray for, and when you are
done, qualify your prayer with, "This or better." In doing so, you
acknowledge to God (and, more important, to yourself) that your
vision is not all-encompassing, and in the event that something you
have requested is not in your highest interests, you are open and
willing to receive an even better result.

It is important to know how and when to pray, but it is equally important to know how and when to stop praying. It is not true the more

faith . **HOPE** . love . mind . **BODY** . *spirit* .

you pray, the greater your chances of your prayers being answered. As in all arts, sciences, and disciplines, prayer has a point of diminishing return; success is not a matter of working harder- it is about working smarter. You cannot truly claim to have mastered the art of prayer until you have mastered the art of releasing prayer.

You must release your prayers so God can answer them. It may even be said that the whole purpose of prayer is to get to the point where you turn your intentions over to the universe.

Holding on to prayer beyond its due time is an affirmation of lack of faith and will bear negative results. After you have gotten clear on what you want, affirmed your worthiness to have it, and asked God for help, any more energy you invest will only backfire. When you overpray, you are saying, in effect, "I don't believe that God has heard my request or that He will answer it. So I had better keep badgering Him until I get what I want."

♥

Of all that we do, our prayer life requires the most nurturing, for in it we summon the power of God to build the life we would choose. Do not broadcast your prayer intentions to everyone you meet; that will not give them power. Tell your prayers only to a few close friends whom you know will support and empower them to come true. One or two good prayer partners is all you need. To build your powers of manifestation, match your friendships with your visions.

♥

"Affirmations such as the peace of God is shining in me now"; "All things are working together for good"; "or I am the beloved child of God, perfect, free, and whole" will sink deeper into your subconscious, remind you of that truth, and reprogram negative imprinting. Any idea that brings you joy and happiness is a good one to digest. Biblical prayers were also spoken in a loud voice because the ancients knew about the dynamics of sound: That every spoken word

. faith . HOPE . love . mind . BODY . spirit .

has tremendous power; and that by certain arrangements of words, such as in an affirmative decree, a tremendous vibratory force could be set up in the invisible which profoundly affected substance and produced the specific results decreed. The power of the spoken word was used for healing long before biblical times.

♥

Passage Matthew 21:22:
And all things, whatsoever ye shall ask in prayer, believing, ye shall receive.

Many people have not employed the power of prayer because they have the erroneous idea that it is wrong to pray for things. Jesus did not mean that praying for things was the only form of prayer, or even the highest form of prayer, when He made this promise. But he knew that if you pray first for things, you will learn the power of prayer as a means of communing with God and his goodness.

♥

THIS OR SOMETHING BETTER, FATHER, LET THINE UNLIMITED GOOD APPEAR, is all that is needed to get results – either the result you had in mind or a far better one. Remind yourself often that if it were not for God's good will for you to experience fulfillment of the deep desires of your heart, you would not desire them in the first place. Selfish, human-limited, surface desires do not last.

♥

If you don't know what to ask for directly, pray for guidance. Say, "Father, what is the truth about this?
The people of the Bible called it "asking for a sign."

When Solomon asked for wisdom to discern between the true and the false, he was asking for guidance, and that guidance brought him all the blessings of life. Paul pointed out the power of simply asking for guidance and wisdom to meet life victoriously when he promised.

faith . **HOPE**. love . mind . **BODY** . *spirit* .

Passage James 1:5:
If any of you lack wisdom, let him ask of God, that giveth to all men liberally, and upbraideth not; and it shall be given him.

♥

Contrary to what most people think, to declare that God's will is being done in a situation is the highest form of prayer and always brings perfect, happy, satisfying answers for all involved. This is true because God is a God of love, so His will for his children is always the highest and best. A heavenly Father would hardly want less for his children than would an earthly father.

♥

Among the most powerful prayers of decree you can ever pray, ones which often bring almost instantaneously happy surprises are: "NOT MY WILL BUT THINE BE DONE, FATHER." "GOD WORKS IN ME TO WILL AND TO DO WHATEVER HE WISHES DONE, AND GOD'S GOOD WILL CANNOT FAIL!" "GOD WORKS IN THIS SITUATION TO WILL AND DO WHATEVER HE WISHES DONE AND GOD CANNOT FAIL!"

♥

Order is heaven's first law, and by affirming "divine order" you somehow release a heavenly form of order to manifest in your mind, body and affairs. Answered prayer inevitably manifests when things get into divine order.

One of the most powerful forms of affirmative prayer is the decree of faith. Jesus promised, "All things whatsoever ye shall ask in prayer, believing, ye shall receive.

♥

(Matthew 21:22).

One of the most powerful ways to invoke the miracle consciousness is to affirm "the peace of Jesus Christ." A prayerless person usually repels his good by his repelling vibrations. He scares away his good with a sense of rush, worry, force or agitation, whereas a

faith . **HOPE** . love . mind . **BODY** . *spirit*

Chapter 8 - Prayer

prayerful person attracts his good by his quiet, peaceful, powerful vibrations. A prayerful person is magnetic to his good and unconsciously draws it to him. A tranquility of bearing, a facial and bodily repose, are usually observed in those whose inner lives are enriched through prayer. Prayer quiets your mind, body, emotions, vibrations. In that peaceful, prayerful state of mind, you unconsciously draw your good to you.

♥

Don't miss your good by praying a situation almost all the way through and then become discouraged when it doesn't quite materialize. It is simply waiting for you to seal the results by affirming "the finished works of Jesus Christ." This is the miracle prayer that can quickly "wrap up" situations that have lingered on the brink of results. Often the decree of completion is all that has stood between you and answered prayer!

♥

Whoever you are, wherever you are, Jesus in His spiritual consciousness is waiting for your mental recognition. Whatever your objective, He will show you how to attain it, if you will only invite His help and presence into your life. The early Christians proved this. As you read the Book of Acts of the Apostles, you will discover that that book is not so much a record of the acts of the Holy Spirit as it is a record of the acts of the Holy Spirit through the apostles. Thus, historians have described the Acts as "The Gospel if the Resurrected Christ" acting through the apostles. It is very interesting that the physician Luke wrote both the Gospel of Luke and the Book of Acts. His first book (Luke's Gospel) related the resurrected Christ's spiritual power while on earth. His second book (Luke's Acts) related the resurrected Christ's spiritual power as this Christ presence poured forth His power from the ethers through the early apostles. By affirming the name "Christ Jesus," you will find a far

faith . **HOPE** . love . mind . **BODY** . *spirit* .

different vibration is aroused by intoning these two names. When you affirm over and over "Jesus Christ, Jesus Christ, Jesus Christ," a vibrant, alive, warm, electric feeling comes alive within you and within your circumstances, producing almost instantaneous results of good. Whereas when you affirm over and over "Christ Jesus," you will find it invokes a far more impersonal vibration, which seems to work more quietly, more slowly, and more universally.

Creative imagination is a form of prayer. Jesus was speaking of creative imagination when he said, "What things so ever ye desire, when ye pray, believe that ye receive them, and ye shall have them." In other words, if you can imagine receiving your desires, they will come into your experience.

In the same way we are all creating our heaven and earth through our inner beliefs about ourselves. So let's give thanks for the wonder and glory of the perfect power within, realizing that we are given tools to use. Creative imagination is one of the most wonderful tools of all when we use it rightly.

♥

I realize that the information on "How to" prayers for some might seem a bit overwhelming. But it is not meant to be overwhelming, it is meant to show you that with God and prayer all things are possible. Always go to God first with your problems. Try not to wait until they have manifested into a crisis. You can get answers to all of your issues if you just pray.

♥

Tennyson poetically expressed the power of praying for things in his line, "More things are wrought by prayer than this world dreams of!"

♥

Emmet Fox once described the power of praying for things:
Prayer does change things: Prayer does make things to happen quite

faith . HOPE . love . mind . BODY . *spirit* .

Chapter 8 - Prayer

differently than they would have happened had the prayer not been made. It makes no difference at all what sort of difficulty you may be in. It does not matter what the causes may have been that led up to it. Enough prayer will get you out of your difficulty, if only you will be persistent enough in your appeal to God.

♥

The most powerful position leaders assume is when they kneel.

♥

It is their prayer life that determines their effectiveness.

Albert Einstein, one of the most illustrious geniuses in history, noted, "There is really only one question that science seeks to answer: Is the universe a friendly place?" If the universe is dangerous by nature, you had better stow away in the mail truck and pray forever, for you cannot trust life to take care of you, and you had better do it all yourself. On the other hand, if there is a loving Force operating behind the scenes, you can relax and trust other people and God to help you in ways that you cannot help yourself.

♥

Dr. Billy Graham once said, "The man who has never discovered the power of prayer in a spiritual sense has never really lived."

♥

Prayer is the one supreme instrument given to man by God for all attainment.

♥

The most powerful prayer Jesus ever uttered – the Lord's Prayer.

♥

A great philosopher once said, "The difference between prayer and prophesy is that in prophesy God initiates the contact. And in prayer it is the man that summons God, man initiates the contact."

faith . HOPE . love . mind . **BODY** . *spirit* .

"A tear is the sweat of the soul and the gates of heaven open before tears."
In the busyness of the everyday, we hide our face-and our souls-with our hands. But in prayer we move them and reveal ourselves.

♥

Sooner or later, there will come a time in each of our lives when we realize that we have been watching the movie but missing the show. When that happens, at that moment we will ask for help from a higher power. It doesn't matter whether we say the words out loud or just hold the thought in our mind. We pray with our being.
Have you ever been in a situation where you have just said or thought: "God help me?" Most often these are times of crisis or turmoil in our lives.
It is also during these times that many people will find their way back to God. However, it is also during some of these times, when the outcome of the situation did not go as we had hoped, that many people turn away from God.

God is not going to take away our lessons. As I have said before, we are here to learn. What he will do, if you ask, is give you the answers that you are looking for to go through the situation at hand and come out of it stronger and wiser. He will not take away the lessons we need to learn, or the issues that we must face. He will give you strength, hope and love to endure them as you go through them.
A strong relationship with God will lead you to awareness that you are not alone, you will learn, and this too shall pass.
The purpose of prayer is not to attain a quick fix and then go back to living in the consciousness that led to our need to pray in the first place. The function of prayer is to lift our soul into a new consciousness, one aligned with our well-being and our soul's purpose, so that our life becomes new.

♥

faith . **HOPE** . love . mind . **BODY** . *spirit* .

Chapter 8 - Prayer

When we pray we have a transformation of the mind; we are shifting our attitude. We are seeking to raise our mind above any fears or limitations that are holding us back or causing us pain. If you will pray I promise you that you will begin to see the world through new eyes. Prayer is not just a tool or a routine that you practice; it is an art and a way of life. When Jesus told us to pray without ceasing, he was telling us to keep our minds in tune and linked with the infinite power of the Lord. Prayer is not an obligation; it is an opportunity for you to stay in touch with your soul. True prayer will join the hearts of human beings with the heart of God. The consistent prayer of your heart will yield you only more love, aliveness and peace. Prayer is our way of "phoning home" and being reunited with our Lord and maker. Prayer is the only action that we can take that will make things different for us from the inside out. Any form of mental action will help you release the highest form of energy. Prayer changes your mentality; it changes your thinking and calms you down. Prayer releases the highest form of energy that links you with God.

No matter what your life situations are, you will always find that there is a way that you can pray, no matter what your circumstances may be. There is a method inside all of us that will get the job done. There is no better way in this world to secure all your blessing of life, the blessings that are your divine heritage.

♥

The practice of prayer is the ultimate secret to success in all that you will do in this life. Talk to God, tell him your hopes and dreams, share your sorrows and thank him for your blessings. Start with what you have, and then talk to him each and every day. Tell him that you are ready for more and why you feel that you can handle more. You don't have to worry about how God will help you in your life; you just have to believe that he will. A strong connection to God starts in your mind, you must move it to your heart and then show it in your actions each and every day.

faith . **HOPE** . love . mind . **BODY** . *spirit* .

♥
PRAYING FOR THE DEAD

One spring, while my brothers and I were staying at Grandma's, she had to attend a funeral service for someone that she was very close to. She did not take any of us with her, probably because she did not want to deal with us and what we might get into.

I was approximately 9 years old at that time, and although my Grandma had shown me many things in her spiritual shoebox, I did not really grasp the meaning of most of it. The morning after the funeral, I came in from the pool to the kitchen and my Grandma was kneeling at her little altar in the kitchen. She had a single kneeler placed in front of a window. On the window ledge were 2 African violets, a statue of Mary and a rosary. (I keep that same statue of Mary in my kitchen window!) I stopped and asked her what she was doing, she looked at me and said, "I'm praying for the dead." I scratched my head and went back outside to play. When I got outside, I told my brothers and my uncle that Grandma was in the kitchen praying to the dead?! They started making gruesome noises like they were monsters and chased me around the pool. The next day at about the same time, I wandered into the kitchen. Once again, there was Grandma at her little altar. I stopped again and asked her what she was doing. "Honey, I am still praying for the dead." I know that my eyes opened really wide, I put my hands on my hips, and said "Really?" Once again, I went outside to play with my brothers and my uncle. And you can bet, once again I remember telling them, "Hey, Grandma's in the kitchen praying to dead people again!" One of my brothers said to me "yeah, she's praying that one of those dead people will come and get you!"

The next day, at about the same time, I came into the kitchen to ask

. *faith* . **HOPE** . love . mind . **BODY** . *spirit* .

my Grandma a question and she was not there. I found her and four of her sisters kneeling in front of the couch in her living room. I stood for just a couple of seconds and looked at them. They were all saying the same thing out loud. I walked up behind my Grandma, tapped her on the shoulder and I whispered in her ear, "Granny, what are you doing?" Her answer was the same as the previous 2 days. "Honey, we are praying for the dead." I looked at her and said "OK" and went back outside to play with the boys. This time I told them, "Hey, now Grandma and her sisters are all kneeling in front of the couch and they are all saying the same thing at the same time and it's all for dead people." My brothers and my uncle quietly sneaked into the house and got out some scary Halloween masks. They put them on and went into the living room where Granny and her sisters were praying and tried to scare them! They all got a 30-minute time-out! Forty years later, I discovered that my Grandma, Alta (Christopher) Williams, and her sisters, Mamie (Christopher) Hardin, Genevieve Christopher, Rachael (Christopher) Reando, and Nell (Christopher) Snyder were all praying for their cousin who had just passed, James Nathan Christopher. The following is the novena they were praying in his memory, just as their faith had taught them.

Prayers for the Dead

(With Novena)

MARIANNHILL MISSION SOCIETY

P. O. Box 87A   Detroit, Michigan

The Catholic religion, in my own personal opinion, and I am sure that Grandma would say the same, is an extremely beautiful, powerful, and thought-provoking study of spirituality and Christianity. The rituals that are done by Catholics are not without purpose. It is a religion that teaches us about God, Jesus, Mary, the Holy Spirit, and so much more. It takes you back to the birth of our Lord, Jesus Christ, and it follows his teachings and his life.

Carrying the Viaticum to the Dying...

After reading this, in my mind I can picture the Catholic churches in years gone by, ringing their church bells and families gathering to prepare for the journey home for a special loved one. I can see people coming out of the fields, and from their homes to gather at the church to light candles, say prayers, practice their faith. Oh, what a beautiful faith, Catholicism. It doesn't matter to me, the wrongs or errors of the humans; it's the beauty of the faith.

Chapter 9

Everybody Matters

When God created the world and all of mankind to live in it, he also set down some rules that we were all supposed to be following. Rules like the Ten Commandments, the Golden Rule (do unto others as you would have them to do unto you), and then all of the wonderful sayings of Jesus that you can find in the Bible.

♥

We tend to view others in regard to how they fulfill or frustrate our needs and goals. This view of the universe represents a basic misunderstanding. With this view of the universe, it is easy to perceive ourselves as victims.

You are who you are, and you are where you are right now because of your choices. Change your life. Then you can change your choices.

♥

Our most upsetting relationships offer us our greatest opportunities. Share them!

♥

What I hold in my heart is mine to share with whomever I decide. I can either share my life, or dwell somewhere else.

I can make a difference in this world, even if it comes through the lives of others, for then I will know that that was God's plan.

I can teach my children the lessons I have learned, and I can teach my grandchildren too! I should always be available to someone in need.

I can rise above the troubles that life may throw my way. I can always see the good in people. No one will ever take that away from me no matter how hard this world may try.

I have learned many lessons the hard way, as have many others. But I realize that life is about surviving and sharing, surviving to help others grow so that they too can find their way.

Everybody really does matter. Learn this lesson and learn it well.

faith . HOPE . love . mind . BODY . *spirit* .

Grandma's Shoebox

Don't ever let someone else tell you that you cannot do something; find out for yourself, for you just might find that you can.

I am not telling you anything that you have not heard a thousand times before. What I hope that I am doing is to help you find a way to open up your heart and let the message in and realize that those things are true.

The greatest knowledge you can gain about yourself and your fellow beings is that one person's thinking and acting constructively in any situation cannot fail to produce good results. All mankind is hungry for constructive attitudes, actions, and reactions, and quickly responds to them.

Thank God that His goodness does not stop at the limits of our human vision. Keep steady, keep your faith, and keep your courage; Remember that God opens ways where, to human sense, there is no way!

...true accomplishments come from "daring to be different," through expressing your distinct individuality.

As Charles Fillmore has written, however, "If you are educated and molded after the ordinary pattern of the human family, you may live an average lifetime and never have an original thought."

♥

There are 4 different ways we have to listen:

1st. We must listen to other people, really listen. Everyone has a story to tell, and we must learn to listen with true interest and without interrupting them. By doing this, we compliment the other person and raise his or her self-esteem. At the same time, we are increasing our own self-esteem.

faith . **HOPE** . love . mind . **BODY** . *spirit* .

Chapter 9 - Everybody Matters

2nd. We must listen to what is going on in the world around us. It is important to be alert for positive items in the media, and for true stories of heroism and how people have overcome adversity. We attract whatever it is we think about, and by instilling these positive attributes of the people we read about we will attract more positives into our lives.

3rd. We need to listen to ourselves. Observe yourself in your different interactions with others. Are you exhibiting high or low self-esteem?

4th. Most important, we must listen to our spirit our soul, that still small voice inside of us. Everywhere we go we take with us someone who wants us to do well, who is urging us on to success all the time. We need to pause and listen to what this voice is telling us. We may feel that our guide is taking away all our fun when they tell us to do something that other people are not doing. In fact the advice our guides provide us will always be correct. Your guide will never give you advice that will ever hurt another living soul. Your guide is there to help and support you, but they also care for life.

It is a wonderful fact that we have the power within us to change and become the people we were meant to be.

♥

While it is important to be centered on yourself and know who you are, making your life a priority, it is also important to be aware of your effect on other people. You are more powerful when you can understand the effect your actions have on others, and then choose what actions you want to take.

We all touch each other in one way or another. It is not for you to understand or question why. But the Bible says, "Do unto Others"; you have heard it a million times. If you are still doing things you shouldn't be doing, STOP IT! Right now, you have the choice, you have free will. Take your problems home, ask your Father for help. He will guide you.

faith . **HOPE** . love . mind . **BODY** . *spirit* .

What if every time you found fault with others, or thought of something you could do better or should be paying attention to, you asked instead, "How does my criticism of other people apply to me?" Even if you think there are no ways your observations of others apply to you or your life, be willing to explore how they might. Think of the other person as representing an aspect of yourself. Ask, "Is there anyway I am doing what I am criticizing the other person for?" Examine your life carefully. The essence of what you criticize another for is usually a quality you are working on developing in yourself. You may have that trait to a lesser degree, or expressed in another way.

Praise and acknowledge people when they demonstrate qualities and behaviors you like. People will often do better at what you praise them for. Emphasize the good and you will have even more good things come to you.

♥

You can discover new ways to love by exploring how much time you want to spend with others, and how much time you want to spend by yourself. It is important to spend time alone to hear your inner self and to feel balanced. It is in moments of silence, when you are alone, that your soul can best work with you to send you energy and ideas. Pay attention to your impulses to be alone, for these can be times when your soul is calling to you to receive its light, joy, will, presence, power, love, or any qualities that will enhance your life.

Give other people permission to do whatever they want to do with their time and life. "Give all the people in your life permission to live in their soul's rhythm and to do whatever they need to do to feel balanced and to recharge themselves."
We are all dancing to the beat of a different drum!

♥

. *faith* . **HOPE** . love . mind . **BODY** . *spirit* .

Chapter 9 - Everybody Matters

There is absolutely nothing that God did not put in his plan for you that you are not experiencing. "Learn the lesson" is a very important message. Everybody needs to stop thinking only of themselves. There is not one perfect person living on this earth. Never treat anyone like you are better than they are. This is a lesson that you should be passing down from generation to generation. If you have not taught this to your children, will you be teaching it to your grand-children? We should be leading by example. A perfect example would be to know that it is never too late change. It is what you feel in your heart that matters. As you enter that next phase of life what will you do as an elder? What wisdom do you plan to share, what lessons will you be passing on to those in your heart? Will you take the time to pass them on and make sure that your grandchildren understand the importance of how they should really be treating other people?

Children can be very cruel. That's a saying that dates way back. They look at another child and simply say the first thought that pops into their mind. They ridicule without thought, they pick on the less fortunate, and they whisper and tell secrets behind another child's back. They make fun of what other children wear, they push and shove. Let's just face it, the saying fits the lifestyle of many of our children. They think only of themselves, they want to be number one, they want to be the best, and they want to win. Who is taking the time to teach them that when you cheat, lie, steal, and make fun of others less fortunate than you, that you are not winning, you are not number one, and God really is watching everything that you do? If God really knows when one little sparrow falls to the ground, then he knows what you are doing.

It's one thing to be a part of a team and try to win at a sporting event, it's another thing to do this by cheating, tripping others, and causing others to fail. That's not winning.

We were given games as a source of enjoyment; we took them into the area of competition. The goal is, and has always been, just to do the best you can: "It doesn't matter if you win or lose, and it's how you play the game."

♥

Emotions are experiences that are chosen, not experiences to which you are subjected. This is not something that is widely understood. In an effort to simplify I will try to give you an example. You can be in a situation where someone is being very cruel to you. You have choice on how to handle that situation. Maybe you begin thinking along the lines of, "I really hate this person," or "I can't believe that this person has the nerve to do this to me," or possibly you begin to say hateful or cruel things back in response. What ever you do is your choice. You can choose to simply walk away and go on with your day, or you can choose to try and diffuse the situation with kindness. But the point is whatever emotion you feel will be chosen by you.

♥

God uses our feelings to communicate to us and through us. Feeling is the language of the soul. If you really want to know what's true for you about something, look to how you are feeling about it. Hidden in your deepest feelings is your highest truth. The goal is to get to those feelings.

Thoughts and feelings are not the same. Words are merely utter-ances: noises that stand for feelings, thoughts and experience. Words may help you to understand something, but experience will allow you to know it.

It is very important that we are in touch with our feelings.

♥

The highest feeling is the experience of unity with all that is. This

faith . **HOPE** . love . mind . **BODY** . *spirit* .

Chapter 9 - Everybody Matters

is the great return to truth for which the soul yearns. This is the feeling of perfect love. Perfect love is to feeling what perfect white is to color. White is every other color that exists, combined.

Love is the summation of all feeling. It is the sum total. The aggregate amount. The everything. Thus for the soul to experience perfect love, it must experience every human feeling.

♥

It is very important that we learn to trust and honor our deepest needs and feelings. It is in our desires that we will find the way in which our soul will be guided along our path in this life.
Whenever you feel an inner sense that it's time to take better care of something, someone, or yourself, the source of this guidance is God. Whenever you feel an urge to serve the world, this desire comes from heaven.

♥

One man may "sharpen" another, but you have to get close enough to let sparks fly. That implies openness, honesty, vulnerability, and the willingness to receive constructive criticism.

An anxious heart weighs a man down, but a kind word cheers him up. Be sure the words you say to others are kind and encouraging.

♥

Bad things happen in this world. We have all seen and heard many horrible tales. When we see people hurting, when we see children being lured into evil things, if we just simply sit idly by and we don't get angry, or if we don't weep for them, then something is wrong deep inside of us.

(Ephesians 4:27) Do not give the devil a foothold…

faith . HOPE . love . mind . BODY . *spirit* .

When you see pain and suffering if your heart is compelled, then follow your heart and do something.

Life is uncertain. No one knows what tomorrow will bring. Be a part of this life. Don't just sit back and watch things happen, especially if those things are wrong. Get up and do something.

♥

Play by the rules, and let God take care of the results.

God gave us two ears and one mouth so that we would listen twice as much as we talk.

♥

A good name is more desirable than great riches; to be esteemed is better than silver or gold. (Proverbs 22:1)

Of all the gifts we can give to our children, none is greater than the gift of a good name.

When you leave this earth there are two things that people will remember about you, one is character and the other is relationships. What kind of person were you and how did you treat other people?

♥

Train a child in the way he should go, and when he is old he will not turn from it. Proverbs 22:6

To raise a child "in the way he should go" is to teach him to choose the path of righteousness and to reject the path of evil.

Children make many mistakes in the course of life, but those raised in a Godly home will be inclined toward righteousness.

The best thing parents can do for their sons or daughters is to give them an example worth following. By God's grace, the pattern of sin

. faith . HOPE . love . mind . BODY . spirit .

Chapter 9 - Everybody Matters

can be broken and godly heritage established.

♥

"The fear of the Lord is the beginning of knowledge." If you have four advanced degrees but don't have the fear of the Lord, you would be better off as an uneducated reader of the Bible who at least believes in God. I am in favor of education that bows the knee to Jesus Christ. If you have to make a choice, choose the fear of the Lord, for without it you're still in spiritual kindergarten.
Many are the plans in a man's heart, but it is always the Lord's purpose that will prevail.

♥

God never intended that you should live the Christian life by yourself. He intended that as you join your life with other people, they would help you and you would help them. We are not meant to go through this life alone. God never intended that we face all of our hardships alone. That's why he gave us family and friends. We are all supposed to be there for each other.

♥

The term "heart" in the Bible generally refers to the innermost part of life. It is the decision-making center, the source of motives, seat of passions, and the center of the conscience. It is the true place "where life makes up its mind."
Proverbs has a great deal to say about the heart. It is our source for wisdom and understanding. It is the origin of both deceit and joy. Your heart may trust in God or take the long road and live a life of hardship and pain.

Passage Proverbs 2:10:
   10When wisdom entereth into thine heart, and knowledge is pleasant unto thy soul.

faith . HOPE . love . mind . BODY . *spirit*.

Passage Proverbs 8:5:
    5 O ye simple, understand wisdom: and, ye fools, be ye of an understanding heart.
Passage Proverbs 6:14:
    14 Forwardness is in his heart, he deviseth mischief continually; he soweth discord.
Passage Proverbs 15:30:
    30 The light of the eyes rejoiceth the heart: and a good report maketh the bones fat.
Passage Proverbs 14:14:
    14 The backslider in heart shall be filled with his own ways: and a good man shall be satisfied from himself.
Passage Proverbs 17:3:
    3 The fining pot is for silver, and the furnace for gold: but the LORD trieth the hearts.

♥

"For out of the overflow of the heart the mouth speaks." This verse cuts both ways. Whatever is on the inside will eventually come out - whether good or bad. If a person's heart is dirty, he cannot produce purity in his life.

What goes in must come out. Sooner or later your thoughts translate into reality. You're not what you think you are, but what you think, you are.

• If you focus on the truth, you will speak the truth.
• If you look on noble things, nobility will mark your life.
• If you seek out lovely things, your life will be lovely to others.
• If you dwell on the right, the wrong will seem less attractive to you.
• If you look for virtue, you will find it.
• If you search for higher things, you will elevate your own life.

faith . **HOPE** . love . mind . **BODY** . *spirit* .

Chapter 9 - Everybody Matters

Passage Proverbs 3:5:
  5Trust in the LORD with all thine heart; and lean not unto thine own understanding.
Proverbs 6:16-19 tells us seven things the Lord hates. Two especially deal with the lack of honesty: a lying tongue and the false witness who pours out lies. Proverbs 14:25 tells us that "a truthful witness saves lives, but a false witness is deceitful." According to Proverbs 12:19, "Truthful lips endure forever, but a lying tongue lasts only a moment."

♥

Many years ago, we all began making choices on our own. The choices that we have made to this date are the choices that have put us where we are today. We are where we are because of our thinking. Our thinking dictates our decisions. Our decisions are our choices.

Our future is in our hands. It will be what we decide we want it to be. Other people, places and things are not responsible for us. We are where we are because of the choices that we made.
When someone says, "It's not my fault," they really need to think about what they are saying. If you are in a situation, and it's not your fault, how did you get involved in the situation? There are consequences for all the choices that we make. It doesn't matter if they are large or small; there are consequences.

♥

It is so vitally important that we seek wisdom. It is imperative that we keep learning, keep researching long after we get out of school.

♥

Our way of thinking creates a pathway to our success or failure. If we are not taking responsibility for our current situations, we are limiting ourselves for what will come to us in our future.

♥

Our thoughts should always be constructive and never destructive,

faith . **HOPE** . love . mind . **BODY** . *spirit* .

Our minds should be focused on solutions when we have problems, and not on the problems themselves.

We control our thoughts 100% of the time. We control our emotions 100% of the time. We should not be asking "Why me?" we should be asking "Why not me?" The sky is the limit to what you can accomplish. If you set your mind to something, and you find that you really enjoy doing it, then why not you? Why not keep doing it? You can be whatever you want to be. We do not all need or want to be filthy rich. What we really want is to be happy, joyous and comfortable.

♥

If you enjoy long walks on the beach, then live near a beach. If you love all 4 seasons of the year, then live in the Midwest, some place like DeSoto, Missouri. Life was not meant to be difficult. We are supposed to be happy. Being happy is a choice, a personal choice! We can all be going through some difficult times and/or situations. But those are lessons. We should be doing research and studying to find our solutions, but they were not meant to take away all of the rest of the joy that is in our lives.

♥

I realize that sometimes our crisis situations or issues of turmoil can overwhelm us. They can consume our thoughts day in and day out. We have all heard that we should let it go, but letting go of something that has you very upset or disturbed is not an easy task to do. It's OK to get depressed about issues that are going on in your life, as long as you do not stay depressed for long. During the more difficult times of our lives, if you feel yourself falling into depression the best way out is to fall into prayer…

♥

When I was going through major issues with my ex-partner and being faced with a potential federal lawsuit, I can honestly tell you

. *faith* . **HOPE** . love . mind . **BODY** . *spirit* .

Chapter 9 - Everybody Matters

that I was not a happy camper. I didn't want to do anything, I didn't want to go anywhere, and I didn't feel like talking to anyone. I would come home from work and just sit in my room. Although I was sitting in my room alone, and many people were very concerned for me, I allowed myself to be sad about the situation. But I did not allow myself to stay sad or depressed for very long. I told myself, "You have 30 days to take it all in, get out all of your "female emotions," scream, yell, cry, mope…whatever you feel the need to do, but after that you must find the solution to your problems."

I'm very lucky that I have read all of the books that you see in my bibliography. Although I gave myself 30 days of alone time to the outside world, I had 30 days of long talks with the Lord. I prayed for solutions and answers and he gave me hope, and he gave me help, and he gave me answers.

I have faced many serious situations in my life, from issues with my children, parents, friends, family ,you name it. I have seen some trauma, and I have lived in trauma. I'm hoping that for a while my traumatic experiences will come to an end. But one thing I know for sure is that when there is trauma in my life I know how to handle it. I always handle it with prayer.

♥

To my children,
My gift to the world…

I hope that you always stand up for yourself and testify that you know true love.
For I will always, always love you.

With just a little faith, your love really will move mountains.

faith . **HOPE** . love . mind . **BODY** . *spirit* .

And someday you will face a mountain that you must move.

Everyone wants a chance to be with that special someone.
That person that makes you whole.
You will know, my special ones, that you have found that special
someone when you reach clear around your heart and they are
standing there.
Then you will spend the rest of your life both here and in eternity
with them.
For you will have given them the true gift of your heart.
Your Love.
♥
Remember, my precious ones, the power in your words, and use them
with kindness and respect.
♥
Mindy…you put the blue back in my sky.
Bradley…you are the silver lining in my clouds.
Christopher…you put the red back in my rose.

When I am with the 3 of you and I look into your eyes, I see the color
of the stars in the sky.
♥
Melinda…Mindy, Minder Winders, My Little Miss Sunshine Girl,
The Grace of my Life, My Little Princess, My Dear Sweet Beautiful
Girl, Now a woman. When I remember my dreams, I know that it is
you that made them all come true.

Bradley…Baby Dumpling, My Pal always, Mommy's Little Man, the
Apple of My Eye, the Answers to My Prayers, Bradder Fradder,
Daaaden, My Little Angel. With you in my life I will always have
paradise.

Christopher…Chrissee Joe, Critter Bug, Little Gritz, Mommy's Boy

faith . **HOPE** . love . mind . **BODY** . *spirit*.

Chapter 9 - Everybody Matters

always, Mommy's Baby of Joy, My Little Guy, Christpher Joseph Gorman, what are you doing? You, my son, will always be my baby.

On this day I give you the book of my heart.
I will always walk this path with you.
You are the 3 Loves of my life.
Mom

These are lessons that I hope that you will learn.

Although you perceive yourself as weak and frail, with wasted hopes and devastated dreams, born but to die, to weep and suffer pain, hear this: "All power is given unto you in Earth and Heaven. There is nothing that you cannot do."

Nothing can hurt you unless you give it the power to do so.

Stop thinking about the past and put the present into God's kind hands.

One very important lesson that I have learned after 50 years on this earth is that it is really important that you balance your days. Too much of any one thing is not good for you. Working for 16-hour days might help you financially, but it will definitely hurt you with your friends and family. The time that you take away from them to spend at your job is time that you will never get back again. If you take too much time away from them, they might just stop calling.

My Grandma used to say "There are times when the days seem to drag on, but yet the years always seem to fly by." Try really hard to the days seem to drag on, but yet the years always seem to fly by. Try really hard to do what you love, and love what you do. But always take time to be with the ones whom you love and who love you.

♥

Did you know it is estimated that the average human being uses only a small portion of his potential mental capacity? The remainder lies dormant until he applies his mind to the task of self-improvement.

God wants you to be ambitious; He is expecting you to be determined, and strive to succeed. After all, it was He who put the desire into your heart. So it only goes without saying that he would surely see to it that your desire will be fulfilled to the extent that you are ready for it.

From the place of power will come the source for every need, the support for all of your problems, and the answer to all of your ambitions! God wants you to have success in your undertakings, as long as they are honest and forthright.

When you begin to devote your time and energy to self-improvement, this cannot be done without finding your way to God. For that is the "self" that most needs improvement in all of us. Once you begin this journey you will never want it to stop. It will lead you to the answers to all the questions that you have wondered about for most of your life.

Did you know that God wants you to "whistle while you work?" Well, in a sense, he wants you to be happy in the work that you are doing. For every ten people who are in the wrong type of work there are 1000 people who are in the right kind of work but are not happy because they long for the wrong kind of work. Sometimes the only thing that is holding you back, the thing that is keeping you from realizing your dreams, is "your own attitude" toward work!

♥

faith . HOPE . love . mind . BODY . *spirit* .

Chapter 9 - Everybody Matters

Such thoughts as regret, disappointment, anger, frustration, or despair over yesterday's happenings will to be responsible for the negative conditions that originally caused them and then shadow your appreciation of today's opportunities for growth. Therefore, it is wise to release the past. Let the past bury its dead. Life is only in the self -perpetuating present. This very moment is priceless to you for it is forming the next and the next. Learn to think and live in the present now.

♥

God always says it's a good morning, a beautiful day. Count your blessings and you will know why.

♥

The qualities that lead to success are stretched. We concentrate on developing them. To fit in we cut ourselves off from what is not valued by others and lose part of our souls in the process. What we reject in ourselves, we bury alive in the unconscious.
Begin to find yourself, find your virtues, and move on from there.

♥

Time can take a lot of things away from you, but it can never steal what you hold valuable in your heart.

♥

Difficulties present choices: We can either waste away from our wounds or use them to grow our souls. The choice will always be yours.

♥

God wants you to find joy in every day. Count your blessings at the end of the day. Keep your life in balance. But always know that there is joy out there for you when you find your way.

♥

Times of crisis are God's message to us to start paying attention. Wake up. Pay attention. Look at what is important and seek where

faith . **HOPE**. love . mind . **BODY** . *spirit*.

you can add to the world rather than take away.

♥

There is a reason for every life on this earth. Every life has a purpose. There is a reason that you were born into your family.

♥

Never take it for granted that you have only one way to go. As you open your mind to consider your numerous opportunities, new ideas will come to you.

Remember that God has to work through someone else to answer most of our prayers. In the same manner, he has to work through you to answer somebody else's.

Understand this and start listening. When you hear a song out there on the radio that makes you stop and think, then do just that; because God is sending you a message. The deeper thought is that he is sending it out across the airways; he is trying to reach more than just you with his message. Are you sharing it? Are you listening? Don't you think it's time you did?

Let's talk about casting out some stones. I get so tired of hearing about people's faults on TV and reading about them in print. Whatever happened to "if you don't have anything good to say about someone then say nothing," especially across the airways. Good "Lord" evil spreads evil. Let's just pass it around, for heaven's sake. Someone should be grounded! Maybe we could start to divide the newspaper into 2 sections, good news and bad news. I don't know about anyone else but I'm only reading the good. I've had enough of the "bad." I am not going to bless them with my time. But that is what the world seems to have done. Share the bad, pass it around,

. *faith* . **HOPE** . love . mind . **BODY** . *spirit* .

Chapter 9 - Everybody Matters

and make sure everybody gets some. Please, tell me more about what matters, that someone saved the life of another, that there really are angels on this earth that live among us. Lord, let me be one of them. Let me walk the right path for my children to follow, let me light a big enough blaze in their heart that they will follow the right path when I am gone.

Give me the wisdom that I need to understand this world! Somehow let us all figure out how to say NO to bad things at the same time! Then let us stay that way. Oh, what a wonderful world it would be if there were no more BAD!

But I know this: I can make a difference.   One chooses to be BAD, I know that as well as others.

I can make a difference by living my life this way knowing those facts, but I can make a bigger difference by teaching it to those I love.

♥

True joy contains within it all the forces for good. If you will cultivate joy, you will find your life and affairs being arranged accordingly. But the great secret of the power of joy is this: Just getting the feeling or realization of joy is all that matters. Everything else will follow. When you can get a realization of joy, when you can stir up warm feelings of joy from within yourself, then you have released the greatest power of heaven and earth to solve your problems, as well as bring forth new good.

Often that realization of joy will come when you are thinking of other things and you least expect it. You may be in a quiet, prayerful, meditative state, and when that feeling of joy wells up within you, you can know your problems are being solved. The good is at work for you. Joy is divine, and it is bringing divine results to you. It is that sublime, divine power of good you are feeling that is being translated as a joyous realization. When this happens, there is nothing more to be anxious about. Your good is at hand.

faith . **HOPE** . love . mind . **BODY** . *spirit* .

No matter what you are going through, don't forget to laugh; don't forget to smell the roses. In other words, count your blessings. Write them down if you must! But always be grateful for that which you do have. It could all be taken away from you in an instant. You could blink and it could all be gone.
All that you have is a gift, remember that! Cherish it for all the right reasons.

♥

When a mother wants to leave behind a valuable lesson for her children she knows that she must reach to the heart of the child. It is only through the heart that these lessons will be learned.

♥

Your birth is simply a sign that your journey has begun.

♥

Affirmations – Their value and why they work
Affirmations are positive, constructive statements phrased in the first person. They are used in order to establish in the individual a new order of thinking. Sometimes we precede the affirmation with a denial of the old order of thinking.
You have to feel them and accept them in order for them to be effective.
Sell yourself on the idea that there is a new order of thinking for you and then it will become your experience.
Within you is all that you will ever need to bring about prosperity – the wisdom, the intelligence, the power, the ideas. Everything you need begins in your mind.

Every one of us is endowed with the gift of creative imagination. Creative imagination is using the imagination creatively to envision that which you desire. Allow yourself to see it happening.

Creative imagination is a form of prayer. Jesus was speaking of

faith . HOPE . love . mind . BODY . *spirit* .

Chapter 9 - Everybody Matters

creative imagination when he said, "What things so ever ye desire, when ye pray, believe that ye receive them, and ye shall have them." In other words, if you can imagine receiving your desires, they will come into your experience.

♥

Much of the fruit we call good deeds grows from the root of religious belief. Even those with no particular faith or creed find themselves compelled toward some sort of decency. And so they participate (or at least feel guilty when they don't). In big and small ways we all do something we consider good because we want to fix what we consider bad. Doing good is not meant to be random acts of kindness. We are all supposed to do good everyday. Give the man with the cardboard sign a dollar or two! Teach your children; help them stay on the right path. Be there for each other when times are difficult. Take home a lost pet, or at least take it to a shelter.

You have to want to do your good for good reasons. It's OK to repent, as long as you stop doing whatever caused you to repent.

♥

If there were such a thing as sin, this would be it: to allow yourself to become what you are because of the experience of others. This is the "sin" you have committed. All of you! You do not await your own experience, you accept the experience of others as gospel, and then, when you encounter the actual experience for the first time, you overlay what you think you already know onto the encounter. Experience it for yourself, see what you get out of it.

♥

Now, having seen the differences between where you are and where you want to be, begin to change, consciously change, your thoughts, words, and actions to match your grandest vision.

This is a call to stop such unconscious living. It is a challenge to

faith . **HOPE** . love . mind . **BODY** . *spirit*

which your soul has called you from the beginning of time.

♥

That which you think, speak and do becomes obvious in your reality.
1. To think, speak, and do something that you do not truly believe is impossible. Therefore, the process of creation must include belief, or knowing. This is absolute faith. This is beyond hoping. This is the knowing of a certainty ("By your faith ye shall be healed"). Therefore, the doing part of creation always includes knowing. It is a gut-level clarity, a total certainty, a complete acceptance as reality of something.
2.   This place of knowing is a place of intense and incredible gratitude. It is thankfulness in advance. And that, perhaps, is the biggest key to creation: to be grateful before, and for, the creation. Such taking for granted is not only condoned, but encouraged. It is the sure sign of mastery. All masters know in advance that the deed has been done.

If there is some aspect of creation you find you do not enjoy, bless it and simply change it. Choose again. Call forth a new reality. Think a new thought. Say a new word. Do a new thing. Do this magnificently and the rest of the world will follow you. Ask it to. Call for it to. Say, "I am the life and the way, follow me."

♥

"I am," is the strongest creative statement in the universe. Whatever you think, whatever you say, after the words "I am" sets into motion those experiences, calls them forth, brings them to you.

The universe responds to "I am" as would a genie in a bottle. It is all a matter of discipline. It is a question of intent.

Study this, master this, and learn this. You are what you think you

. faith . HOPE . love . mind . BODY . spirit .

Chapter 9 - Everybody Matters

you are. But you still have to look at yourself and live with yourself every day.

***

When you catch yourself thinking negative thoughts – thoughts that negate your highest idea about a thing - then think again! I want you to do this, literally. If you think you are in a state of unhappiness or despair, and no good can come of this, think again. If you think the world is a bad place, filled with negative events, think again. If you think your life is falling apart, and it looks as if you'll never get it back together again, think again. You can train yourself to do this. Think about it!

♥

Faith is that attribute of divinity in man that enables him to draw upon this invisible energy source and bring it forth into tangible or visible form. It's as simple as that.
Faith is therefore the key that unlocks all the doors leading to success, health and prosperity.

If you can establish faith strong enough within your consciousness, all things become easy for you to achieve. It is the law that Jesus referred to when he said: "To him that believeth, all things are possible." (Mark 9:23)

"Before they call, I will answer." (Is. 65:24)
Faith is therefore the key that unlocks all doors leading to success, health and prosperity.

Faith is the activating motive of the intellect. It is a virtue…

From moment to moment, you are always facing unproven experiences, and it is your complete confidence in their outcome that makes your going on possible. "We walk by faith, not by sight." (II Cor. 5:7)

faith . **HOPE** . love . mind . **BODY** . *spirit* .

You inherit the Kingdom when you have established your oneness with the Father and you think and act accordingly. (Matt: 25:34) That is faith. To repeat, it is the confident knowledge, the inner conviction, the unfaltering trust in things that truly exist, even though they are not visible to the physical eye.

To sum it all up, faith may be defined as the creative power of God acting through the subconscious mind of man. Faith is therefore man's use of his own inherent God power; and it is controlled by his own free will. Faith helps us project into reality that which originates in imaginative thinking.

"According to your faith Be it unto you." (Matt. 9:29)
♥
When the Bible says we walk by faith, it is not kidding. There are days that our faith is tested to the point that we shiver. At some points in your life you will feel like "all is right with my little world." Then there will come the times that you feel as though if one more bomb is dropped on you, you hope it falls directly on you and takes you out of your misery and/or pain. Well that, my friend, is called a "wake-up call." This is when your "faith is being tested."
Life on earth is a "class." We go from grade to grade as we get older and closer to going home. The class that we all have in common and are trying to learn is the one that takes us home. Deep in everyone's heart is the final lesson. There is a God, or a higher place.

When your faith is being tested, you are being sent a message. Search your heart for that message, because in the end what really mattered the most to you in this life? Now, stop and think about that. Was it what you did? Or was it who you were doing it with? The answer is who your were doing it with.

faith . **HOPE** . love . mind . **BODY** . *spirit* .

Chapter 9 - Everybody Matters

Because when you're smiling, and laughing, and feeling happy and joyous it's because your soul is in the presence of other souls that you love and care for. That is why you feel joyous. When they suffer, you suffer, because your soul aches for them. "That's love!" "That's Life."

When it comes to wisdom, which is "The lesson," you just need to remember something: "The harder the lesson the greater the gift of knowledge." What does this mean? When you get through the lessons; God has blessed you tenfold for passing them. For when you do, you have found your way home, and you will truly know that what lies and waits for you is heaven on earth! Understand those words; feel joyous every day. Talk to the person who matters most; go to the one who can really help you. Go deep, deep within, and you will shiver. Because you are finding your way home.
Just know that when the ending says : "this too shall pass," it is true. All things do come to an end.

Eventually we will all die, and it will be all over. Or will it? So, now what do you think? Is there a heaven? Wouldn't you like to go there? I really think I would! Because when my life is "good," it is really good. We have all had "good" times, the days when we smile, and laugh, and get up and just look forward to the day - the ones where we say, "thank you, God" for giving me this day, this glorious beautiful day. You think about all the good things that happened that day and you feel blessed. When this happens, don't take it for granted. Be sure that you are saying "thank you" for those blessings, so that they will be magnified for you and they will continue. We are entering our next level of teaching, which is called "grand parenting." We have watched our parents with our kids, and now our babies are having babies. It really is the next generation. The question is, are you going to sit back and enjoy the ride? Or are you going to fight

faith. **HOPE**. love. mind. **BODY**. *spirit*.

Grandma's Shoebox

this kicking and screaming? It's coming; this is your first lesson! Are you getting it? Find your way, my child; mom and dad won't always be here.

The "Take your head out of the sand" lesson. When you get it, you really get it. You know what matters in the end, it was always the same thing: who you loved, who loved you, who did you make happy, and enjoying your day! But you, alone, set your levels. "Hence, we walk by faith and not by sight." If you believe in God you must have faith. The Bible has told this to all of us for what seems like forever! We walk by faith and not by sight. If you are getting this point, your lives are a lot easier, because then we really do believe that this too shall pass. You have to believe with all of your heart!

♥

From moment to moment you are always facing unproven experiences and it is in your complete confidence in their outcome that makes your ongoing possible. "We walk by faith, not by sight." (IICor. 5:7)

There is no need to analyze or rationalize the truth. It defies analysis. "It is." All great demonstrations are brought forth by a deep and steadfast faith. Divine intelligence will only do for you what it can do through you, and your state of consciousness determines the measure of your demonstration.
Therefore be genuine in your thought and actions and avoid deception.
According to your faith be it unto you. (Matt 9:29)

The truth is an ever-present reality in your life. You must accept it and apply it in everything you do. Your faith will then release you from the burden of the past, and "the truth will make you free." (John 8:32)

. *faith* . **HOPE** . love . mind . **BODY** . *spirit* .

Chapter 9 - Everybody Matters

♥

The Angel of wisdom teaches us that nothing happens without a reason. No guidance from any angel is unconsidered. We are always given what we need, we are never given more than we can handle.

Sorrow and sadness can come to you in many ways, not always through death. Sometimes it is just through the hard lessons that life has dealt you. When you kneel to pray, you are drawing upon a power from the deepest most intimate depths of your being, from the kingdom within you. This is the only power that can help you overcome sorrow and sadness. Once you put your troubles into the gentle, kind hands of God, you have only one thing to look forward to, "My peace I give unto you."

Everything that you are experiencing is in a plan set forth by God. You are here to "learn the lesson" that is is his message. "Everybody," and he means "everybody" - there is not one perfect person on this earth. So don't ever treat anyone like you are better than they are; because you are not. Now, if you didn't teach that to your children, are you going to teach it to your grandchildren? Because you should have taught it by example; that is the deeper lesson. Go even deeper and you really do know it's never too late to change; it is what you feel in your heart that matters. Now as you enter that "next" phase of life, what will you as an "elder", what "wisdom" will you take the time to pass down to your grandchildren? Think long and hard about your answers, because as a child if you were blessed, truly blessed with wonderful parents, and grandparents, you will pass it on. You will verbally give the child the preparation that it needs impressed into its head through its heart where it truly learns from. There really is heaven on earth! It is our duty to pass down our wisdom and to pass it down with pride. I am no better or worse than anyone else in

faith . **HOPE** . love . mind . **BODY** . *spirit* .

God's eyes. We are all His creatures, and he really does love us all the same; for in His eyes, we really are all one!!

♥

If you listen to country music and you hear that song that talks about blinking, and all the things in life you could miss with a blink, when you have faith you feel the deeper message of the song! What do you think?

My Grandma used to say "God will do his work through the voices of his angels." He will get to you any way that he can. So, if nothing happens without a reason, stop and think of those possibilities. It could boggle your mind.

♥

When I go to sleep at night, I am not asking for forgiveness for too many wrongs of that day. I don't toss and turn after I give my problems to God; he takes them off my shoulders for the night so I can rest. I know now that in order to solve my problems I must use my "mind" and I must think and listen to find the solution! In situations where my faith is being tested, it's not hard to know what to do. I simply follow my inner most feelings.

♥

Recognize the beliefs you acquired from your parents and consciously decide if you want to keep them. Forgive your parents for any beliefs they may have taught you that you no longer want. Realize that they did the best they knew how.

After you discover a belief that is holding you back, let go of it and create a new belief. Share your lessons with your parents and all the other loving souls in your life. You might be able to spark a flame (light) in their hearts.

♥

Your integrity leads you to those choices and situations that are prosperous for you. Honor your integrity and you will be repaid

. faith . HOPE . love . mind . BODY . spirit .

Chapter 9 - Everybody Matters

many times over with increased prosperity. It is important to feel good about everything you do, to act upon your values, to be honest with the people you deal with, and to come from your truth. Your integrity challenges you to look at what is real and important to you, and to choose that over illusions, promises, and glamour. Come from your highest ideals, follow your own wisdom over another person's, and do things in ways that honor you and feel right to you. Honor everyone you deal with and hold everything you do up to the light of your soul. For every experience that you had, you also had an experience that was nearly its opposite.

♥

As you make your way in this world, always know that you are a part of God. He will always be here for you. Share your wisdom that you have learned along the way.

God's love for you will always be strong and true. There is nothing that you could ever do to change the love that He feels for you.

Someday you will understand why I have told you to praise God for the life that he has given you.

Leave behind your own message. Write down the days that have touched your heart. Tell your future loved ones why you are who you are.

♥

Before you know it, your children are all grown. What you taught them about God is a part of what they will pass down to your grandchildren. Know what you will say when they ask the question "why." Keep your family information close to your heart. Keep God in your life every day.

♥

. *faith* . **HOPE** . love . mind . **BODY** . *spirit* .

Grandma's Shoebox

Chapter 10

A Call from Your Heart

♥

There is a longing deep down inside all of us. It starts in our soul. We all long for home. Home really is where the heart is. Our hearts belong to the Lord. So our hearts long to be with him. There are times in all of us when we just feel like there is something missing in our lives. It's a feeling that stirs inside you. You sometimes feel like you just can't quite put your finger on it, but it still longs deep inside you. I believe that is your heart longing for what it has always known.

When you want to try to figure out what that longing is for, that is when you start your search. You begin to search your soul. When I started that journey, I had lots of questions. I began my search looking for answers. I didn't really know what answers I was looking for, but I knew that I was on a mission.

Early in my marriage, I began looking for answers. I had once read a book that said if God wants you to know something he will put a longing for it in your heart, and he will leave it there until you do something about it. If there is a book that you should read, many times your Angels will lead you to the book.

I have attached a Bibliography at the end of this book. These are the books that I have read that are still in my possession. I have given away a lot of books to family and friends. When I am inspired by something in a book, sometimes I will think of a friend or loved one who I think could benefit by the book. I would pass it on to them. After many years of passing on my books and never getting them back, I finally started just buying a new one that I could pass on.

♥

It is rare that I would ever read a book and not find something in there that helps the longing in my heart. It's also rare that I would not

faith . **HOPE** . love . mind . **BODY** . *spirit* .

Grandma's Shoebox

pass that information on to another. If it's a really good book, I will buy multiple copies and give them as gifts. It's funny because I give books to people all the time, I don't even know if they enjoy reading or if they ever read the books that I give them. But someday, maybe, just maybe, their heart might find its way to that book and they will find the gift inside the pages that were meant for them. I don't believe that I would have given them the book if they weren't supposed to have it. There really are no coincidences. Everything in this life happens for a reason.

Discovering the reasons is just part of the journey. It's how we find our way home.

♥

In all the books that I have read, there has never been one that did not tell me that my faith was what will keep me strong and help me solve my problems.

Faith is the answer to your problems. When you finally take this to heart and really understand this great truth, then your life will become very different.

You will be able to overcome any problem that life may send your way with confidence, the confidence that comes with true abiding Faith in God's love for you.

When "fate" takes a hand in your life it usually leads you to a deeper understanding of "faith." We all have issues that we are dealing with everyday of our lives. These issues get a little easier to handle as you develop a stronger "faith" in the person up above. You can begin to relax and share in all the blessings that God has provided out of his great love for his children. It really is simple. You just have to "keep the faith in Him and with Him" alive in your heart.

♥

faith . **HOPE** . love . mind . **BODY** . *spirit* .

Chapter 10 - A Call from Your Heart

Your thoughts have incredible power, and they manifest everything that happens in your life. What are you thinking about? Have you ever noticed that when you are thinking bad thoughts, or unpleasant thoughts, your emotions change? You have to be very careful with what you allow to stay in your mind. It's one thing to think of unpleasant things, it's another thing to let them dwell in your mind. If you allow them to stay there, then you are allowing them to control you. Only you have control over what you let enter your head…

That which you think about you draw to you. Don't ever think that you can't change things, because you surely can. Maybe just one decision that you make could change the world as you know it.

♥

Your heart has a special purpose. It was put inside of you before your soul was placed in your mother's womb. Some people find that purpose early in their life and they seem to be able to live their life's purpose throughout their entire life. Then there are others who spend many years looking for what their heart is longing for. When they discover it, they realize it was right in their heart the whole time they were looking. For some, it's a feeling that is similar to looking for a missing pair of reading glasses and then finding them on the top of your head. When you finally figure it out, the lights in your head come on. Your thoughts change, you are suddenly motivated, and your life improves drastically.

Some people have more lessons to learn in this life than others. While we are here, all of life is a discovery process. If you spend too much time discovering your way into trouble, doing things that you know are wrong, hurting or causing pain to others, life is not going to be on your side. You are always going to feel as though life is out to get you. In fact it is. We all have choices that we make about the paths that we take. We have always had the choice of doing right or wrong. We have been told for generations, do unto others, honor your parents, keep God first in your life, do not steal. I believe that every home should have the Ten Commandments hanging where you are reminded every day of the rules of life.

You may know someone who never seems to have many issues that they are struggling with, then know someone else who seems to find difficulty around every corner. It's highly likely that the man with fewer problems has a better relationship with God than the one who struggles everyday. The importance of everyone's lesson is to search your heart for your answers. Go back and right your wrongs, mend your fences, find forgiveness, and move along on your journey. That is one thing that we all have in common. Our final destination on this journey of life is what we are all striving for.

You can have days when you feel as if it's heaven on earth, but this is not heaven. This is still earth, and there are things that you must deal with in order to earn your way into heaven. Our journey will always lead us home. Home is where our hearts want to be. But you won't get home if your heart is not in the right place.

If you dwell on your problems, you will keep them close to you, but if you give them up to the Lord every night when you say your prayers, he will surely give you a peaceful night's sleep and fill your heart with hope for tomorrow. Your heart will always be filled with answers from above if you just allow yourself to go within and find them.

When it's time for you to make changes in your life and live the purpose that is in your heart, God will often put roadblocks along your path. If necessary, he will stop you cold in your tracks. He will

. *faith* . **HOPE** . love . mind . **BODY** . *spirit* .

put a strong desire into your heart and soul to come back on the path that he put in your heart. When you are on the wrong path, you will know it. Life will be hard everyday. Nothing will come easily to you. You will struggle with almost every issue of life: home, family, friends, and work. In order to get back on the right path all you have to do is ask for his guidance. He will surely lead you back home again. His heart longs for you as you long for him.

Your soul always longs for what it already knows. That is its purpose. It will always lead you home. You have to be able to tune into its messages and then follow it when it speaks to you. Your soul speaks to you through the longings you feel in your heart.

♥

When changes occur in your life that lead you back on the right path, you will begin to notice that thoughts come into your mind much more easily. You find solutions to your problems without having to stress over them. Proper mental exercise will increase your chances for happiness, good health, wealth, and all the things that you want in this life.

By telling yourself that you cannot do something, this will surely stop you from doing it. Instead, start asking yourself how you can accomplish this task. The universe will hear your words and things will begin to change.

It is far easier to change yourself than it is to change everyone else in this world.

♥

Your heart puts only good thoughts and solutions into your mind. You have to take the time to listen and then think about it, and then move forward with your solutions. Your solutions should never be harmful to others. The way out of any of life's problems is through your mind. Keep using your brain, and soon you will be shown ways of solving whatever problem you are dealing with.

♥

It's not easy to put into words a description of how to follow your heart, but it's important enough for me to try. You were born with the gift of knowing right from wrong, good from bad, love from hate. When you do something that causes pain or problems for someone else you are not following what your heart is telling you. When you do the wrong things, the still small voice inside you starts questioning you. Then things in your life stop adding up; nothing seems to be going your way. All the good that you already have in your life seems to start slipping away.

It is so vitally important that you pay attention to the things in your life when your heart and soul are trying to reach you. Your physical body will begin to give you signs.

We are all born with a natural beauty that shines from within us. If you are right with the world, you can stare into your own eyes and see the beauty in your soul staring back at you.

When you go within for the answers, you will soon be given opportunities that will seem to manifest right before your eyes. Once you learn how to spot these opportunities, they will be placed before you for the rest of your life. God never stops giving us his blessing when we are living our lives the way he planned for us to.

It's a long, long way from here to where we are going. However, it's very important that we stay on the right path if we want to get to the final destination that was placed in our heart and soul.

♥

We all know someone who instead of trusting their own inner psyche or good judgment will follow the crowd just so they can fit in. For

. *faith* . HOPE . love . mind . BODY . *spirit* .

Chapter 10 - A Call from Your Heart

some reason people feel that it is so important to "fit in," when really what is important is to get along with each other. We do not need to try to fit ourselves into someone else's life. We just need to let nature take its course. If a person is supposed to be a part of your life, they will be. If they are not, they never will be. But trying to just fit in, and doing things that go against our better judgment, is not what our hearts would really have us do. It would just be better to blend in with the crowd than to force yourself to fit in.

Trust your insight; it is one of the many gifts you were given at birth. Use your brain and start thinking. The single most powerful asset that we all have is our "mind." Control your own thoughts, guide your own ship. Do what you know is best for you and right for you.

♥

It is extremely important that you know how to hear from your heart. If you have ever had God answer one of your prayers, then you know already how to hear from your heart. Remember, God's laws are simple; they are the paths that you must follow to get you to your final destination, no matter what that destination is. If it is prosperity, peace, happiness, you must obey these laws. He has placed every good thing in this world here for you. He asks only that you follow his laws. He has also placed the power to gain these things in your heart.

You should always be in touch with God. You should make time for him everyday, just like you make time to eat and sleep. If you want goodness in your life then, you must first be grateful for all the good that you have now, and you must say thanks. It's no different than thanking a friend for opening a door for you. It takes only a moment to offer up your thanks giving to the Lord, just a moment.

Scripture tells us that God hears our prayers and all our requests. It only makes sense that if he hears our prayers, we should be able to receive his answers to those requests.

. faith . **HOPE** *. love . mind .* **BODY** *. spirit .*

1 Chronicles 5:20
They were helped against them, and the Hagrites and all who were with them were given into their hand; for [2 Chr 14:11-13] they cried out to God in the battle, and He answered their prayers because [Ps 9:10; 20:7, 8; 22:4, 5] they trusted in Him.

1 John 4:6
[John 8:23; 1 John 4:4] We are from God; [John 8:47; 10:3-ff; 18:37] he who knows God listens to us; [1 Cor 14:37] he who is not from God does not listen to us By this we know [John 14:17] the spirit of truth and [1 Tim 4:1] the spirit of error.

God wants you to be ambitious. He is expecting you to be determined and striving to succeed. After all, it was He who put the desire into your heart.

So it only goes without saying that He would surely see to it that your desires will be fulfilled to the extent that you are ready for them. From the place of power will come the source for every need, and the support for all your problems, and the answer to all of your ambitions! God wants you to have success in your undertakings, as long as they are honest and forthright.

Genesis 22:14
Abraham called the name of that place The LORD Will Provide, as it is said to this day, "In the mount of the LORD [Gen 22:8] it will be provided."

Exodus 16:8
[The LORD Provides Meat] Moses said, "This will happen when the LORD gives you meat to eat in the evening, and bread to the full in the morning; for the LORD hears your grumblings which you grumble against Him. And what are we? Your gramblings are [1 Sam 8:7; Luke 10:16; Rom 13:2, 1 Thess 4:8] not against us but against the LORD."

faith . **HOPE** . love . mind . **BODY** . *spirit* .

Chapter 10 - A Call from Your Heart

Psalm 34:1
[The LORD, a Provider and Deliverer.] [A Psalm of David when he feigned madness before Abimelech, who drove him away and he departed.] I will [Eph 5:20; 1 Thess 5:18] bless the LORD at all times; His [Ps 71:6] praise shall continually be in my mouth.

♥

When one thinks, "There is so much to say," then one forgets to listen. Be restrained in what you say. Be attentive in your listening. Where you are is where you are supposed to be. The path to follow to all changes will be shown to you if you will but be attentive. If you follow the way that is shown to you, all uncertainty will end. Uncertainty is where difficulty lies. Confidence and ease will surely go together. There are no more decisions for you to make. There is only a call for a dedicated and devoted will, a will dedicated to the present moment, to those who are sent to you and to how you are to guide and respond to them. One will be a teacher; another, a student. The difference will be clear if you listen with your heart.

Deuteronomy 11:28
and the [Deut 28:15-68] curse, if you do not listen to the commandments of the LORD your God, but turn aside from the way which I am commanding you today, by following other gods which you have not known.

Judges 2:19
But it came about when the judge died, that they would turn back and act more corruptly than their fathers, in following other gods to serve them and bow down to them; they did not abandon their practices or their stubborn ways.

1 Samuel 6:12
And the cows took the straight way in the direction of [1 Sam 6:9] Beth-shemesh; they went along [Num 20:19] the highway, lowing as they went, and did not turn aside to the right or to the left. And the

faith . **HOPE** . love . mind . **BODY** . *spirit* .

lords of the Philistines followed them to the border of Beth-shemesh.
2 Kings 6:19
Then Elisha said to them, "This is not the way, nor is this the city;
follow me and I will bring you to the man whom you seek." And he
brought them to Samaria.
Job 31:7
"If my step has [Job 23:11] turned from the way, Or my heart
followed my eyes,Or if any [Job 9:30] spot has stuck to my hands,
Job 34:27
Because they [1 Sam 15:11] turned aside from following Him, And
[Job 21:14] had no regard for any of His ways;
Isaiah 26:8
Indeed, while following the way of [Is 51:4; 56:1] Your judgments, O
LORD,We have waited for You eagerly; [Is 12:4; 24:15; 25:1; 26:13]
Your name, even Your [Ex 3:15] memory, is the desire of our souls.
Isaiah 65:2)
" [Rom 10:21] I have spread out My hands all day long to a [Is 1:2,
23; 30:1, 9] rebellious people,Who walk in the way which is not
good, following their own [Ps 81:11, 12; Is 59:7; 66:18] thoughts,
Acts 16:17
Following after Paul and us, she kept crying out, saying, "These men
are bond-servants of [Mark 5:7] the Most High God, who are
proclaiming to you the way of salvation."
2 Peter 2:2
Many will follow their [Gen 19:5-ff; 2 Pet 2:7, 18; Jude 4] sensuality,
and because of them [Acts 16:17; 22:4; 24:14] the way of the truth
will be [Rom 2:24] maligned;
2 Peter 2:15
forsaking [Acts 13:10] the right way, they have gone astray, having
followed [Num 22:5, 7; Deut 23:4; Neh 13:2; Jude 11; Rev 2:14] the
way of Balaam, the son of Beor, who loved [2 Pet 2:13] the wages of
unrighteousness;

faith . **HOPE** . love . mind . **BODY** . *spirit*.

Chapter 10 - A Call from Your Heart

Genesis 24:5
The servant said to him, "Suppose the woman is not willing to follow me to this land; should I take your son back to the land from where you came?"

Genesis 24:39
" [Gen 24:5] I said to my master, 'Suppose the woman does not follow me."

Genesis 44:4
They had just gone out of [Gen 44:13] the city, and were not far off, when Joseph said to his house steward, "Up, follow the men; and when you overtake them, say to them, 'Why have you repaid evil for good? ?

Exodus 11:8
" [Ex 12:31-33] All these your servants will come down to me and bow themselves before me, saying, 'Go out, you and all the people who follow you,' and after that I will go out " [Heb 11:27] And he went out from Pharaoh in hot anger.

Numbers 14:24
"But My servant Caleb, [Num 14:6-9] because he has had a different spirit and has followed Me fully, [Num 26:65; 32:12; Deut 1:36; Josh 14:6-15] I will bring into the land which he entered, and his descendants shall take possession of it."

Numbers 32:11
"[Num 14:28-30] None of the men who came up from Egypt, from twenty years old and upward, shall see the land which I swore to Abraham, to Isaac and to Jacob; for they did not follow Me fully, "

Deuteronomy 4:3
" [Num 25:1-9] Your eyes have seen what the LORD has done in the case of Baal-peor, for all the men who followed Baal-peor, the LORD your God has destroyed them from among you."

. *faith* . **HOPE** . love . mind . **BODY** . *spirit* .

Deuteronomy 7:4

"For they will turn your sons away from following Me to serve other gods; then the anger of the LORD will be kindled against you and [Deut 4:26] He will quickly destroy you.

Joshua 14:8

"Nevertheless my brethren who went up with me made the heart of the people melt with fear; but [Num 14:24; Deut 1:36] I followed the LORD my God fully.

Judges 4:14

Deborah said to Barak, "Arise! For this is the day in which the LORD has given Sisera into your hands; [Or has not the LORD gone...?] behold, [Deut 9:3; 2 Sam 5:24; Ps 68:7] the LORD has gone out before you." So Barak went down from Mount Tabor with ten thousand men following him.

Judges 6:35

He sent messengers throughout Manasseh, and they also were called together to follow him; and he sent messengers to Asher, [Judg 4:6, 10; 5:18] Zebulun, and Naphtali, and [Judg 7:3] they came up to meet them.

Judges 8:5

He said to the men of [Gen 33:17] Succoth, "Please give loaves of bread to the people who are following me, for they are weary, and I am pursuing Zebah and Zalmunna, the kings of Midian."

Judges 9:49

All the people also cut down each one his branch and followed Abimelech, and put them on the inner chamber and set the inner chamber on fire over those inside, so that all the men of the tower of Shechem also died, about a thousand men and women.

Ruth 1:16

But Ruth said, "Do not urge me to leave you or turn back from following you; for where you go, I will go, and where you lodge, I will lodge. Your people shall be my people, and your God, my God."

faith . **HOPE** . love . mind . **BODY** . *spirit* .

Chapter 10 - A Call from Your Heart

1 Samuel 15:11

" [Gen 6:6, 7; Ex 32:14; 1 Sam 15:35; 2 Sam 24:16] I regret that I have made Saul king, for [Josh 22:16; 1 Sam 13:13; 1 Kin 9:6, 7] he has turned back from following Me and has not carried out My commands " And Samuel was distressed and [Ex 32:11-13; Luke 6:12] cried out to the LORD all night.

1 Samuel 25:42

Then [Gen 24:61-67] Abigail quickly arose, and rode on a donkey, with her five maidens who attended her; and she followed the messengers of David and became his wife.

1 Samuel 30:21

[The Spoils Are Divided] When [1 Sam 30:10] David came to the two hundred men who were too exhausted to follow David, who had also been left at the brook Besor, and they went out to meet David and to meet the people who were with him, then David approached the people and greeted them.

2 Samuel 2:21

So Abner said to him, "Turn to your right or to your left, and take hold of one of the young men for yourself, and take for yourself his spoil." But Asahel was not willing to turn aside from following him.

2 Samuel 2:22

Abner repeated again to Asahel, "Turn aside from following me. Why should I strike you to the ground? [2 Sam 3:27] How then could I lift up my face to your brother Joab?"

2 Samuel 20:2

So all the men of Israel withdrew from following David and followed Sheba the son of Bichri; but the men of Judah remained steadfast to their king, from the Jordan even to Jerusalem.

2 Samuel 20:11

Now there stood by him one of Joab's young men, and said, "Whoever favors Joab and whoever is for David, [2 Sam 20:13] let him follow Joab."

. *faith* . **HOPE** . love . mind . **BODY** . *spirit* .

1 Kings 9:6
" [2 Sam 7:14-16; 1 Chr 28:9; Ps 89:30-ff] But if you or your sons indeed turn away from following Me, and do not keep My commandments and My statutes which I have set before you, and go and serve other gods and worship them,"

1 Kings 14:8
and [1 Kin 11:31] tore the kingdom away from the house of David and gave it to you-- [1 Kin 11:33, 38] yet you have not been like My servant David, who kept My commandments and who followed Me with all his heart, [1 Kin 15:5] to do only that which was right in My sight;

1 Kings 19:20
He left the oxen and ran after Elijah and said, "Please [Matt 8:21, 22; Luke 9:61, 62; Acts 20:37] let me kiss my father and my mother, then I will follow you." And he said to him, "Go back again, for what have I done to you?"

1 Kings 20:10
Ben-hadad sent to him and said, "May [1 Kin 19:2; 2 Kin 6:31] the gods do so to me and more also, if the dust of Samaria will suffice for handfuls for all the people who follow me."

♥

Are you a guide, a student or a teacher? Where are you? What are you? Are you getting it? Or are you still struggling to find your way? As you grow old in this world, you will grow young in the next, for you will be starting over again, taking with you only that which you learn to carry in your heart. Your Heart is your "true mind." There you learn that when you follow the plan that was set out for you, life gets a little easier as you go. Learn to think from the heart, because you are bringing this wisdom with you when you leave. The only way for you to transport your wisdom is through your heart. How you feel lives on and on.

♥

faith . **HOPE** . love . mind . **BODY** . *spirit* .

Chapter 10 - A Call from Your Heart

Transform me with the truth. There are five ways to do this: You can receive it, read it, research it, remember it, and reflect on it. It all takes you to the same results. Follow your heart, do what you know is right.

♥

What is hope but a feeling of optimism, a thought that says things will improve, it won't always be this bad, there is a way to rise above the present circumstances. Hope is an internal awareness that you do not have to suffer forever, and that somehow, somewhere, there is a remedy for despair that you will come upon if you can only maintain this expectancy in your heart.

Job 8:13
"So are the paths of [Ps 9:17] all who forget God; And the [Job 11:20; 13:16; 15:34; 20:5; 27:8] hope of the godless will perish,"
Job 11:18
"Then you would trust, because there is hope; And you would look around and rest securely."
Job 11:20
"But the [Deut 28:65; Job 17:5] eyes of the wicked will fail, And there will [Job 27:22; 34:22] be no escape for them; And their [Job 8:13] hope is [Job 6:9] to breathe their last."
Job 27:8
"For what is [Job 8:13; 11:20] the hope of the godless when he is cut off, When God requires [Job 12:10] his life?"
Psalm 9:18
For the [Ps 9:12; 12:5] needy will not always be forgotten, Nor the [Ps 62:5; 71:5; Prov 23:18] hope of the afflicted perish forever.
Psalm 31:24
[Ps 27:14] Be strong and let your heart take courage, All you who hope in the LORD.

♥

faith . HOPE . love . mind . **BODY** . *spirit* .

It is your knowing because of your direct experience and nothing more that gives you "Faith."

♥

Job 39:12
"Will you have faith in him that he will return your grain And gather it from your threshing floor?"

Psalm 143:1
[Prayer for Deliverance and Guidance.] [A Psalm of David.] Hear my prayer, O LORD, [Ps 140:6] Give ear to my supplications! Answer me in Your [Ps 89:1, 2] faithfulness, in Your [Ps 71:2] righteousness!

Psalm 146:6
Who [Ps 115:15; Rev 14:7] made heaven and earth, The [Acts 14:15] sea and all that is in them; Who [Ps 117:2] keeps faith forever;

Proverbs 12:22
[Rev 22:15] Lying lips are an abomination to the LORD, But those who deal faithfully are His delight.

♥

It is the higher plan of the universe for all beings to have lives of beauty, harmony and abundance. The principles of "allowing" are very important. You can increase the good you bring into your life by simply learning how to allow yourself to have what you want. You must allow the Lord in your heart. All though you are always in his, you must put him in yours. Once you learn this, you have found the Kingdom within. You will know Heaven on Earth. You will be at peace with all things in your life. You will be facing your problems one day at a time and living life to its fullest. Just allow Him in, and let it happen. There is no forcing. When He enters He is just like any other Father: gentle, kind, and caring, and He loves you.

♥

Mark 2:8
Immediately Jesus, aware in His spirit that they were reasoning that

faith . HOPE . love . mind . BODY . *spirit* .

Chapter 10 - A Call from Your Heart

way within themselves, said to them, "Why are you reasoning about these things in your hearts?

Mark 8:17
And Jesus, aware of this, said to them, "Why do you discuss the fact that you have no bread? [Mark 6:52] Do you not yet see or understand? Do you have a hardened heart? "

Mark 10:5
But Jesus said to them, " [Matt 19:8] Because of your hardness of heart he wrote you this commandment."

Luke 5:22
But Jesus, aware of their reasoning's, answered and said to them, "Why are you reasoning in your hearts?"

Luke 9:47
But Jesus, [Matt 9:4] knowing what they were thinking in their heart, took a child and stood him by His side,

John 14:1
[Jesus Comforts His Disciples] " [John 14:27; 16:22, 24] Do not let your heart be troubled; [Or you believe in God] believe in God, believe also in Me."

Acts 8:37
[Early mss do not contain this v] And Philip said, "If you believe with all your heart, you may." And he answered and said, "I believe that Jesus Christ is the Son of God."]

Acts 21:13
Then Paul answered, "What are you doing, weeping and breaking my heart? For [Acts 20:24] I am ready not only to be bound, but even to die at Jerusalem for [Acts 5:41; 9:16] the name of the Lord Jesus."

Romans 10:9
that [Matt 10:32; Luke 12:8; Rom 14:9; 1 Cor 12:3; Phil 2:11] if you confess with your mouth Jesus as Lord, and [Acts 16:31; Rom 4:24] believe in your heart that [Acts 2:24] God raised Him from the dead, you will be saved;

. *faith* . HOPE . love . mind . **BODY** . *spirit* .

1Philippians 4:7
And [Is 26:3; John 14:27; Phil 4:9; Col 3:15] the peace of God, which surpasses all comprehension, will [1 Pet 1:5] guard your hearts and your [2 Cor 10:5] minds in [Phil 1:1; 4:19, 21] Christ Jesus.

1 Thessalonians 3:13
so that He may [1 Cor 1:8; 1 Thess 3:2] establish your hearts [Luke 1:6] without blame in holiness before [Gal 1:4; 1 Thess 3:11] our God and Father at the [1 Thess 2:19] coming of our Lord Jesus [Matt 25:31; Mark 8:38; 1 Thess 4:17; 2 Thess 1:7] with all His saints.

♥

Times of uncertainty are also times of new possibilities. When your soul takes control you must open your mind to receive its messages.

♥

Genesis 42:21
Then they said to one another, " [Gen 37:26-28; 45:3; Hos 5:15] Truly we are guilty concerning our brother, because we saw the distress of his soul when he pleaded with us, yet we would not listen; therefore this distress has come upon us."

Genesis 49:6
" [Ps 64:2] Let my soul not enter into their council; Let not my glory be united with their assembly; Because in their anger they slew men, And in their self-will they lamed oxen."

Leviticus 16:29
[An Annual Atonement] "This shall be a permanent statute for you: [Lev 23:27; Num 29:7] in the seventh month, on the tenth day of the month, you shall humble your souls and not [Ex 31:14, 15] do any work, whether the native, or the alien who sojourns among you;"

Leviticus 16:31
"It is to be a sabbath of solemn rest for you, that you may [Lev 23:32; Ezra 8:21; Is 58:3, 5; Dan 10:12] humble your souls; it is a permanent statute."

faith . HOPE . love . mind . **BODY** . *spirit* .

Chapter 10 - A Call from Your Heart

Leviticus 17:11
"For [Gen 9:4; Lev 17:14] the life of the flesh is in the blood, and I have given it to you on the altar to make atonement for your souls; for [Heb 9:22] it is the blood by reason of the life that makes atonement."

Leviticus 23:27
"On exactly [Lev 16:29; 25:9; Num 29:7] the tenth day of this seventh month is [Ex 30:10; Lev 16:30; 23:28; Num 29:7-11] the day of atonement; it shall be a holy convocation for you, and you shall humble your souls and present an offering by fire to the LORD."

Leviticus 23:32
"It is to be a sabbath of complete rest to you, and you shall humble your souls; on the ninth of the month at evening, from evening until evening you shall keep your sabbath."

Leviticus 26:11
"[Ex 25:8; 29:45, 46; Ezek 37:26] Moreover, I will make My dwelling among you, and My soul will not reject you."

Leviticus 26:15
if, instead, you [Lev 26:11; 2 Kin 17:15] reject My statutes, and if your soul abhors My ordinances so as not to carry out all My commandments, and so [Lev 26:9] break My covenant,

Leviticus 26:16
I, in turn, will do this to you: I will appoint over you a [Deut 28:22; Ps 78:33] sudden terror, consumption and fever that will waste away the eyes and cause the [1 Sam 2:33; Ezek 24:23; 33:10] soul to pine away; also, [Judg 6:3-6; Job 31:8] you will sow your seed uselessly, for your enemies will eat it up.

There is a difference between being and doing, and most people have placed the emphasis on the doing. Doing is a function of the body; being is a function of the soul. So be the best person you can be. Every soul has a purpose. God placed the purpose in everyone's soul

faith . **HOPE** . love . mind . **BODY** . *spirit* .

before birth.

♥

When people speak of nourishing the soul, they mean opening the heart to the subtle whispers in the mind.

♥

Your heart holds the answer to resolving any and all problems in your life.

An adage says that the three truly difficult things to do in life are: Returning love for hate; including the excluded; and saying "I was wrong." It is the first and most difficult item, returning love for hate, that I will explore here.

You might as well just let it go. Until you can remove harsh feelings about others from your life, you will be stuck. Just let it go! Forgive and forget, and then move on.

One who knows the scriptures but does not live by them does not share in the bounty of a Holy Life. He is like the cowherd who counts someone else's cattle. One who knows a few lines from the scriptures and lives by them, harboring good thoughts, banishing hatred and delusion, wanting nothing from this world or the next, he reaps the full bounty of a Holy life.

♥

Your heart will aid you in replacing thinking with remembering. In this way, remembering can be experienced as the language of the heart. To remember is to recall from your memory, to know who you really are.

♥

Your Heart is calling you. How will you get from here to there?

♥

If God brings you to it, He will most assuredly bring you through it. In happy moments, praise God.

. *faith* . **HOPE** . love . mind . **BODY** . *spirit* .

Chapter 10 - A Call from Your Heart

In difficult moments, seek God.
In quiet moments, worship God.
In painful moments, trust God.
Every moment, Thank God.

Don't let life just pass you by. Stand up and be accounted for. Do something for yourself and for others. Make a difference in this world.

You were born to be somebody. You are a special gift to this world. We all have a purpose. Life on this earth is too short to live your life with regrets. It's never too late to start over again.

God has His reasons for all the things that you have and will experience in this world. We might not always understand them, or agree with them, but we will always be a wiser person for experiencing them and learning from His wisdom.

♥

Every now and then, when your heart longs for home, you can feel the softest breath upon your skin. It's like leaning over and kissing your baby as it sleeps. They are not awake to see you there, but their body is in tune to feel you there. Love was designed to reach across eternity. God's love for us can easily be felt through our senses. It was He who designed us that way. Just as your baby knows that you are there, so does your heart know that God is there. That is Faith. It is a simple knowing that you are loved.

♥

A little more time is what we all need. Just a little more time with those that we love, just a little more time. When it comes to your heart you should never put off expressing your love. Never put off today and try for tomorrow. Life is too short, and you never know what's next. God doesn't tell us our future. We live with our past, and today is his present to us. We all need to take the present and

faith . HOPE . love . mind . **BODY** . *spirit*.

enjoy the blessing. Every day that you wake up and you know that you are loved, really loved, you are truly blessed. If you have love in your life then everything in life is worth living for.

If you are experiencing some of life's difficulties, just remember that something really better is coming your way. If you thought that life was good before, prepare yourself for something better. You have to believe that it is coming your way. You have to feel it in your heart. And then, you can expect it. Follow your heart; it will take you where you need to be for all of God's blessings.

♥

We all fall down; it's the getting back up that really counts. We live and we learn. We help someone else up when it's their turn. Your feet won't always be on the ground. So, I know what you are going through when your heart is aching. Really, you are never alone with what you are feeling inside. When you love and have others love you in return, you feel God's blessing to you.

♥

Look inside your heart. Trust the feelings inside your heart. You will find God there. When you feel that there is something missing from your life, all you have to do is look inside your heart. It will always lead you back on to the path. There will just be a feeling that you get inside that somehow tells you that what ever it is your experiencing that is causing you pain or heart ache will soon pass. Everything happens for a reason. Our place is not to question why, just simply learn and move on.

♥

Learn to feel the word "Forever." It's not just a word, it's an expression of God's love for us, all of us. It's all or nothing at all. You either believe or not. If you say that you believe, then you should believe completely, with all of your heart, mind and soul, the same way you want someone to fall in love with you. When you go out in this world and you are looking for a mate, you want to

. faith . HOPE . love . mind . BODY . spirit .

Chapter 10 - A Call from Your Heart

find someone who you can say, "I will love you forever."
There are a lot of divorced couples out there who obviously didn't
know what forever meant. Love doesn't get anywhere when you are
walking away from it. You have to go toward love to make it work.
Moments of weakness should make your love stronger, and when you
look back after 50 years you can tell your loved ones that it really
does get easier all the time. When you know how good you have it,
even when you are experiencing some really hard times…just
remember love doesn't get anywhere when you are walking away.
You have to stay and work it out. It's God's way of teaching us
patience, kindness and understanding and what true love really is all
about.
Never forget how you were raised. If you were born into a loving
family, remember how lucky you really are. And if you were born
into a not so loving family, then you know how it made you feel. You
didn't like it so don't repeat it.

♥

There is a call in your heart. God gently placed it there when he sent
you here. It never goes away. But you do have to find it in order to
understand and feel it.

♥

Chapter 11

It Takes a Tribe

faith . **HOPE** . love . mind . **BODY** . *spirit* .

When I was growing up, my Grandma used to say "It takes a tribe to raise a family." For years I was not really sure what she meant. Now that I am 50 years old, I know exactly what she meant.

When life gets hard, it usually means that it is time for a lesson. Depending on what area of your life you are struggling with, that will give you the first clue as to what lesson you should be working on.

When you go through any of life's troubles, you need to be able to face them with a strong faith so that you can come out of them a better person for what you have learned.
You need to hope for a brighter tomorrow and know that the love you have for our Lord will be there with you all the way through.
When you go through any eye-opening life lesson, or any lesson that was difficult for you, it would benefit your family in the future if you would write these lessons down for them. It's very simple: You just write what you are going through, when you are going through it, being sure to include the prayers that you said. It's very important that our family learns how to get through the hard times from some-one who loves them and has their best interests at heart. As you work through your issues, be sure you write down how the ideas to solve your problems came to you. Did you feel as though you were being guided to the solution? Were random thoughts popping into your head? Give the details. It is so very important that we share these lessons with our "tribe." There are people in your life who can learn from you. You are filled with special gifts, gifts that you were born to share. It might very well be that your great-great-grandchild someday reads your story and chooses a different path because of the story you left behind. You have a message in your heart; it's very important that you share that message with your tribe.

♥

faith . **HOPE** . love . mind . **BODY** . *spirit* .

Grandma's Shoebox

You always give comfort to those you love through your heart. It's important that you give your heart's message to them also. If expressing your love can spare your children from one single heart-ache or one major crisis, then by all means teach your children what you have learned. When you write in your journal, you are leaving behind the lessons of your heart. You are leaving behind the story of your life and the history of your family. These words will live on and on for generations to come. You will always be there for them, even when you are gone. When God answers your prayers, he always does this through your heart. Leave those answers behind for all those whom you love. Let them know how you knew God was there for you, and how he is also there for them.

♥

When you feel your soul stirring, then you know that you are getting ready to make a change in your life. When you start doing any "soul searching," you are about to receive a message, and things in your life are about to change. It is critical that you are praying at those points in your life. Although you should be praying every day, when your heart starts longing and your soul starts stirring, you had better start praying.

The Bible tells us to ask in the name of Jesus Christ. It is through him that all things will come.
Acts 10:48
And he [1 Cor 1:14-17] ordered them to be baptized [Acts 2:38; 8:16; 19:5] in the name of Jesus Christ. Then they asked him to stay on for a few days.

John 20:31
but these have been written [John 19:35] so that you may believe that Jesus is the Christ, [Matt 4:3] the Son of God; and that [John 3:15] believing you may have life in His name.

.*faith* . **HOPE**. love . mind . **BODY** . *spirit* .

Chapter 11 - It Takes A Tribe

Acts 2:38
Peter said to them, " [Mark 1:15; Luke 24:47; Acts 3:19; 5:31; 20:21]
Repent, and each of you be [Mark 16:16; Acts 8:12, 16; 22:16]
baptized in the name of Jesus Christ for the forgiveness of your sins;
and you will receive the gift of the Holy Spirit.

Acts 3:6
But Peter said, "I do not possess silver and gold, but what I do have I
give to you: [Acts 2:22; 3:16; 4:10] In the name of Jesus Christ the
Nazarene--walk!"

Acts 4:10
let it be known to all of you and to all the people of Israel, that [Acts
2:22; 3:6] by the name of Jesus Christ the Nazarene, whom you
crucified, whom [Acts 2:24] God raised from the dead--by this name
this man stands here before you in good health.

Acts 8:12
But when they believed Philip [Acts 1:3; 8:4] preaching the good
news about the kingdom of God and the name of Jesus Christ, they
were being [Acts 2:38] baptized, men and women alike.

Acts 10:48
And he [1 Cor 1:14-17] ordered them to be baptized [Acts 2:38; 8:16;
19:5] in the name of Jesus Christ. Then they asked him to stay on for
a few days.

Acts 15:26
men who have [Acts 9:23; 14:19] risked their lives for the name of
our Lord Jesus Christ.

Acts 16:18
She continued doing this for many days. But Paul was greatly
annoyed, and turned and said to the spirit, "I command you [Mark
16:17] in the name of Jesus Christ to come out of her!" And it came
out at that very moment.

1 Corinthians 1:2
To [1 Cor 10:32] the church of God which is at [Acts 18:1] Corinth,

faith . **HOPE** . love . mind . **BODY** . *spirit* .

to those who have been sanctified in Christ Jesus, saints [Rom 1:7; 8:28] by calling, with all who in every place [Acts 7:59] call on the name of our Lord Jesus Christ, their Lord and ours:

1 Corinthians 1:10

Now [Rom 12:1] I exhort you, [Rom 1:13] brethren, by the name of our Lord Jesus Christ, that you all agree and that there be no [1 Cor 11:18] divisions among you, but that you be made complete in [Rom 12:16; Phil 1:27] the same mind and in the same judgment.

1 Corinthians 6:11

[1 Cor 12:2; Eph 2:2; Col 3:5-7; Titus 3:3-7] Such were some of you; but you were [Acts 22:16; Eph 5:26] washed, but you were [1 Cor 1:2, 30] sanctified, but you were [Rom 8:30] justified in the name of the Lord Jesus Christ and in the Spirit of our God.

Ephesians 5:20

[Rom 1:8; Eph 5:4; Col 3:17] always giving thanks for all things in the name of our Lord Jesus Christ to [1 Cor 15:24] God, even the Father;

2 Thessalonians 1:12

so that the [Is 24:15; 66:5; Mal 1:11; Phil 2:9-ff] name of our Lord Jesus will be glorified in you, and you in Him, according to the grace of our God and the Lord Jesus Christ.

2 Thessalonians 3:6

Now we command you, brethren, [1 Cor 5:4] in the name of our Lord Jesus Christ, that you [Rom 16:17; 1 Cor 5:11; 2 Thess 3:14] keep away from every brother who leads an [1 Thess 5:14; 2 Thess 3:7, 11] unruly life and not according to [1 Cor 11:2; 2 Thess 2:15] the tradition which you received from us.

1 John 3:23

This is His commandment, that we [John 6:29] believe in [John 1:12; 2:23; 3:18] the name of His Son Jesus Christ, and love one another, just as [John 13:34; 15:12; 1 John 2:8] He commanded us.

faith . HOPE . love . mind . BODY . *spirit*.

Chapter 11 - It Takes A Tribe

Asking in the name of Jesus is really a very simple lesson. God put all of us on this Earth with a divine purpose; Jesus is the "go-to" guy to get to God.

♥

John 14:6
Jesus saith unto him, I am the way, the truth, and the life: no man cometh unto the Father, but by me.

♥

When you hear the saying, "it takes a tribe," that means not just that we were all sent here to learn and make our way, but that we were sent here with other souls who will play a very important part in our lives. We were never sent here to be alone. Keeping things bottled up inside us has never been a healthy way to deal with all of our issues. You need a tribe to share, vent, laugh, cry, learn, etc. We all belong to a tribe. We all have a role to play in that tribe.
Sometimes when I think of that saying, I immediately think of all the women in my life, the close friends that I go to no matter what is going on in my life. There are people out there who love you, and they want you to be safe and happy. I have a tribe of girlfriends, aunts, and cousins who have always been near and dear to my heart. The friends that you keep through out your life are worth their weight in gold. These are the friends who really will be there for you no matter what you are facing. These are not the ones who run as soon as they don't get their way, and trust me there will be those who run when the going gets a little rough. Don't be discouraged when this happens; just realize that they were never meant to walk your entire journey with you.
We need our tribe. There are lessons that we learn from each other, and the members of the tribe are always available to step in at a moment's notice should you need their talents or their heart.

♥

faith . **HOPE** . love . mind . **BODY** . *spirit* .

Give up selfish rewards and pleasures and start to devote your thoughts to helping others. The Bible clearly tells us, "Whosoever will save his life shall lose it…whosoever will lose his life shall save it." What do you honestly think that means?

Matthew 16:25
For whosoever will save his life shall lose it: and whosoever will lose his life for my sake shall find it.

Mark 8:35
For whosoever will save his life shall lose it; but whosoever shall lose his life for my sake and the gospel's, the same shall save it.

Luke 9:24
For whosoever will save his life shall lose it: but whosoever will lose his life for my sake, the same shall save it.

Luke 17:33
Whosoever shall seek to save his life shall lose it; and whosoever shall lose his life shall preserve it.

Start putting the past behind you forever. Write it down. Share the lessons that you have learned, but give your problems up to God every night and I promise you, when you wake in the morning, you will awaken to a bright new day.

Stop thinking about the past and put your present issues into God's kind hands. "Him that cometh to me I will in no wise cast out…Behold I will make all things new again."

Mark 8:38
Whosoever therefore shall be ashamed of me and of my words in this adulterous and sinful generation; of him also shall the Son of man be ashamed, when he cometh in the glory of his Father with the holy angels.

faith . **HOPE** . love . mind . **BODY** . *spirit*.

Chapter 11 - It Takes A Tribe

John 12:13
Took branches of palm trees, and went forth to meet him, and cried, Hosanna: Blessed is the King of Israel that cometh in the name of the Lord.

♥

No matter how far off the path we may appear, we are always headed home. The more we can share with each other the deadened paths we have been down, the more we can help lead each other more quickly there.

♥

Remember that God has to work through someone else to answer most of our prayers. In the same manner, he has to work through you to answer someone else's prayer.
Have you ever been told by someone that you were the answer to their prayers? Think about it.

♥

If you are a parent, then by all means when your children start to go down the wrong path you have the "Father's" permission to get them back on the right one. If you have children, they were one of your "gifts" from God. You are supposed to be cherishing that gift and teaching them all that you know about him. "Teach them early." When they can't read, you read it to them. What stories do you really want them to remember? The story of Jesus or that of a mouse? One must come first. You must always keep Him alive in your home. That is your responsibility as parents. Even more so as grandparents! In today's world it still takes a village to raise a child. Where one person lacks, another will step in to teach what he or she knows.

It's like tutoring, except it's really the beginning of Bible study. Give them what they need to know so that they will pass it on. Pay attention to all the ducklings, for in God's heart they are all the same. By all means, keep your children in line. Try to keep them on the right path. When they do veer off the path, it is OK to grab them and pull them back, but do this by talking to them. Get to their heart; you can always reach them there.

No child should ever be beaten by his parents. God does not send us any gifts and then condone our beating them up. If you talk to your children, let them know how strong your love for them really is. You will reach them from the heart.

If you can't reach them, and they are using their free will to make the wrong choice, just know that eventually they will come back to you. Your job then is to be there for them and never stop talking. Help them with their lessons.

♥

Each of you has a personal map of reality or truth: your own assumptions, a unique philosophy about life, and a personal belief system. One of the challenges I will offer you is to look at your map. What is a personal map? For one person a map may say, "There is not enough love in the universe" For another, their map may say, "Every time I open up to another person I get hurt." Your maps are based on your childhood and lifetime experiences. They are based on your experiences of how your life has gone, how your energy has flowed out, and how you have been received by others, especially those you loved or wanted love from.
Start reading your map. Would you take a road trip without directions? You will find directions in many different books. Pick one, start reading, start looking, and know where you are going.

♥

. faith . HOPE . love . mind . BODY . spirit .

Chapter 11 - It Takes A Tribe

You will find the truth when you learn to go within.

♥

Deuteronomy 15:7
If there be among you a poor man of one of thy brethren within any of thy gates in thy land which the LORD thy God giveth thee, thou shalt not harden thine heart, nor shut thine hand from thy poor brother:
1 Samuel 25:37
But it came to pass in the morning, when the wine was gone out of Nabal, and his wife had told him these things, that his heart died within him, and he became as a stone.
Psalm 36:1
The transgression of the wicked saith within my heart, that there is no fear of God before his eyes.
Psalm 51:10
Create in me a clean heart, O God; and renew a right spirit within me.
Ezekiel 11:19
And I will give them one heart, and I will put a new spirit within you; and I will take the stony heart out of their flesh, and will give them a heart of flesh:
Ezekiel 36:26
A new heart also will I give you, and a new spirit will I put within you: and I will take away the stony heart out of your flesh, and I will give you an heart of flesh.

♥

The scriptures are full of tribal messages. We have always been a member of a tribe.
Genesis 49:16
Dan shall judge his people, as one of the tribes of Israel.
Genesis 49:28
All these are the twelve tribes of Israel: and this is it that their father

faith . HOPE . love . mind . BODY . *spirit* .

Grandma's Shoebox

spake unto them, and blessed them; every one according to his blessing he blessed them.

Exodus 24:4

And Moses wrote all the words of the LORD, and rose up early in the morning, and builded an altar under the hill, and twelve pillars, according to the twelve tribes of Israel.

Exodus 28:21

And the stones shall be with the names of the children of Israel, twelve, according to their names, like the engravings of a signet; every one with his name shall they be according to the twelve tribes.

Exodus 31:2

See, I have called by name Bezaleel the son of Uri, the son of Hur, of the tribe of Judah:

Exodus 31:6

And I, behold, I have given with him Aholiab, the son of Ahisamach, of the tribe of Dan: and in the hearts of all that are wise hearted I have put wisdom, that they may make all that I have commanded thee;

Exodus 35:30

And Moses said unto the children of Israel, See, the LORD hath called by name Bezaleel the son of Uri, the son of Hur, of the tribe of Judah;

Exodus 35:34

And he hath put in his heart that he may teach, both he, and Aholiab, the son of Ahisamach, of the tribe of Dan.

Exodus 38:22

And Bezaleel the son Uri, the son of Hur, of the tribe of Judah, made all that the LORD commanded Moses.

Exodus 38:23

And with him was Aholiab, son of Ahisamach, of the tribe of Dan, an engraver, and a cunning workman, and an embroiderer in blue, and in purple, and in scarlet, and fine linen.

faith . **HOPE** . love . mind . **BODY** . *spirit* .

Chapter 11 - It Takes A Tribe

Exodus 39:14
And the stones were according to the names of the children of Israel, twelve, according to their names, like the engravings of a signet, every one with his name, according to the twelve tribes.

Leviticus 24:11
And the Israelitish woman's son blasphemed the name of the Lord, and cursed. And they brought him unto Moses: (and his mother's name was Shelomith, the daughter of Dibri, of the tribe of Dan:)

Numbers 1:4
And with you there shall be a man of every tribe; every one head of the house of his fathers.

Numbers 1:5
And these are the names of the men that shall stand with you: of the tribe of Reuben; Elizur the son of Shedeur.

Numbers 1:16
These were the renowned of the congregation, princes of the tribes of their fathers, heads of thousands in Israel.

Numbers 1:21
Those that were numbered of them, even of the tribe of Reuben, were forty and six thousand and five hundred.

Numbers 1:23
Those that were numbered of them, even of the tribe of Simeon, were fifty and nine thousand and three hundred.

Numbers 1:25
Those that were numbered of them, even of the tribe of Gad, were forty and five thousand six hundred and fifty.

Numbers 1:27
Those that were numbered of them, even of the tribe of Judah, were threescore and fourteen thousand and six hundred.

Numbers 1:29
Those that were numbered of them, even of the tribe of Issachar, were fifty and four thousand and four hundred.

Numbers 1:31
Those that were numbered of them, even of the tribe of Zebulun, were fifty and seven thousand and four hundred.
Numbers 1:33
Those that were numbered of them, even of the tribe of Ephraim, were forty thousand and five hundred.
Numbers 1:35
Those that were numbered of them, even of the tribe of Manasseh, were thirty and two thousand and two hundred.
Numbers 1:37
Those that were numbered of them, even of the tribe of Benjamin, were thirty and five thousand and four hundred.
Numbers 1:39
Those that were numbered of them, even of the tribe of Dan, were threescore and two thousand and seven hundred.

None of us can make it all alone. We were not sent here to be alone.

I don't have any sisters. I have only experienced the sister relationship through others who have them. My Grandma had 4 sisters. I was lucky to be able to be around them all the time. Several times when I was a little girl, my Grandma told me the story of the day that my Dad was born. But she also reminded me of the story after I had lost my first child, and when I was pregnant with my daughter, Mindy.

My Grandmother had also lost her first child. When she was pregnant with my dad, it was a very difficult pregnancy. My father was born February 3, 1934. My Grandma was out at my Great Grandmother's farm (her mother-in-law) and she was 7 months along with her pregnancy. It was snowing and very cold. She went into labor, and there was nothing to do to stop it. My Great Granny put her upstairs in her bed and sent my grandpa into town to get her sisters.

faith . **HOPE** . love . mind . **BODY** . *spirit* .

Chapter 11 - It Takes A Tribe

When the sisters arrived the prayers started. The novenas began, and the rosaries were held tightly in everyone's hand. The sisters were all on their knees on the floor in the same room as my Grandmother. My Great Granny and her daughter, my Great Aunt Gin (Virginia), were preparing for the birth. The baby was coming.

My Great Aunties prayed nonstop to the Blessed Mother. They knew that if my Grandma lost this child, she would be brokenhearted. She loved children so much, and she really wanted one of her own.

My Grandma was in Granny's bed, and she (Granny) was about to deliver her own first grandchild. She had helped a lot of animals on the farm with birth, so she was familiar with the process, but she was not a doctor nor was she a midwife. But she was there and she was ready. When my father was born he weighed 1.5 pounds. He was very, very small. But he had 10 fingers and 10 toes and a room full of women praying for him.

My Great Granny delivered him easily enough, but he wasn't breathing. So she put her mouth to his and filled his lungs with air, and then he cried, a faint tiny little noise. She instructed her husband and son (my grandpa) to increase the wood in the kitchen stove and bring her a bucket of snow.
She took the baby down to the kitchen with her daughter (Aunt Gin) and they placed him in a large mixing bowl filled with snow. Then they moved him near the stove. They continued doing this for several days: in the snow, in the warmth; in the snow, in the warmth.

The little guy was so tiny everyone feared for the worst, but my Great

faith . HOPE . love . mind . BODY . *spirit* .

Grandma's Shoebox

Aunties remained on the floor on their knees and they just kept praying. They believed with all their hearts that when two or more gather in his name with the same request, your prayers will be heard much faster. They placed my Grandma's rosary in her hand as she lay in bed, and she began to pray also.

I remember that my Grandma told me the prayers went on for 9 days. While two sisters slept, the others would pray. They prayed around the clock. My Great Granny and Aunt Gin were doing all that they could to keep life in the child downstairs in the kitchen by the big woodstove.

Each day my dad got a little bigger and a little stronger. It was nothing short of a miracle. It was the first example of the power of prayer that my Grandma shared with me. There was a tribe of women there to make sure that he was going to be around for a long, long time.

Maybe that explains why my father was so close to his Aunts all his life. He has always stopped what he was doing whenever one of them was in need. He has cared for each and every one of them throughout his entire life. As they grew older and weaker, he was the man who took them to all of their doctor's appointments, shopped for them, rushed to them in the middle of the night whenever they called his name. I believe that his heart had a special bond with each one of those special women. They were the women in my Grandma's tribe.

Today my father sleeps every night in the same bed that he was born in. That bed is filled with his life. Every night when he lays his head down to rest, I believe they are all still watching over him. His life has not been easy, but his heart has always been filled with their love.

. *faith* . **HOPE** . love . mind . **BODY** . *spirit* .

Chapter 11 - It Takes A Tribe

♥

The Women in my Life…My Tribe

♥

My gift to the girls.
A part of my heart, a gift of my love is always within you.

Please take this message and put it in your hearts.
Know in your heart that it is me, always loving you, and always thinking of you.

Don't ever be afraid to give away a piece of your heart.
It grows back double in size.

When words are not enough, that is when you know love.
It will stay with you forever, because it has no beginning and no end.

Forever in your heart,

Debbie

♥

faith . **HOPE** . love . mind . **BODY** . *spirit* .

"Time passes.
Life happens.
Distance separates.
Children grow up.
Love waxes and wanes.
Men don't do what they're supposed to do.
Hearts break.
Parents die.
Colleagues forget favors.
Careers end.
BUT – Girlfriends are there no matter how much time and how many miles are between you.
A girlfriend is never farther away than needing her.
When you have to walk that lonesome valley and you have to walk it by yourself, the women in your life will be on the valley's rim, cheering you on, praying for you, pulling for you, intervening on your behalf, and waiting with open arms at the valley's end.
Sometimes, they will even break the rules and walk beside you, or Come in and carry you out.
Girlfriends, daughters, granddaughters, daughters-in-law, sisters, Sisters-in-law, mothers, grandmothers, aunties, nieces, cousins and Extended family all bless our life.
When we began this adventure called womanhood, we had no idea of the incredible joys or sorrows that lay ahead, nor did we know how much we would need each other.
Every day, we need each other still."

Anonymous

faith . **HOPE** . love . mind . **BODY** . *spirit* .

Chapter 11 - It Takes A Tribe

♥

Women have always told each other stories. Throughout women's history, they have always shared each other's stories. Weaving together experiences and insights, analyzing the important relationships and challenges in our lives, is how we discover our wisdom. This is also how we keep our sanity.

It doesn't matter who you are or how old you are, women need women in their lives to help them keep it together. It's much easier to forgive your husband when you have a kind shoulder to cry on when he really gets under your skin. Women help other women stay married. In a room full of women, it's hard not to laugh at the daily trials and tribulations of marriage and children. We all have our stories to share. It is very important that we are there for each other to share them.

♥

I have spent a lot of time with most of the women in my life. There has only been one good friend that I thought was a good friend and she ended up not being much of a friend. The rest of the women in my life have all been there for years and years. I thought it would be best if I shared some of our memories in this book, and some of our experiences as mothers. I have always enjoyed taking "girls' vacation trips." There is so much laughter on these trips that you can hardly wait until the next trip comes around.

♥

On one of our "girls' vacations," we were driving to Bald Head Island. There were 8 women going on the trip: 2 were flying there and the other 6 of us were driving. We had small little walkie talkies that we brought along with us so that we could stay in touch with each other in the 2 cars that we were driving. With 6 women in 2 cars it was rare that we ever came close to running out of gas. We always filled up when we had to make a "potty stop."

faith . HOPE . love . mind . **BODY** . *spirit*.

From St. Louis to Bald Head was about a 14 to 16-hour drive -- or 18 depending on our bladders. On this particular trip, we had 3 women in each car: Sue E., Sue Y, Kim, Holly, Lana, Me. As we were driving down the highway Kim made an announcement that she brought her little pistol. She had it in her purse. She recently obtained her conceal and carry license. We all just kind of looked at her and we all got a little chuckle out of it. The little pistol was all of maybe 3 or 4 inches. Obviously it didn't pack a lot of power, but we really didn't think too much about it. We left St. Louis around noon and we were headed for our favorite beach setting.

We had made several stops along the way for food and gas, every time we needed to take a potty break. At about 2:00 in the morning, we were somewhere in South Carolina. Sue E. needed another potty break so we sent a message to the other car of women that we would be getting off at the next exit for gas and potty time. All 6 women exited the cars. Two started pumping the gas in the cars and 4 of us went into the building to use the restroom. We had absolutely no idea where we were. All we knew was what the signs were telling us, "Welcome to South Carolina." Lana was in the men's room, and Sue Y. was in the ladies' room Sue E, Kim, and myself were waiting our turns.   All of a sudden a man came running into the building, robbed the store, and ran back out of the building, as Sue E and I are standing there thinking what the _ _ _ _? Kim started digging around in her purse. I could not at that point figure out what she was doing. Then it dawned on me: she's going for the gun! I looked at her and said "Please leave that little cap gun in your purse." We were loading up the girls and were going to finish our business a couple of exits down. I looked over at "PP Sue" and she was about to wet her pants. Holly came running in from the pumps to see what was going on, and about the same time the "little Asian man" behind the counter

faith . **HOPE** . love . mind . **BODY** . *spirit* .

Chapter 11 - It Takes A Tribe

grabbed his "Nunchucks" and started chasing the man who had just robbed his store. Lana came out of the rest room and we told her what just happened. Then a few seconds later, the store man came back into the building and told us that his store gets robbed almost every single night. OBVIOUSLY we were not in the best of neighborhoods. We quickly finished paying for our gas and we moved farther down the highway before we made any more stops.

As we were driving down the highway, I looked over at Kim and I started laughing. It was just simply uncontrollable laughter. I then looked at her and I asked her, "what was up with you and that gun? You are all of 5 foot tall…you are searching in your purse for your pistol… wouldn't you put that thing somewhere where you know where it is??? It doesn't mean conceal it from yourself." As I continued laughing, the chatter started from the other car. They were also laughing uncontrollably over what we had just witnessed. When we arrived at our next stop, breakfast before the island, we all 6 compared stories. The man who robbed the gas station was probably 6 foot 6 inches or taller, and he was a very large man, in what appeared to be very good physical condition.

I asked Kim at breakfast how many bullets were in her gun. She said "1." I looked at her and I said I guess you weren't planning on missing. Then PP Sue ran to the bathroom again.

We all 6 knew that it was a very dangerous situation that we witnessed, but it was also something that could have come directly from an "I LOVE LUCY" episode. It was also agreed that we would not tell our husbands this story for a minimum of 2 years. We didn't want them to try to limit our vacation destinations.

♥

Once we arrived to our location, we had to make a trip to Wal-Mart and the liquor store. When we entered Wal-Mart, it was a divide-and-conquer mission. We each took a part of our list and a basket and went in search of the items we needed to take over on the ferry to the Island. Sue Y. had mentioned that she needed to grab a pair of flip-flops for the beach. Sue E. and I were in the beach chair section because we knew we would need some lounge chairs for the beach. When we looked over, we saw Sue Y looking at the flip flops, but she was in the "men's section." She reached up and took the first pair that seemed to be within sight. We walked over and Sue E. said, "Do you realize that you are looking at men's shoes?" She calmly looked at us both and said she would just take the scissors and cut them to fit her.

Sue E asked her why she would do that when we were sure that Wal-Mart would definitely sell her size in flip-flops in the section for women. She said she was just going to grab the first pair she saw and make them work. We took her over to the "women's" flip-flops and encouraged her to buy a pair that fit her. We had many laughs over that!

Sue Y. was in desperate need of a vacation. She needed some quality time with the girls. She had given birth to a little boy, Alexander - "Alex." Alex was born in 2004 and he died in 2006. Sue Y. was under a great deal of emotional stress. Her little boy didn't even come home from the hospital until he was over a year old. And when he did, it was required that 24-hour care be provided for him.

♥

Many people will come in and out of your life, but only your friends will leave their footprints on your heart.

♥

faith . **HOPE** . love . mind . **BODY** . *spirit* .

Chapter 11 - It Takes A Tribe

The following final words were the hardest words that I have as of this date, had to pull from my heart and say them from my mouth. This is the eulogy that I wrote for Alexander Y, the 2-year-old son of a very dear friend, Sue Y.

♥

"Today we gather in the quiet of this sanctuary to pay our last tribute of respect to the life of this beautiful child of God, Alexander Y. I would like to share a special poem with you that is fitting for the Alex that will always be in our hearts:

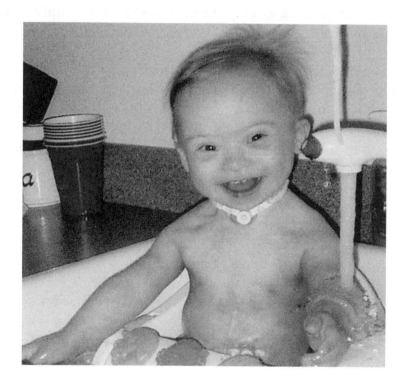

faith . **HOPE** . love . mind . **BODY** . *spirit* .

God's Very Special Child

"A meeting was held quite far from earth.
'It's time again for another birth,'
Said the angels to the Lord above,
'This special child will need much love.'

'His progress may seem very slow,
Accomplishments he may not show;
And he'll require extra care
From the folks he meets down there.

'He may not run or laugh or play,
His thoughts may seem quite far away.
In many ways he won't adapt
And he'll be known as handicapped.

'So let's be careful where he is sent;
We want his life to be content.
Please, Lord, find the parents who
Will do a special job for you.

'They may not realize right away
The leading role they are asked to play.
But with this child sent from above
Comes stronger faith and richer love.

'And soon they'll know the privilege given
In caring for this gift from Heaven.
Their precious charge, so meek and mild
Is Heaven's very special Child.'

faith . **HOPE** . love . mind . **BODY** . *spirit*

Chapter 11 - It Takes A Tribe

"The best use of life is love – the best expression of love is time. Alex didn't get to spend enough time with us. It's never enough time! But Alex knew love. He gave his love freely to everyone he met, and Alex met a lot of people. His list of admirers was actually quite long.

"There are 3 words written by Saint Paul in his letter to the Corinthians, 'love never fails.' What happens outwardly in your life is not as important as what happens inside you. On July 9, 2004, Alex was born, and nothing was ever easy again. But love stepped in. The purest, most unconditional love that we see in this world is a mother's love for her child. I know that I and many others watched Sue as she faced each day not knowing what it was going to bring. I am so proud of her for being so strong, so loving, so caring, so nurturing, so gentle, so kind, such a wonderful mother to Alex. Her love never failed him.

"There is not a moment in your lifetime without meaning. Each breath you take has purpose. Every time you sang 'Itsy Bitsy Spider' to Alex it brought him joy, it made him smile. Every minute you gave him was a gift that he will cherish for eternity.

"Sue gave her life to be with Alex – it was pure devotion. This love will last forever.
"I'll close for now with a simple little prayer for Alex:

> "Jesus loves me this I know
> For the Bible tells me so
> Little children ask no more
> For love is all they're looking for
> And in a small child's shining eyes
> The Faith of all the ages lies.

faith . **HOPE** . love . mind . **BODY** . *spirit* .

Grandma's Shoebox

"And tiny hands and tousled heads
That kneel in prayer by little beds
Are closer to the dear Lord's heart
And of his Kingdom more a part.
Than we who search and never find,
The answers to our questioning mind.
For faith in things we cannot see
Requires a child's simplicity."

♥

When I read these words at Alex's funeral I promised myself I would do it with honor, because it was an honor to be asked to do so. I was there the day he was born, and the day that he died, and so many days in between.

Life is not always easy. We don't learn much when things are easy. We learn and grow from our pain and troubles. We get through those hard times by being there for each other.

♥

When Alex died, you can just imagine the pain and anguish that filled Sue's heart. She became an emotional basket case. But those of us who love her and loved Alex stepped up to the plate to help her on her road to healing her heart and recovering her life. For anyone who has ever been through this, you will know that this is not an easy task to perform. But it does become easy to do when you really love someone.

Tragic Events as Major Crossroads. These events are watershed events in our lives, and their power to change us is immense. These events will always cause us anguish for a period of time, and pain perhaps forever. However, it is our choice whether, in the end, they have darkened our spirit or have become milestones and added greater purpose and peace to our lives.

faith . HOPE . love . mind . BODY . *spirit* .

Chapter 11 - It Takes A Tribe

We will tend to blame ourselves or the others involved.
The ability of these tragic events to crush the human spirit is no greater than their ability to elevate it. These events are often the beginning of a lifelong examination of previously held beliefs. The result of this subsequent inner search is often greater peace of mind and sense of purpose. Though the pain of the "tragedy" may linger, we often feel it created changes in our lives for which we are grateful. The tragedy tends to refocus our priorities and remind us of what is truly important in life.

♥

In some instances, the intense pain becomes a catalyst for a life's work or calling. Many service organizations, such as those to prevent alcohol-related accidents or locate missing children, were founded by people who had directly experienced the pain these tragedies can cause and subsequently decided to devote their lives to help prevent others from having to experience them.

♥

There is no one "right" way to grow. There are many paths to enlightenment and God. See what is beautiful in every person's path, in every religion, and in every belief system. Honor other people's paths even if they are different from yours. Be inclusive and loving, and look beyond the form of people's beliefs to the essence. There is no one right way; there is only the way that is right for you. There is something unique, perfect, and beautiful in every culture, in every system of belief. Look for what you have in common with others and accept and love those who are on different paths.

Christ came to earth to be an example of what you might become—a peaceful, loving, compassionate, and wise being.

♥

Our capacity to recognize universal values in life's experiences is what we call "wisdom." Wisdom also lies in the selectivity of the

faith . **HOPE** . love . mind . **BODY** . *spirit* .

discriminating intelligence. You thereby choose and follow that which you discern as truth in the myriad circumstances of everyday living. In fact, wisdom is the mastery of all knowledge.
It is the ability to discern inner qualities and insights. The wise men taught that it was a wise course of action in attitude and beliefs. Wisdom is often considered to be a trait that can be developed by experience.
In practical matters it is prudence. Wisdom is a virtue, a sense of knowing.
Virtue is the moral excellence of a person. Virtue is a trait valued as good. It signifies courage. The 4 cardinal virtues are: Justice, Courage, Wisdom and Moderation. The 3 supernatural virtues are: Faith, Hope, and Love.

♥

There is a group of women in my life who have been the rock of support for each other for many years. When one person is in need, the rest of us are there. There is no shame in any of the tears that we have cried while we were together. Life is not always going to be easy, but it is much easier to deal with when you have the comfort of your girlfriends. Mere words could never express how I truly feel about these women. We have truly shared the good, the bad, the crazy, the heartaches and the sorrows. We have been there for each other for many years. So I decided to show my appreciation with one of Grandma's beautiful pictures. I have dedicated one special picture to each of them.
These pictures were Grandma's art; the art that lived in her heart and soul. These are the pictures of her life in faith. Her expression of her faith in the Lord was truly beautiful. She lived her life knowing what was ahead of her on her path with the Lord.
I hope that you will see the beauty that both Grandma and I see in them.

♥

faith . **HOPE** . love . mind . **BODY** . *spirit* .

Chapter 11 - It Takes A Tribe

Grandma
♥
Alta Christopher Williams

. *faith* . **HOPE** . love . mind . **BODY** . *spirit* .

My Mom

♥

Jacqueline Gehrs Williams

. *faith* . **HOPE** . love . mind . **BODY** . *spirit* .

My Mother-in-Law
♥
Ann Gorman

faith . **HOPE** . love . mind . **BODY** . *spirit* .

Grandma's Shoebox

My Daughter
♥
Melinda "Mindy" Gorman

Christmas Blessings

faith. **HOPE**. love. mind. **BODY**. *spirit*.

Chapter 11 - It Takes A Tribe

My Aunt
♥
Joan Gehrs Bins

faith. **HOPE**. love. mind. **BODY**. *spirit*.

My Cousin

♥

Cheryle "Cherry" Roussin

faith. HOPE. love. mind. BODY. spirit.

Chapter 11 - It Takes A Tribe

My Grandma
♥
Gerturde "Gertie" Gehrs

. faith . **HOPE** *.* love *. mind .* **BODY** *. spirit .*

My Sister-in-Law
♥
Helen Williams

. faith . **HOPE** *. love . mind .* **BODY** *. spirit .*

Chapter 11 - It Takes A Tribe

My Sister-in-Law
♥
Lynne Gorman Owens

faith . **HOPE** . love . mind . **BODY** . *spirit* .

Melinda Swingle Bobbitt

♥

. *faith* . **HOPE** . love . mind . **BODY** . *spirit* .

Chapter 11 - It Takes A Tribe

Carleen Gentemann

. *faith* . **HOPE** . love . mind . **BODY** . *spirit* .

Grandma's Shoebox

Karen Arnold

♥

.faith. **HOPE.** |ove. mind. **BODY**. *spirit.*

Chapter 11 - It Takes A Tribe

My Sister-in-Law
♥
Mary Kay Gorman Stecich

faith . **HOPE** . love . mind . **BODY** . *spirit* .

My Sister-in-Law

♥

Stacy Williams

. *faith* . **HOPE** . love . mind . **BODY** . *spirit* .

Chapter 11 - It Takes A Tribe

My Sister-in-Law

♥

Donna Gorman

a blessed christmas

. faith . HOPE . love . mind . BODY . spirit .

Grandma's Shoebox

My Aunt
♥
Nancee Williams

. *faith* . **HOPE** . love . mind . **BODY** . *spirit* .

Chapter 11 - It Takes A Tribe

My Aunt

♥

Becky Williams

faith . **HOPE** . love . mind . **BODY** . *spirit* .

Grandma's Shoebox

My Aunt
♥
Mary Ann Gehrs

. faith . **HOPE** *. love . mind .* **BODY** *. spirit.*

Chapter 11 - It Takes A Tribe

My Cousin

♥

Tracee Williams Bone

A Blessed Christmas

. *faith* . **HOPE** . love . mind . **BODY** . *spirit* .

Debbie Holborow

faith . **HOPE** . love . mind . **BODY** . *spirit* .

Chapter 11 - It Takes A Tribe

My Goddaughter

♥

Lauren Holborow Smith

faith. **HOPE**. love. mind. **BODY**. *spirit*.

Sue Elsenrath

faith. **HOPE**. love. mind. **BODY**. *spirit*.

Chapter 11 - It Takes A Tribe

Sue Young

♥

faith . **HOPE** . love . mind . **BODY** . *spirit* .

Lynne "Evelyn" Hammerstone

. *faith* . **HOPE** . love . mind . **BODY** . *spirit* .

Chapter 11 - It Takes A Tribe

Debbie Rathgeber

♥

. *faith* . **HOPE** . love . mind . **BODY** . *spirit* .

Grandma's Shoebox

My 2nd Mom
♥
Lorene Gorman

.*faith*. **HOPE**. love. mind. **BODY**. *spirit*.

Chapter 11 - It Takes A Tribe

Lana Shepherd

♥

faith . **HOPE** . love . mind . **BODY** . *spirit* .

My Cousin
♥
Sarah Williams

faith . **HOPE** . love . mind . **BODY** . *spirit* .

Chapter 11 - It Takes A Tribe

My Cousin

♥

Concetta Williams Lawrence

faith. **HOPE**. love. mind. **BODY**. *spirit*.

Grandma's Shoebox

Ellen Owens
♥

. *faith* . **HOPE** . love . mind . **BODY** . *spirit* .

Chapter 11 - It Takes A Tribe

Holly Brander

♥

Merry Christmas

. faith . **HOPE** _. love . mind . _ **BODY** _. spirit ._

Kate Fuszner

♥

. *faith* . **HOPE** . love . mind . **BODY** . *spirit* .

Chapter 11 - It Takes A Tribe

Katie Roberts

. *faith* . **HOPE** . love . mind . **BODY** . *spirit* .

Grandma's Shoebox

Rhonda Rogers

♥

. *faith* . **HOPE** . love . mind . **BODY** . *spirit* .

Chapter 11 - It Takes A Tribe

Aisha Thomassen

♥

. faith . HOPE . love . mind . BODY . spirit .

Kim Curtis

♥

. *faith* . **HOPE** . love . mind . **BODY** . *spirit* .

Chapter 11 - It Takes A Tribe

My Great Aunt Gin
♥
Virginia Coleman

faith . **HOPE** . love . mind . **BODY** . *spirit* .

My Great-Granny

♥

Margaret Elanor Williams

. *faith* . **HOPE** . |ove . mind . **BODY** . *spirit* .

Chapter 11 - It Takes A Tribe

My Great Aunt

♥

Genevieve Christopher

faith . **HOPE** . love . mind . **BODY** . *spirit* .

Grandma's Shoebox

My Nieces

Amy, Alex, Abbi, Andrea, Kristin, Tammy, Cassie, Ashley, Molly, Nikki, Sheila, Shannon, Casey

faith . **HOPE** . love . mind . **BODY** . *spirit* .

Chapter 11 - It Takes A Tribe

My God Daughter
♥
Judee Williams Gaeta

. *faith* . **HOPE** . love . mind . **BODY** . *spirit* .

Grandma's Shoebox

Michelle Deierman
♥

. *faith* . **HOPE** . love . mind . **BODY** . *spirit* .

♥

Laughing at our mistakes can lengthen our own life. Laughing at someone else's can shorten it.

♥

No act of kindness, no matter how small, is ever wasted.

♥

I expect to pass through this world but once; any good thing therefore that I can do, or any kindness that I can show to any fellow creature, let me do it now; let me not defer or neglect it, for I shall not pass this way again.
Ettiene De Grellet

♥

Guard well within yourself that treasure, kindness. Know how to give without hesitation, how to lose without regret, how to acquire without meanness.
George Sand

♥

To be able under all circumstances to practice five things constitutes perfect virtue; these five things are gravity, generosity of soul, sincerity, earnestness and kindness
Confucius

♥

Misfortune shows those who are not really friends.
Aristotle

♥

When the character of a man is not clear to you, look at his friends.

♥

Adversity does teach who your real friends are.

♥

. faith . HOPE . love . mind . BODY . spirit .

Chapter 12

Home for the Holidays

My Grandma loved the winter Holidays. When Thanksgiving came around there was always a feast prepared at her home. I cannot remember any holiday that everyone wasn't at Grandma's house for Thanksgiving and Christmas. We all went to her home for those very special days.

Through out my life she made sure that all the Holidays were special. It wasn't in the gifts, even though there were gifts, it was how she brought joy to the hearts of everyone in our family. There was always music…someone was always playing the piano or organ and the rest of the crowd was singing and dancing. Everyone took piano lesson…it was just something that we all did when we were young. Some of us made it longer with the lessons than others. Grandma thought it was important so we all tried.

Every year at Thanksgiving after dinner it was her tradition that we would all decorate her Christmas Tree. It was no secret that for her Christmas was the most wonderful time of the year. Everyone spent extra time with the family, shopping, visiting, but most of all sharing. During all of our family dinners at Grandma's house there were always memories being shared throughout the entire meal. The rooms were always filled with laughter, and everyone's faces were always filled with smiles.

I have said before that my Grandmother was not financially wealthy, but she was surely the richest woman that I ever knew when it came to love. There was hardly ever a time that I was around her that someone wasn't being hugged. Children took an immediate liking to her. It was almost like she was magical with them. If a baby was crying in her home it would never be for long, because Granny always went and picked it up, and held it in her arms. Whenever she

. *faith* . **HOPE** . love . mind . **BODY** . *spirit* .

Grandma's Shoebox

would take the baby into her arms there was always an instant silence. I have actually seen her do this in stores. I was in the check out line with her one day when I took her shopping, there was a young mother in front of us and her baby was wailing out of control. My Grandma tapped her on the shoulder and said, "My name is Alta, this is my Granddaughter Debbie with me, and if you would like, I will hold your baby for you until you finish with your check out and get your bags into your car." The young mother handed my Grandma her baby. I watched her as she gently cradled the baby near her heart, and suddenly there were no more tears and no more noise.

The young mother looked at my Grandma and said, "How did you do that?" Grandma said it was her gift. When she said that I wasn't exactly sure what she meant, it wasn't until we got back to her house then I asked her.
When you told the young mom at the store that being able to make anyone's baby stop crying was your gift, what exactly did you mean?

She reminded me of the story of my father's birth. She said that while she was praying with her sisters she promised in her prayers that she would never ever just let her baby cry for no reason. That she would always hold that baby close to her heart and let him know that he was so loved. She told me that she held my father so much when he was tiny that he was in her arms more than he was ever in his bed. When God grants you the blessing of a child it is truly a blessing. It's the most wonderful gift you can ever receive. Life is short, hold your babies!

She said she was never going ignore a blessing. So she never ignores a crying child. She always told me, if your baby cries just pick it up. Give it all the love that you have, because days might seem to drag on, but years fly by really fast. Don't miss an opportunity to hold

faith . **HOPE** . love . mind . **BODY** . *spirit*.

Chapter 12 - Home for the Holidays

your baby in your arms when they cry. You should always think that when they cry, they are crying for you. They want you to hold them, they want to feel your love. Then when you pick up the infant the tears usually stop, because they feel your love.

♥

I asked my Grandma why she loved Christmas so much, and here is what she said: "When God gives you the blessing of a child, it is truly a miraculous thing. When I was pregnant with your dad, I wasn't sure he was going to make it. My sisters and I prayed for days, we said novena's to the Blessed Mother. We said our novena's to her for a reason. She was a mother, she has a mother's heart. While I was praying that my little child would live I told her in my prayers that if she would allow me to become a mother I would worship her on the day of the birth of her child for the rest of my life. So when Christmas comes around every year, I know that we are celebrating the birth of Jesus, but I also know that we are celebrating the day that Mary became a mother, that was the day that her heart changed to the heart of a mother. I knew in my heart and soul that she would understand the cries of my heart when I asked her to please grant me a miracle and let my baby live. When I prayed to her I asked her to please allow me the joys of motherhood I knew that she would understand." Then she went into her bedroom and once again she went to her shoe box. She put the box down on the kitchen table and she started showing me all the beautiful pictures of Mary. She said that whenever she received a picture of Mary or her family into her home she kept it in her box. That box was her soul. She never threw away any pictures of Mary or her family. She told me that she saved each and everyone that she ever got because they were all beautiful to her.

. faith . HOPE . love . mind . BODY . spirit .

Matthew 1:25
And knew her not till she had brought forth her firstborn son: and he called his name JESUS.
Luke 2:7
And she brought forth her firstborn son, and wrapped him in swaddling clothes, and laid him in a manger; because there was no room for them in the inn.

♥

My Grandma believed everyday of her life from the moment of my father's birth until her death that he was her miracle baby; that the Blessed Mother heard her prayers and answered them. After I lost my first child, she told me to pray to her, she gave me the same novena that she said for my father. I now have my daughter, she came to this world via the same prayers as my father. The prayers that my grandma knew would be answered because they were answered for her.

To me it is a tradition…Christmas is truly the most wonderful time of the year, not just because Jesus was born, but because without the heart of the Blessed Mother my father would not be here, I would not be here, and I don't believe that my daughter would be here.

♥

Christmas at my house is now very much like Christmas at Grandma's. I will carry on her tradition, I will continue the promise of Thanking the Blessed Mother for our Children until the day I die, and I can only hope and pray that my children will carry on the same tradition for me.
I will always love being home for Christmas…Grandma can count on me.
I always hope for snow and hang the mistletoe, but I always say the novenas that were passed down to me.

♥

.*faith* . **HOPE**. love . mind . **BODY** . *spirit*.

Chapter 12 - Home for the Holidays

I hope that you will enjoy the following beautiful pictures that were such an important part of my Grandma's shoebox.

♥

The Pictures in Grandma's Heart

♥

. faith . HOPE . love . mind . BODY . spirit .

Chapter 12 - Home for the Holidays

christmas greetings

. faith . **HOPE** . love . mind . **BODY** . spirit .

faith . **HOPE** . love . mind . **BODY** . *spirit* .

Chapter 12 - Home for the Holidays

CHRISTMAS BLESSINGS

faith . **HOPE** . love . mind . **BODY** . *spirit* .

Grandma's Shoebox

CHRISTMAS
Greetings

faith . **HOPE** . love . mind . **BODY** . *spirit* .

Chapter 12 - Home for the Holidays

One Solitary Life

He was born in an obscure village, the child of a peasant woman. He grew up in still another village, where He worked in a carpenter shop until he was thirty. Then for three years He was an itinerant preacher.

faith . **HOPE** . love . mind . **BODY** . *spirit*.

Grandma's Shoebox

A Little Town

It was just a quiet little town
In the stillness of the night
Till the moment
when the Christmas Star
Sent down its brilliant light
Then the shepherds on the hillside
And the Wise Men from afar
Came to kneel in adoration
At the manger 'neath the star
And the angel choirs sang joyously
Of "peace on earth, good will"
While a mother's loving murmurs
Kept the tiny infant still
Yes, it was just a little town
Like so many here on earth
Until the glorious moment
Of Our Holy Saviour's birth!

faith . **HOPE** . love . mind . **BODY** . *spirit* .

Chapter 12 - Home for the Holidays

314

faith . **HOPE** . love . mind . **BODY** . *spirit* .

Grandma's Shoebox

. faith . **HOPE** *.* love *.* mind *.* **BODY** *. spirit .*

Chapter 12 - Home for the Holidays

Christmas Greetings

. *faith* . **HOPE** . love . mind . **BODY** . *spirit* .

Grandma's Shoebox

Come Let Us Adore Him —

. faith . **HOPE** *. |ove . mind .* **BODY** *. spirit .*

Chapter 12 - Home for the Holidays

CHRISTMAS WISHES

Greetings

.faith. HOPE. love. mind. BODY. spirit.

.*faith*. **HOPE**. |ove. mind. **BODY**. *spirit*.

Chapter 12 - Home for the Holidays

Christmas Greetings

J OY TO THE WORLD

. *faith* . **HOPE** . love . mind . **BODY** . *spirit* .

Grandma's Shoebox

A Christmas Remembrance

. *faith* . **HOPE** . love . mind . **BODY** . *spirit* .

Chapter 12 - Home for the Holidays

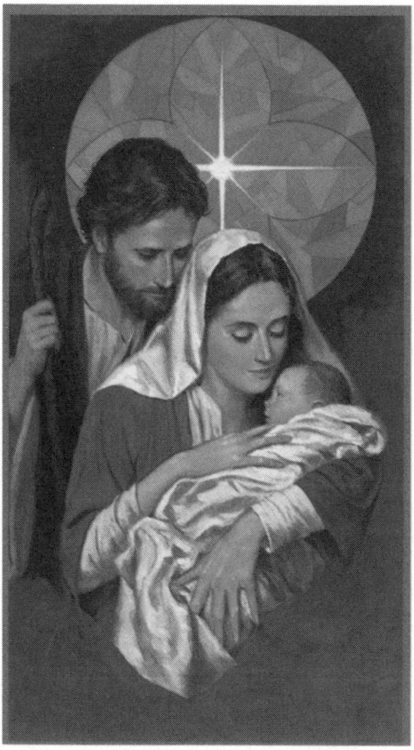

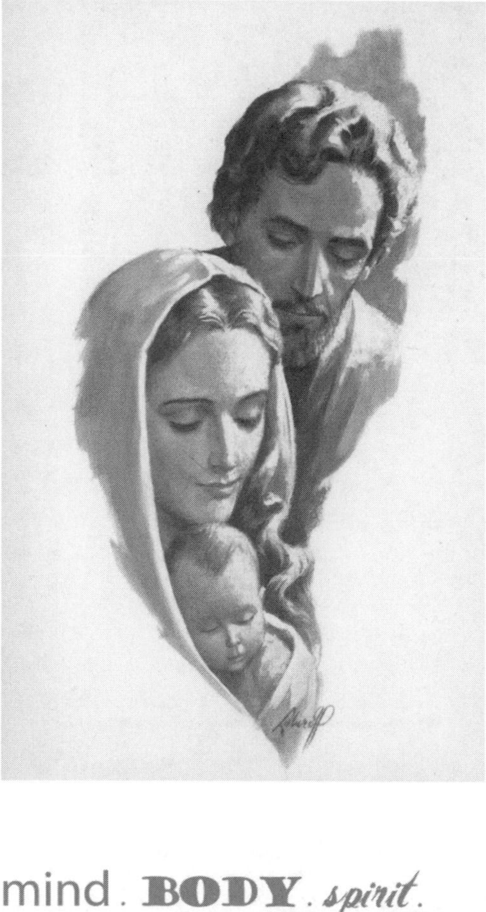

. faith . **HOPE** *. love . mind .* **BODY** *. spirit .*

Chapter 12 - Home for the Holidays

Merry Christmas

CHRISTMAS PEACE

. *faith* . **HOPE** . love . mind . **BODY** . *spirit* .

faith . **HOPE** . love . mind . **BODY** . *spirit* .

Chapter 12 - Home for the Holidays

. *faith* . **HOPE** . love . mind . **BODY** . *spirit* .

Final Thoughts

The choice of how you live your own life is ultimately your own responsibility. The results you experience are also of your own choices. Your action or inaction in response to the circumstances of your life is also your responsibility. A person who truly knows who they are, is not threatened by the beliefs of others.

♥

Fear is caused by resistance to the truth and misunderstanding it. The understanding of fear cures fear.

♥

Don't get "hung up" on the kind of person that you think you are. Don't get all caught up and concerned with thoughts of whether you are better or worse than other people. Try to know yourself as the kind of person you are and the kind of person you would really like to be.

♥

Whatever your present condition, just realize the need for more construction. When you look at a new home being built, you don't condemn it because it's not finished yet. You don't say it is inferior to other homes; and during the construction period you are not really concerned with its appearance. You realize it still needs additional work.

When you adopt a new way of thinking about the person you really want to be, then be patient with yourself. Also be aggressive about building toward the person that you really want to be.

Our self-worth comes from within. That's why it's called "self worth" and not "my worth from others."

faith . HOPE . love . mind . BODY . *spirit* .

Discover your own weaknesses and you will also discover your own strengths. Everything that you can learn about yourself will only help you to discover all the good within you.

♥

A wise person is always willing to give a piece of coal in exchange for the beautiful diamond that lies within. Take a good look at what you are denying yourself by not learning the truth about yourself. Never think that you are wrong for wanting to be all that you are designed and destined to become. Your diamond is within you.

♥

When you discover and learn that you are separate from what you have and what you do, you can transcend what is happening in your life. You will realize that what is happening in your life is only temporary. Life, including yours, is always changing. (This too shall pass.) Nothing but love lasts through eternity.

♥

Your higher self is changeless. When you allow yourself to identify with what is really only temporary in your life - things like financial struggles, illness, etc. - then you allow your beliefs to turn into what you are feeling at the time that feels "real" to you. This could be the biggest error that we can make in our lives.

To really experience your own "powerful" seed means that you must be able to separate what you have and what you do from "who you really are." Separate the performance from the "performer."

♥

Your only authority figure is within you. When you honestly start to look at your life you will come to the point of reality that this is truth. We may at times look to others to tell us what we should do, but the only person who will ever know what is right for our lives is ourselves.

faith . **HOPE** . love . mind . **BODY** . *spirit* .

Some people struggle to understand why things happen to them. They need to realize that this happens because they give it the power to happen and they don't want to accept their responsibilities. They have but 1 lesson to learn from this mistake.

If you allow others to do it "for" you, then you also allow them to do it "to" you. When you allow others to have responsibility for your life, then they are in control of your destiny.

♥

The secret is to live in this world, yet not to let the world live in us. We want our boats in the water, but we surely don't want water in our boats. If that were to happen, our boat may sink.

♥

People and events never really do anything to us. They simply trigger a feeling that exists already within us. Our basic life principle tells us that nothing happens in our world that we do not permit deep within our consciousness. It has been said many times and in many ways that "it is done unto you as you believe." You are who you are because that is who you want to be. Make no mistake: The only person responsible for you is you. You must be totally honest with yourself in order to change yourself. You can't fix what's outside yourself until you have taken the time to fix what is within. You need to learn to accept the truth about yourself, that you are not what you have and you are not what you do. Realize that you are spiritually whole, complete and perfect. When you accept this truth, your success and happiness will always be in direct proportion to your ability to know your true self.

♥

It is a demonstrated fact of life that we do not behave in accordance with the reality of what we can do, but in actuality of what "we believe" we can do. So, if you change the things you believe you can do, you can change your entire life.

faith . **HOPE** . love . mind . **BODY** . *spirit* .

Final Thoughts

As humans, we think in a 3-dimensional form – emotions, pictures, and words. Thinking is a process by which we allow words to trigger pictures that brings about our emotions. We do not always see what is really happening in our lives; we see what "we think" is happening. Our interpretation of our situations in life is what shapes our person. One single thought does not form our image of self. It takes a vast accumulation of thoughts and experiences to build our self-image.

♥

Our key to freedom is to be able to control the things we allow ourselves to think about and our perception of them. Other people will come in and out of our lives. We can allow them to build us up or tear us down if we allow our belief system to accept what they say as truth. There is only one truth for all of us, and it lies within us. It's the diamond in the coal waiting to be found. God placed this truth in each of us the same as he gave us our breath of life. There is something beautiful hidden deep within every one of us. It is our responsibility to bring out our beauty and let it shine for the entire world to see, but also as an example for the entire world to know that we can all do this. God did not give his gift to just a few. We were all created equal in his eyes. He is sitting back, waiting with great anticipation to see what each one of us will be.

♥

Life is a discovery process. When you are seeking out the truth, you must be careful because often we operate in accordance with the truth as we may see it and not as it really is. Our entire life is supposed to be a learning process, discovering truth along the way. That's why we must keep our thoughts open to allow for growth and change. We should never hold onto attitudes or beliefs that no longer serve us in our path to be all that we were meant to be. Our most important lesson is to grow, learn, and expand our knowledge from what is within us and to keep growing in our beliefs each day of our lives.

. *faith* . HOPE . love . mind . BODY . *spirit* .

Grandma's Shoebox

What we can and will do with our lives will always be of our own doing. We all talk to ourselves in our minds. We tell ourselves who we are and we allow ourselves to experience our emotions. Our self-image is an accumulation of our thoughts, attitudes and opinions. We began as small children and we continue throughout our whole lives to be the makers of our own thoughts and deeds. We are who we are because of who we let ourselves become.

♥

When we imagine an experience, we record it in our subconscious and we leave it there until we choose to change what we believe about ourselves. The impact that our thoughts and emotions has on us is extremely powerful. Our subconscious believes that what we tell ourselves consciously is true, whether in fact it is or is not the truth. Every statement you make in life has an effect on you. You must be extremely careful about what you allow yourself to say and think about yourself, then about others. What you think about your-self is what determines your own self-image.

♥

Our level of expectation determines our outcome. As soon as we set our minds onto any preconceived notion of how we think things will be, we then begin to create the exact situation that we expect.

This ability can be used either to make our lives better or worse. If you constantly see only what the negative is, you will constantly experience the negative. However, if you see yourself succeeding, you will eventually succeed. If at first you don't succeed, then try, try again. In order to have you true success in your life, you and only you have to see it there, because only you can put it there. Learn from your mistakes. The only proof that you need that this really works is the results you will experience if you do it.

faith . HOPE . love . mind . BODY . _spirit_ .

Final Thoughts

God gave us all the ability to play the game of life with balance and harmony. He also gave us universal rules that must be followed in order to truly succeed. The Laws of God's Universe are totally dependable and they are also unchangeable. In essence, God is our universal source of power and will never let you down if you play by his rules.

We control our universal powers through our own ideas and beliefs. The laws of cause and effect are impersonal. They simply must be understood. The universe that we live in can either support us or destroy us. It is our interpretation and use of these laws that will determine the effects they will have on us. We can only receive the knowledge that our minds are capable of accepting.

We may curse in our minds others who have more than us…but the universe clearly shows us curse and you will be cursed. Universal laws are simple, so simple that many do not believe that they can actually be true.

♥

God's abundance is there for everyone. When you go to the waters to gather what you need for your life, you must take along a reliable vessel to carry back all that you will need to sustain your life. You won't want to take a small cup when you need a large bucket. Open your mind to receive just what you ask for. The universal power of your spoken words will be reflected in your actions in the universe. What we take from this life is up to us. Our only limitation is in our minds. The universal truth, the truth for all, is that we can have anything we want, if we just give up the belief we have about ourselves that says we can't. It really is that simple.

If you plant a seed, and continue to water it and give it sunshine, it is eventually going to sprout and grow. Once you learn to accept that, you can have an idea whose time has come. Just as that seed grows, so can your idea!

♥

The goal of all the wonderful teachers of this world is to awaken the universal truths within us and the awareness that we do create our own reality. We are solely responsible for everything that happens to us, the good, the bad, and the ugly.

♥

If you believe that someone or something outside of yourself is the cause of your problems, then you will always be looking outside of yourself for your solution. In order to find our true answers and solutions, we must look within ourselves. That is the universal law. When you realize this and look within for the answer, your life will change and that still small voice that lies within all of us will also guide you to your solutions. Our current external situation is in many ways a reproduction of our inner world. Change what you have inside and all the world becomes your playground for life. No amount of determination or willpower will solve our problems if we look outside ourselves for the answer. That is God's universal law. No one lives beyond any of God's universal laws. Like attracts like.

♥

You don't need to fully understand the law of gravity to know that its universal effects work. What goes up eventually comes down. Our mind attracts whatever it is familiar with. Fear attracts more fear, confusion attracts more confusion. We attract what we allow ourselves to think about. Your subconscious mind doesn't think for itself, it only draws to it that which you allow in it: your beliefs, nothing more, nothing less. If you tell yourself that you are power-less in your current situation, then you are just that: powerless.

faith . **HOPE** . love . mind . **BODY** . *spirit* .

Final Thoughts

It is when you come to understand that you and only you have the power to change your situation, that only you can create the thoughts that you allow to run through your mind, then the realization comes that you are in fact NOT powerless. You hold all the universal powers necessary to change your current situation. Universal power is simply God's power of creation. It is the impersonal force of life within all of us. The effect will always be equal to the cause. It all comes out of our own thoughts and ideas. Our thoughts direct power. It is done unto you as you believe; not as you want, but as you believe. There is a vast difference between the two. When you put your thoughts out into God's universe, then and only then does he bring you to people, places, and things to help you!

♥

Your higher self is always within you. It's your source of power from Gods universe. That power within you is for your use, for your purpose of creating your world. We all have the ultimate power of the universe within us. God is within the hearts, minds, and souls of all of life's creation. He is our universal one and we are all one with God. If you need more power, then create less resistance toward God's universal rules, and you will soon feel more power flow from within you.

♥

We are and have always been creative beings. We have always had the universal power to create from within. By knowing who we are and the process from which our power comes to us, we can create ourselves to be all that we dream and desire to be. We are limited, not by reality, but by reality as we see it. We must understand God's universal rules for life.

There really is only one way to change ourselves, and the entire universe will someday follow suit. We can only change ourselves

faith . **HOPE** . love . mind . **BODY** . *spirit* .

Grandma's Shoebox

from the inside out. That is also the only way that our entire world can change: one person at a time, changing their own situations and leading the way for others to do the same. The only way anyone can heal the world is to heal themselves first. We must stand up and be accountable for our actions. We must take responsibility for everything that has happened in our lives. By the universal law of attraction, we have participated at some level, and that ultimately makes us responsible and accountable for all of the circumstances of our lives.

Our lives can only get better when we realize the universal truth: that we are who we are because of our natural ability to create from "our power within." Unlimited power lies in our ability to control our own thoughts. So, if we are not creating our lives the way we want them to be, we have no one, absolutely no one to blame but ourselves.

♥

If we want something badly enough, we will soon discover that we must let go and let God help us to dismiss any misconceptions that are keeping us from moving toward our desires. Your life is important to you. We all came here with a purpose, a mission to accomplish. If you will listen carefully from within, that purpose will be revealed to you.

If you really want to take control of your life, you must gain a basic understanding of God and his universal rules and powers. You must have this basic understanding of who you really are. Just as a drop of water has all the qualities of the ocean, you too have all the qualities of our creator within you.

♥

Science, philosophy and religion all teach us in their own way that there really is only "one power" in the universe and that we should be, as we always have been, one with that powerful source.

faith . HOPE . love . mind . BODY . *spirit*.

Final Thoughts

When you realize that you will experience in life what you convince yourself of, you realize that within you is the power, the universal power, the power from God to live your life with his unconditional love. Then you are free: we have a total acceptance of ourselves and then others and we know that we are spiritually perfect and so is everyone else. We all have the power within us to change. We are never meant to be permanently stuck in a rut. We are always and forever destined to change. How we see ourselves will always create our behavior, and our behavior will create our environment.

Do not attach yourself to your accomplishments or your failures; you will never be able to please everyone. Learn to please yourself and enjoy the person you really are. Anger, pain, suffering, and unhappiness in our lives really comes from being disappointed in ourselves for not living up to an expectation we placed on ourselves. We have to learn our lessons and throw away our experiences. We are only here to grow and learn.

♥

We always think that the enemy is someone who can harm us, but the truth is that no one can harm us unless we let them.

As we move along the path of our lives and discovery, we will all make mistakes. The failures or mistakes in our lives are only temporary. We learn from them and then let them go. It will never do you any good to dwell on what is wrong. If you dwell on it, it will only attract more of the same to you.

We are here to live in this world, not to let the world live in us. We all have a story to share. My Grandma experienced many trials and tribulations in her life, but her heart remained forever the same, filled with love and overflowing with her faith.

faith . **HOPE** . love . mind . **BODY** . *spirit*

Alta L. Christopher Williams

When she passed away August 26, 1998, I thought that my life would never be the same again. Now I know that she is forever with me in my heart and soul.

faith . **HOPE** . love . mind . **BODY** . *spirit* .

Final Thoughts

. *faith* . **HOPE** . love . mind . **BODY** . *spirit* .

Grandma's Shoebox

. *faith* . **HOPE** . love . mind . **BODY** . *spirit* .

Final Thoughts

faith . **HOPE** . love . mind . **BODY** . *spirit* .

faith. **HOPE**. love. mind. **BODY**. *spirit*.

Final Thoughts

. *faith* . **HOPE** . love . mind . **BODY** . *spirit* .

Grandma's Shoebox

. *faith* . **HOPE** . love . mind . **BODY** . *spirit* .

Final Thoughts

In
Loving
Memory

Alta L. Williams
July 10, 1913-
August 26, 1998

. *faith* . **HOPE** . love . mind . **BODY** . *spirit* .

Grandma's Shoebox

Bibliography

A Family Treasury of Prayers. New York: Simon & Schuster, 1996.

Addington, Jack and Cornelia Addington. All About Prosperity. Marina del Rey: DeVorss & Company, 1984.

Adrienne, Carol. The Numerology Kit. New York: Penguin Group, 1988.

Adrienne, Carol. The Purpose of Your Life. New York: Eagle Brook, 1998.

Agee, M.J. The End of the Age. New York: Avon, 1987.

Ailes, Roger. You Are the Message. New York: Doubleday, 1995.

Albom, Mitch. The Five People You Meet In Heaven. New York: Hyperion, 2003.

Altenhein, Bonnie. Angel Love. New York: Random House, 1995.

Anderson, George and Andrew Barone. Walking In the Garden of Souls. New York: Berkley, 2001.

Anderson, Ken. Where to Find It in the Bible. Nashville: Thomas Nelson, 1996.

Andrews, Andy. The Traveler's Gift. Nashville: Thomas Nelson, Inc., 2002.

. *faith* . **HOPE** . love . mind . **BODY** . *spirit* .

Andrews, Ted. How To Meet and Work With Spirit Guides. St. Paul: Llewellyn, 2000.

Anthony, Dr. Robert. Beyond Positive Thinking. Newport News: Morgan James, 2004.

Bach, Richard. Illusions: The Adventures of a Reluctant Messiah. New York: Dell Publishing, 1977.

Barrick, Marilyn C. Emotions, Transforming Anger, Fear and Pain. Corwin Springs: Summit University Press, 2002.

Barrick, Marilyn C. Soul Reflections. Corwin Springs, MT: Summit University Press, 2003.

Barton, Ruth Haley. Invitation to Solitude and Silence. Downers Grove, IL: InterVarsity Press, 2004.

Beckwith, Harry. Selling the Invisible. New York: Warner Books, 1997.

Behrend, Genevieve. Your Invisible Power. Los Angeles: Filiquarian Publishing, 2006.

Berendt, John. Midnight in the Garden of Good and Evil. New York: Random House, 1994.

Berg, Michael. The Secret. Los Angeles: Kabbalah, 2004.

Berry, Carmen Renee and Tamara Traeder. Girlfriends. Berkeley, CA.: Wildcat Canyon Press, 1995.

Betts, George Herbert. How to Teach Religion. New York: Abingdon Press, 1919.

Blackaby, Henry and Richard Blackaby. Spiritual Leadership. Nashville: Broadman & Holman, 2001.

Bodine, Echo. A Still, Small Voice. Novato, CA: New World, 2001.

Bowes, Susan. Notions and Potions. New York: Sterling, 1997.

Boyan, Lee. Successful Cold Call Selling. New York: AMACOM, 1983.

Breathnach, Sarah Ban. Simple Abundance: A Daybook of Comfort and Joy. New York: Warner Books, 1992.

Brennan, J.H. Discover Your Past Lives. New York: Sterling, 1994.

Bro, Margueritte Harmon. Every Day a Prayer. New York: Harper & Brothers, 1943.

Browne, Sylvia. Blessings from the Other Side. New York: Penguin, 2000.

Browne, Sylvia. Book of Dreams. New York: Penguin, 2002.

Browne, Sylvia. Conversations with the Other Side. Carlsbad, CA: Hay House, 2002.

Browne, Sylvia. God, Creation, and Tools for Life. Carlsbad, CA: Hay House, 2000.

Browne, Sylvia. Life on the Other Side. New York: Penguin Putnam Inc., 2000.

Browne, Sylvia. Meditations. Carlsbad, CA: Hay House, 2000.

Browne, Sylvia. Past Lives, Future Healing. New York: Penguin Group, 2001.

Browne, Sylvia. Prayers. Carlsbad, CA: Hay House, 2002.

Browne, Sylvia. Soul's Perfection. Carlsbad, CA: Hay House, 2000.

Bruner, Kurt. Inklings of God. Colorado Springs: Zondervan, 2003.

Brussat, Frederic and Mary Ann Brussat. Spiritual Literacy. New York: Touchstone, 1998.

Budapest, ZsuZsanna. The Holy Book of Women's Mysteries. Oakland, CA: Wingbow Press, 1989.

Burg, Bob. Endless Referrals: Third Edition. New York: McGraw-Hill, 2006.

Burkhardt, Margaret A. and Mary Gail Nagai-Jacobson. Spirituality. Albany: Delmar, 2002.

Burlingham, Bo. Small Giants. New York: Penguin Group, 2005.

Burnham, Sophy. Angel Letters. New York: Random House, 1991.

Buzan, Tony. Use Your Perfect Memory. New York: E.P. Dutton,

faith . **HOPE** . love . mind . **BODY** . *spirit* .

Byrne, Rhonda. The Secret. New York: Atria, 2006.

Campbell, Eileen. Love and Relationships. San Francisco: Thorsons, 1996.

Canfield, Jack and Mark Victor Hansen. Chicken Soup for the Soul. Deerfield Beach, FL: Health Communications, Inc., 1993.

Canfield, Jack. The Success Principles. New York: HarperCollins, 2005.

Canfield, Muriel. Broken and Battered. West Monroe, LA: Howard, 2000.

Cannon, Elaine. Count Your Many Blessings. Salt Lake City: Bookcraft, Inc., 1995.

Caples, John. Making Ads Pay. Toronto: General Publishing Company, 1957.

Carlson, Richard. Don't Sweat the Small Stuff. New York: Hyperion, 1997.

Carlson, Richard and Joseph Bailey. Slowing Down to the Speed of Life. New York: HarperCollins, 1997.

Carlton, Josephine. Life Messages. New York: Fine, 2002.

Carnegie, Dale. How to Enjoy Your Life and Your Job. New York: Pocket Books, 1974.

faith . **HOPE** . love . mind . **BODY** . *spirit* .

Bibliography

Carnegie, Dale. How to Win Friends & Influence People. New York: Pocket Books, 1964.

Carter-Scott, Cherie. If Life Is a Game, These Are the Rules. New York: Bantam Doubleday Dell, 1998.

Chapman, Hester W. King's Rhapsody. Boston: Houghton Mifflin Company, 1950.

Choquette, Sonia. Trust Your Vibes. Carlsbad, CA: Hay House, 2004.

Cialdini, Robert B. Influence – The Psychology of Persuasion. New York: HarperCollins, 2007.

Cohen, Alan. Handle with Prayer. Carlsbad, CA: Hay House, 1998.

Cohen, Alan. Heart. Carlsbad, CA: Hay House, Inc., 2002.

Collins, Ace. Stories Behind the Great Traditions of Christmas. Grand Rapids: Zondervan, 2003.

Connell, Janice T. Angel Power. New York: Ballantine Books, 1995.

Connolly, Elieen. Tarot, A New Handbook for the Apprentice. New York: Newcastle, 1979.

Cornell, Judith. Drawing the Light from Within. Wheaton, IL: Theosophical, 1997.

Cornell, Judith. Mandala. Wheaton, IL: Theosophical, 1994.

Covey, Stephen R. The 8th Habit. New York: Free Press, 2004.

Crabtree, Maril. Sacred Feathers. Avon: Adams, 2002.

Crary, Robert Wall. The Still Small Voice. Euclid, OH: Rishis Institute of Metaphysics, 1987.

Crawford, Saffi and Geraldine Sullivan. The Power of Birthdays, Stars, & Numbers. New York: Ballantine, 1998.

Crystal, Ruth. Angel Talk. Gillette, WY: Edin Books, 1996.

Custer, Dan. The Miracle of Mind Power. New York: Prentice, 1960.

Daniel, Alma and Timothy Wyllie and Andrew Ramer. Ask Your Angels. New York: Ballantine Books, 1992.

Davies, Brenda. The 7 Healing Chakras. Berkeley, CA: Ulysses, 2000.

Davis, Patti. Angels Don't Die. New York: HarperCollins, 1995.

Detz, Joan. It's Not What You Say, It's How You Say It. New York: St. Martin's Press, 2000.

Dolnich, Barrie. Simple Spells for Success. New York: Crown, 1996.

Dreher, Diane. The Tao of Womanhood. New York: William Morrow and Company, 1998.

.*faith* . **HOPE** . love . mind . **BODY** . *spirit* .

Bibliography

Dyer, Wayne W. There's A Spiritual Solution to Every Problem. New York: HarperCollins, 2001.

Eason, Cassandra. Crystals Talk to the Woman Within. Berkshire, United Kingdom: Quantum, 2000.

Edward, John. Crossing Over. San Diego: Jodere Group, 2001.

Emerson, Ralph Waldo. The Spiritual Emerson. Boston: Beacon Press, 2003.

Essig, Don. 148 Motivational Minutes. Lombard, IL: Successories, 1994.

Exley, Helen. The Love Between Friends. New York: Exley Publications, 2000.

Exley, Helen. The Love Between Grandmothers and Grandchildren. New York: Exley Publications, 1997.

Ezell, Suzanne Dale. Living Simply in God's Abundance. Nashville: Thomas Nelson, Inc., 1998.

Farrington, Debra K. Hearing With the Heart. San Francisco: Jossey-Bass, 2003.

Fields, Mary Elizabeth. Foundations of Truth. Marina del Rey: Book Graphics, 1980.

Fillmore, Charles. Jesus Christ Heals. Unity Village, MO: Unity Books, 1939.

faith . **HOPE** . love . mind . **BODY** . *spirit* .

Fillmore, Charles. Prosperity. Unity Village, MO: Unity Books, 1998.

Fillmore, Charles and Cora Fillmore. Teach Us to Pray. Unity Village, MO: Unity Books, 1941.

Fillmore, Charles and Cora Fillmore. The Twelve Powers. Unity Village, MO: Unity Books, 1999.

Fincher, Susanne F. Creating Mandalas. Boston: Shambhala, 1991.

Fiore, Edith. You Have Been Here Before. New York: Random House, 1978.

Flach, Frederic M.D. The Secret Strength of Angels. New York: Hatherleigh Press, 1998.

Flesch, Rudolf. The Art of Readable Writing. New York: Macmillan, 1949.

Foster, David. The Power to Prevail. New York: Warner Books, 2003.

Fox, Emmet. Around the Year With Emmet Fox. New York: HarperCollins, 1931.

Fox, Emmet. Diagrams for Living. New York: HarperCollins, 1993.

Fox, Emmet. Find and Use Your Inner Power. New York: HarperCollins, 1992.

faith . **HOPE** . love . mind . **BODY** . *spirit*

Fox, Emmet. Make Your Life Worthwhile. New York: HarperCollins, 1942.

Fox, Emmet. Power Through Constructive Thinking. New York: HarperCollins, 1940.

Fox, Emmet. The Sermon on the Mount. New York: HarperCollins, 1966.

Fox, Emmet. The Ten Commandments. New York: HarperCollins, 1953.

Freeman, Criswell. Fathers Change the World. Nashville: Delaney, 2000.

Freeman, Criswell. Wisdom From The Garden. Nashville: Delaney, 2000.

Gaither, Gloria. Bless This House. Nashville: J. Countryman, 1998.

Gallagher, Winifred. Spiritual Genius. New York: Random House, 2001.

Gawain, Shakti. Creating True Prosperity. Novato, IL: New World Library, 1997.

Gibbs, Terri. Deeper Than Tears. Dallas: Word Publishing, 1997.

Goldberg, Dr. Bruce. Past Lives Future Lives. New York: Ballantine Books, 1982.

Goodman, Sandy. Love Never Dies. San Diego: Jodere, 2001.

Grant, Russell. The Illustrated Dream Dictionary. New York: Sterling, 1996.

Grant, Russell. The Place We Call Home. Virginia Beach: A.R.E. Press, 2000.

Guggenheim, Bill and Judy Guggenheim. Hello From Heaven! New York: Bantam, 1995.

Haanel, Charles F. The Master Key System. Stilwell: Digireads.com, 2006.

Hailey, Arthur. The Moneychangers. New York: Doubleday & Company, 1975.

Haskell, Brent. The Other Voice. Marina del Rey: DeVorss and Company, 1997.

Hausner, Lee. Children of Paradise. New York: St. Martin's Press, 1990.

Hay, Louise L. You Can Heal Your Life. Carlsbad, CA: Hay House, 1984.

Haykal, Muhammad H. The Life of Muhammad. Selangor, Malaysia: Islamic Book Trust, 1976.

Heller, David. Talking to Your Child About God. New York: Bantam, 1988.

Hewitt, William W. Psychic Development for Beginners. St. Paul: Llewellyn, 2000.

Hill, Napoleon. A Year of Growing Rich. New York: Penguin Group, 1993.

Hill, Napoleon. Grow Rich! With Peace of Mind. New York: Ballantine Books, 1967.

Hill, Napoleon. Napoleon Hill's Keys To Success. New York: Penguin Group, 1994.

Hill, Napoleon. Succeed and Grow Rich Through Persuasion. New York: Penguin Group, 1970.

Hill, Napoleon. Success Through a Positive Mental Attitude. New York: Pocket Books, 1960.

Hill, Napoleon. The Master-Key to Riches. New York: Ballantine Books, 1965.

Hill, Napoleon. Think and Grow Rich. New York: Fawcett Crest, 1960.

Hill, Napoleon. You Can Work Your Own Miracles. New York: Ballantine, 1971.

Hillman, James. The Soul's Code. New York: Warner, 1996.

Hoffman, Enid. Develop Your Psychic Skills. West Chester, PA: Whitford Press, 1981.

Hoffman, Enid. Expand Your Psychic Skills. West Chester, PA: Para Research, Inc., 1987.

Hoffman, Enid. Hands, A Complete Guide to Palmistry. West Chester, PA: Whitford Press, 1983.

Hogan, Kevin. The Psychology of Persuasion. Gretna, LA: Pelican Publishing, 1996.

Hogan, Kevin and Mary Lee Labay. Irresistible Attraction. Eagen, MN: Network 3000 Publishing, 2000.

Hogue, John. Nostradamus, The Complete Prophecies. Boston: Element, 1997.

Holmes, Ernest. Creative Mind And Success. New York: Penguin, 1997.

Holmes, Ernest. Love & Law. New York: Putnam Special Markets, 2001.

Holmes, Ernest. The Science of Mind. New York: Penguin Putnam Inc., 1966.

Holmes, Ernest. Words That Heal Today. Deerfield Beach, FL: Health Communications, 1949.

Hoover, Herbert, and Hugh Gibson. The Problems of Lasting Peace. New York: Doubleday, Doran and Company, Inc., 1942.

Hopcke, Robert H. There Are No Accidents. New York: Riverhead Books, 1997.

Houston, June Dimmit. The Faith and The Flame. New York: William Sloane   Associates, 1958.

Hund, Wolfgang. 42 Mandala Patterns. Alameda, CA: Hunter House Inc., 2001.

Hunt, Dave. How Close Are We? Eugene, OR: Harvest House, 1993.

Huyser, Anneke. Mandala Workbook for Inner Self-Discovery. York Beach: Red Wheel/Weiser LLC, 2002.

Illes, Judika. The Element Encyclopedia of 5000 Spells. United Kingdom: Harper Collins, 2004.

Jakes, Serita Ann. Beside Every Good Man. U.S.A.: Warner, 1979.

Jaworski, Joseph. Synchronicity: The Inner Path of Leadership. San Francisco: Berrett-Koehler, 1998.

Jones, Riki Robbins. Negotiating Love. New York: Random House, Inc., 1995.

Jones, Timothy. Celebration of Angels. Nashville: Thomas Nelson, Inc., 1994.

Joyner, Mark. Simple.ology. Hoboken, NJ: John Wiley & Sons, 2007.

Joyner, Mark. The Great Formula. Hoboken, NJ: John Wiley & Sons, Inc., 2006

Kaufmann, Peter. The Temple of Truth. Cincinnati: Truman & Spofford, 1858.

Keenan, Father Paul. Stages of the Soul. Lincolnwood, IL: Contemporary, 2000.

Kemp, Jillian. The Fortune-Telling Book. Hauppauge, NY: Quarto, 1998.

Kimbrough, Lawrence. Men of Character. Nashville: Broadman & Holman, 2003.

King, Larry. Powerful Prayers. Los Angeles: Renaissance, 1998.

Kiyosaki, Robert T. Rich Dad Poor Dad. New York: Warner, 1997.

Kuthumi and Djwal Kul. The Human Aura. Corwin Springs, MT: University Press, 1971.

Komp, Diane M. Breakfast for the Heart. Grand Rapids: Zondervan, 1996.

Kuhn, Hermann. Karma The Mechanism. Incline Village, NV: Crosswind, 1999.

Kushner, Harold S. When Bad Things Happen to Good People. New York: Avon Books, 1981.

faith . **HOPE** . love . mind . **BODY** . *spirit* .

Lallaye, Tim. Sprit Controlled Temperament. LaMesa, TX: Post, 1966.

Lama, Dalai. Transforming the Mind. Hammersmith, United Kingdom: Thorsons, 2000.

Lane, Barbara. 16 Clues to Your Past Lives!. Virginia Beach: A.R.E. Press, 1999.

Larkin, Geraldine A. Woman To Woman. Englewood Cliffs, NJ: Prentice Hall, 1993.

Lawless, Julia. Aromatherapy and the Mind. Hammersmith, United Kingdom: Thorsons, 1994.

Lawrence, Shirley Blackwell. The Secret Science of Numerology. Franklin Lakes, NJ: Career Press, 2001.

Leonard, George and Michael Murphy. The Life We Are Given. New York: Penguin, 1995.

Linn, Denise. Sacred Space. New York: Ballantine, 1995.

Linn, Denise. Soul Coaching. Carlsbad, CA: Hay House, 2003.

Liungman, Carl G. Dictionary of Symbols. New York: W.W. Norton & Company, 1991.

Mahony, Ann. Handwriting & Personality. New York: Henry Holt and Company, 1989.

Marshall, Tom. Understanding Leadership. Grand Rapids: Baker Books, 1991.

Martin, Joel and Patricia Romanowski. Love Beyond Life. New York: Dell, 1997.

Martin, Joel and Patricia Romanowski. We Don't Die, George Anderson's Conversations With the Other Side. New York: Berkley Publishing Group, 1988.

Mathers, S.L. MacGregor. The Greater Key of Solomon. Stilwell, OK: Digireads.com, 2006.

Mathers, S. Liddell MacGregor. The Key of Solomon the King. San Francisco: Red Wheel/Weiser, LLC, 1972.

McLemore, Dr. Clinton W. Toxic Relationships & How to Change Them. San Francisco: Jossey-Bass, 2003.

Meier, Paul and Robert Wise. Windows of the Soul. Nashville: Thomas Nelson, 1995.

Melville, Francis. The Secrets of High Magic. Hauppauge, NY: Barron's, 2002.

Miller, Gustavus Hindman. The Dictionary of Dreams. New York: Fireside, 1984.

Moody Jr., Raymond A. Coming Back A Psychiatrist Explores Past-Life Journeys. New York: Bantam Books, 1990.

faith . **HOPE** . love . mind . **BODY** . *spirit* .

Moore, Thomas. Care of the Soul. New York: HarperCollins, 1992.

Murdoch, Iris. Existentialists and Mystics. New York: Penguin Group, 1997.

Na, An. A Step From Heaven. New York: Penguin Putnam Books, 2001.

Nemeth, Maria. Mastering Life's ENERGIES. Novato, CA: New World, 2007.

Newton, Michael. Destiny of Souls. St. Paul: Llewellyn, 2000.

Newton, Michael. Journey of Souls. St. Paul: Llewellyn, 1994.

O'Bryan, Pat. Your Portable Empire. Hoboken, NJ: John Wiley & Sons, Inc,.2007.

O'Sullivan, Terry and Natalia O'Sullivan. Soul Rescuers. Hammersmith, United Kingdom: HarperCollins, 1999.

Ophiel. The Art & Practice of Creative Visualization. York Beach, ME: Samuel Weiser, 1997.

Osho. Creativity. New York: St. Martin's Press, 1999.

Osho. Meditation. New York: St. Martin's Press, 1996.

Palmer, Jessica Dawn. Animal Wisdom. Hammersmith, United Kingdom: Element, 2001.

Paulson, Genevieve Lewis. Energy Focused Meditation. St. Paul: Llewellyn, 1994.

Paulson, Norman. Christ Consciousness. Buellton, CA: Solar Logos Foundation, 2002.

Peale, Norman Vincent. The Amazing Results of Positive Thinking. New York: Fireside, 2003.

Peale, Norman Vincent. The Power of Positive Living. New York: Ballantine Books, 1990.

Peay, Pythia. Soul Sisters. New York: Penguin Putnam, 2002.

Pitkin, David J. Spiritual Numerology. Ballston Spa, NY: Aurora, 2000.

Pollack, Rachel. Seventy Eight Degrees of Wisdom. Hammersmith, United Kingdom: Element, 1997.

Ponder, Catherine. Dare to Prosper. Marina del Rey: DeVorss & Company, 1983.

Ponder, Catherine. Open Your Mind to Receive. Marina del Rey: DeVorss & Company, 1983.

Ponder, Catherine. The Dynamic Laws of Propsperity. Marina del Rey: DeVorss & Company, 1984.

Ponder, Catherine. The Prospering Power of Love. Marina del Rey: DeVorss & Company, 1983.

faith . HOPE . love . mind . **BODY** . *spirit* .

Ponder, Catherine. The Prosperity Secrets of the Ages. Marina del Rey: DeVorss & Company, 1986.

Powers, Margaret Fishback. Footprints. Grand Rapids: Zondervan, 1998.

Prayers for a Woman of Faith. Grand Rapids: New Life Clinics, 1998.

Price, John Randolph. Angel Energy. New York: Random House, 1995.

Prophet Elizabeth Claire and Mark L. Prophet. Creative Abundance. Corwin Springs, MT: Summit University Press, 1998.

Quinn, Gary. May The Angels Be With You. New York: Random House, 2001.

Rabey, Steve, Lois Rabey, and Claire Cloninger. 101 Most Powerful Prayers in the Bible. New York: Warner, 2003.

Rabey, Steve, Lois Rabey, and Marcia Ford. 101 Most Powerful Promises in the Bible. New York: Warner, 2003.

Redfield, James and Michael Murphy. GOD and the Evolving Universe. New York: Penguin Putnam, 2002.

Redfield, James. The Celestine Prophecy. New York: Warner, 1993.

Redfield, James. The Tenth Insight. New York: Warner, 1996.

Reid, Lori. Sweet Dreamer. Boston: Element, 1998.

Remele, Patricia. Money Freedom. Virginia Beach: A.R.E Press, 1995.

Reynolds, Dana and Karen Blessen. Be An Angel. New York: Simon & Schuster, 1994.

Riso, Don Richard. Discovering Your Personality Type. New York: Houghton Mifflin, 1995.

Roberts, Jenny. An Introduction to the Bible. New York: Quintet, 1991.

Roman, Sanaya and Duane Packer. Creating Money. Tiburon, CA: H J Kramer, 1988.

Roman, Sanaya and Duane Packer. Opening to Channel. Tiburon, CA: H J Kramer, 1987.

Roman, Sanaya. Personal Power Through Awareness. Tiburon, CA: H J Kramer, 1986.

Roman, Sanaya. Soul Love. Tiburon, CA: H J Kramer Inc., 1997.

Roman, Sanaya. Spiritual Growth. Tiburon, CA: H J Kramer Inc., 1989.

Rosen, Eliot Jay. Experiencing the Soul. Carlsbad, CA: Hay House, 1998.

Roskind, Robert. In the Spirit of Business. Berkeley, CA: Celestial Arts, 1992.

faith . **HOPE** . love . mind . **BODY** . *spirit* .

Rothschild, Joel. Signals. Novato, CA: New World Library, 2000.

Ruiz, Don Michael. The Mastery of Love. San Rafael, CA: Amber-Allen Ruiz, 1999.

Runyon, Carroll "Poke". The Book of Solomon's Magick. Silverado, CA: C.H.S., Inc., 2007.

Sasson, Gahl and Steve Weinstein. A Wish Can Change Your Life. New York: Fireside, 2003.

Scheinfeld, Robert. The 11th Element. Hoboken, NJ: John Wiley & Sons, 2003.

Schuller, Robert H. Life's Not Fair, But God Is Good. New York: Bantam, 1979.

Schuler, Robert H. Pearls of Power. Dallas: Word, 1997.

Schwab, Victor O. How to Write a Good Advertisement. New York: Harper & Row, 1962.

Schwartz, Gary E. The Truth About Medium. Charlottesville, VA: Hampton Roads, 2005.

Scott, Steven K. The Richest Man Who Ever Lived. New York: DoubleDay, 2006.

Segriff, Larry, Ed Gorman, and Martin Greenberg. An Anthology of Angels. New York: Glorya Hale Books, 1996.

Sellers, Ronnie. Fifty Things to Do When You Turn Fifty. Portland, OR: Ronnie Sellers Productions, Inc., 2005.

Sheehan, Don. Shut Up and Sell. New York: American Management Associations, 1981.

Sher, Barbara with Annie Gottlieb. Wishcraft. New York: Random House, 1979.

Sherrer, Quin. Miracles Happen When You Pray. Grand Rapids: Zondervan, 1997.

Singer, June. Boundaries of the Soul. New York: Random House, Inc., 1994.

Sire, James W. Learning to Pray Through the Psalms. Downers Grove, IL: InterVarsity, 2005.

Small, Jacquelyn. Awakening In Time. New York: Bantam, 1991.

Smalley, Dr. Gary. Change Your Heart Change Your Life. Nashville, Thomas Nelson, 2007.

Smith, Susy. The Afterlife Codes. Charlottesville: Hampton Roads Publishing, 2000.

Snyder, Rachel. Words of Wisdom for Women. New York.: Barnes & Noble, 1997.

Spangler, Ann. Praying the Names of God. Grand Rapids: Zondervan, 2004.

faith . **HOPE** . love . mind . **BODY** . *spirit* .

Bibliography

Spangler, Ann and Jean Syswerda. Women of the Bible. Grand Rapids: Zondervan, 1999.

Spiller, Jan. Astrology for the Soul. New York: Bantam, 1997.

Stein, Diane. All Women Are Psychics. Berkeley: Ten Speed Press, 1988.

Steiner, Rudolf. Genesis Secrets of Creation. London, United Kingdom: Rudolf Steiner Press, 2002.

Stokes, Penelope J. Simple Words of Wisdom. Nashville: J. Countryman, 1998.

Stone, Joshua David. Soul Psychology. New York: Random House, 1999.

Stone, W. Clement. The Success System That Never Fails. New York: Pocket, 1962.

Swedenborg, Emanuel. Foundation Truths of the Christian Religion. London: Swedenborg Society, 1901.

Taylor, Terry Lynn. Angel Courage. New York: HarperCollins, 1999.

Taylor, Terry Lynn and Mary Beth Crain. Angel Wisdom. New York: HarperCollins, 1994.

Taylor, Terry Lynn. Creating With the Angels. Tiburon, CA: New World Library, 1993.

faith. **HOPE**. love. mind. **BODY**. *spirit*.

Tepperman, Lorne. Choices and Chances. Boulder, CO: Westview Press, 1990.

The Life-Study Fellowship. With GOD All Things Are Possible! New York: Bantam, 1972.

The New American Bible. Wichita, KS: Fireside Bible Publishers, 1995

Thomas, Marlo and Friends. The Right Words at the Right Time. New York: Atria, 2002.

Tirabassi, Becky. Change Your Life. New York: G.P. Putnam's Sons, 1999.

Tolle, Eckhart. Stillness Speaks. Novato, CA: New World Library, 2003.

Tolle, Eckhart. The Power of Now. Novato, CA: New World Library, 1999.

Tucci, Giuseppe. The Theory and Practice of the Mandala. London: Rider, 1969.

Underhill, James. Angels. Rockport, TX: Element, 1995.

Van Praagh, James. Healing Grief. New York: Penguin, 2001.

Van Praagh, James. Heaven and Earth. New York: Pocket Books, 2001.

Van Praagh, James. Talking to Heaven. New York: Penguin Books Ltd., 1997.

Vanzant, Iyanla. One Day My Soul Just Opened Up. New York: Fireside, 1998.

Vaughn, Frances and Roger Walsh. Gifts From a Course in Miracles. New York: Penguin Putnam, 1995.

Virtue, Doreen. Angel Therapy. Carlsbad, CA: Hay House,1997.

Virtue, Doreen. Archangels & Ascended Masters. Carlsbad, CA: Hay House. 2003.

Virtue, Doreen. Divine Guidance. New York: St. Martin's Press, 1998.

Virtue, Doreen. Healing With The Angels. Carlsbad, CA: Hay House, 1999.

Virtue, Doreen. Messages From Your Angels. Carlsbad, CA: Hay House, 2002.

Vitale, Joe. The Attractor Factor. Hoboken, NJ: John Wiley & Sons, 2005.

Vitale, Joe. There's A Customer Born Every Minute. Hoboken, NJ: John Wiley & Sons, 2006.

Vitale, Joe and Ihaleakala Hew Len. Zero Limits. Hoboken, NJ: John Wiley & Sons, 2007.

Walker, Barbara G. The Woman's Dictionary of Symbols and Sacred Objects. New York: HarperCollins, 1988.

Walker, Barbara G. The Woman's Encyclopedia of Myths and Secrets. New York: HarperCollins, 1983.

Walsch, Neale Donald. Applications for Living. Charlottesville: Hampton Roads, 1999.

Walsch, Neale Donald. Communion With God. New York: Penguin, 2000.

Walsch, Neale Donald. Conversations With God. Charlottesville, Hampton Roads Publishing, 1997.

Walsch, Neale Donald. Friendship With God. New York: G.P. Putnam's Sons, 1999.

Walsch, Neale Donald. Holistic Living. Charlottesville: Hampton Roads, 1999.

Walsch, Neale Donald and Dr. Brad Blanton. Honest To God. Stanley, WI: Sparrowhawk, 2002.

Walsch, Neale Donald. Moments of Grace. Charlottesville: Hampton Roads, 2001.

Walsch, Neale Donald. The New Revelations. New York: Atria Books, 2002.

Walsch, Neale Donald. Tomorrow's God. New York: Atria Books, 2004.

Wapnick, Kenneth. The 50 Miracle Principles of A Course In Miracles. Temecula, CA: Foundation for A Course In Miracles, 1985.

Ward, Carol. The Christian Sourcebook. New York: Ballantine Books, 1986.

Wariner, Steve. Holes in the Floor of Heaven. Nashville: J. Countryman, 1999.

Warren, Rick. The Purpose Driven Life. Grand Rapids: Zondervan, 2002.

Webster, Richard. Astral Travel for Beginners. St. Paul: Llewellyn, 2002.

Webster, Richard. Spirit Guides & Angel Guardians. St. Paul: Llewellyn, 1979.

Weiss, Brian. Messages From the Masters. New York: Warner, 2000.

Westcott, Edward Noyes. David Harum. New York: D. Appleton and Company, 1898.

Wheatley, Margaret J. Leadership and the New Science. San Francisco: Berrett-Koehler, 1999.

Wilber, Ken. A Theory of Everything. Boston: Shambhala, 2000.

Wilde, Stuart. Silent Power. Carlsbad, CA: Hay House, Inc., 1996.

. *faith* . **HOPE** . love . mind . **BODY** . *spirit* .

Wilkinson, Bruce. The Prayer of Jabez. Kansas City, MO: Multnomah, 2000.

Williams, A.L. All You Can Do Is All You Can Do. Nashville: Oliver-Nelson Books, 1988.

Williamson, Martha. In the Words of Angels. New York: Fireside, 2001.

Williamson, Martha. Touched By An Angel. Nashville: Thomas Nelson, Inc., 1997.

Wind, Yoram and Colin Crook. The Power of Impossible Thinking. Philadelphia: Wharton School Publishing, 2006.

Wittke, Carl. We Who Built America. New York: Prentice-Hall, Inc, 1939.

Wolf, Fred Alan. Taking the Quantum Leap. New York: Harper & Row, 1981.

Wolff, Virginia Euwer. True Believer. New York: Simon & Schuster, 2002.

Wolman, Richard N. Thinking With Your Soul. New York: Random House, 2001.

Women's Devotional Bible: New International Version. Grand Rapids: Zondervan, 1990.

faith . **HOPE** . love . mind . **BODY** . *spirit* .

Zubko, Andy. Treasury of Spiritual Wisdom. San Diego: Blue Dove Press, 1996.

Zukav, Gary and Linda Francis. The Heart of the Soul. New York: Fireside, 2002.

Zukav, Gary. The Seat of the Soul. New York: Fireside, 1989.